MW00977147

© 2013 Douglas Brinley & David Brinley

All rights reserved. No part of this book may be reproduced in any form whatsoever, whether by graphic, visual, filming, microfilming, tape recording or any other means, without the written permission of the copyright holder, except in the case of brief passages embodied in critical reviews and articles where the title, editors and ISBN accompany such review or article.

All rights reserved under International and Pan-American Copyright Conventions

First Printing: September 2013 V2

ISBN: 978-1-937735-58-6

Digital Legend Publishing Inc. Honeoye Falls, New York

Send Inquiries to: info@digitalegend.com or visit www.digitalegend.com

Book interior layout and cover design by Alisha Bishop

MARITAL 'TUNE-UP KIT'

DOUG & DAVE BRINLEY

DIGITAL
LEGEND

New York

CONTENTS

INTRODUCTION

Anyone who owns a car is familiar with the need for a periodic tune-up. This procedure may involve a change in spark plugs, a check of engine belts, hoses, coils, wires, and other engine components that affect a car's functionality and dependability. This Marital 'Tune-up Kit' is designed with a similar goal in mind: Assist couples to keep their marriages functional and viable with a quick daily tune-up.

Each day of the year contains a quote, usually from a Church authority, a brief commentary, and an application of the principle. The quotes chosen for this 'kit' are primarily based on President Boyd K. Packer's counsel: "True doctrine, understood, changes attitudes and behavior. The study of the doctrines of the gospel will improve behavior quicker than a study of behavior will improve behavior" ("Do Not Fear," *Ensign*, May 2004, 73; see also "Little Children," *Ensign*, Nov. 1986, 17 and "Washed Clean," *Ensign*, May 1997, 9).

What doctrines have that kind of power? Appendix A contains a list of eleven Church doctrines and principles. The list is taken from that used by the Seminary and Institute arm of Church Education— CES. You will notice that these doctrines are the fundamental elements of the plan of salvation. When understood and applied, as

President Packer stated, individuals are more likely to voluntarily bring their behavior into conformity with these doctrines.

The daily quotes are primarily, but not exclusively, from members of the First Presidency and the Quorum of Twelve Apostles. The Lord charged the original quorum of Twelve to "cleanse your hearts and your garments, lest the blood of this generation be required at your hands" (D&C 112:33). Their counsel typically comes to the membership of the Church in the form of articles in the monthly *Ensign* magazine, or in General Conference addresses every April and October. These addresses are then printed in the May and November *Ensign.* They are also accessible on the Church website at *lds.org.*

An application is suggested to encourage couples to *do* something that day to strengthen their companionship. It may involve a brief sharing of thoughts and reflections, a scripture, or to read the entire talk referenced. If the application does not fit a couple's situation (no children), Appendix B provides a list of 'love notes' and 'coupons,' for use instead. Of course, love notes and coupons may be used at any time—birthdays, anniversaries, holidays, etc.

Our promise to you is that by reading and applying the counsel of Church leaders, scripture, and a review of the doctrines of the gospel, your marriage will stay 'in-tune' as you two hit the road of life together headed for your celestial destination!

Our thanks to J. Robert Driggs for helpful editing assistance.

Doug Brinley   *David Brinley*

Provo, Utah   Houston, Texas

2

JANUARY

JANUARY 1

D&C 49:15 "Whoso forbiddeth to marry is not ordained of God, for marriage is ordained of God unto man."

Elder Dallin H. Oaks: "Our theology begins with heavenly parents. Our highest aspiration is to be like them" ("Apostasy and Restoration," *Ensign*, May 1995, 87). Marriage is the crowning ordinance in our Father's plan of salvation for His children. In the premortal life we were brothers and sisters to one another, sons and daughters unto God, but *never* were we husbands or wives, fathers or mothers. Just as mortal parents anticipate the day when their children leave the nest, why wouldn't heavenly parents have similar feelings? Parents yearn to see their children find happiness in the very things that bring them happiness, marriage and parenthood in this instance. We left our premortal home to obtain a body of element that was to be a counterpart to our spirit body. This combination of bodies allows us to 'apprentice' in marriage and parenting roles for the first time in our existence.

Application: A new year causes us to reflect on time. Consider the phrase: 'For time and all eternity.' Just how long is that!? Why is marriage the 'crowning ordinance' of the gospel?

JANUARY 2

"Happiness in family life is most likely to be achieved when founded upon the teachings of the Lord Jesus Christ" (*"The Family: A Proclamation to the World," Ensign*, Nov. 1995, 102).

Jacob taught a simple truth: "Men are, that they might have joy" (2 Nephi 2:25). The entire gospel plan is designed to bring men and women true joy. The Savior's Atonement allows us to repent and to be forgiven of our sins. His resurrection paved the way for couples to live forever as husband and wife because resurrection restores both body and spirit, the soul of man (see D&C 88:15). No longer subject to death, a husband and a wife, sealed by priesthood authority and faithful to their covenants, remain forever sweethearts. Without a Savior and priesthood authority, at death we would return to a state of singleness. Jacob explained that without a Savior, 'our spirits must have become like unto [Satan] and we become devils, angels to a devil' (2 Nephi 9:9). Satan's everlasting punishment? To be limited to a spirit existence, and remain forever impotent, incapable of ever being a husband or a father. No wonder he wages war against marriages and families!

Application: Explain how Jesus Christ makes it possible for you to be eternal companions. What would immortality be like if marriage ended with death?

JANUARY 3

Ezra Taft Benson: "We covenant to live the law of consecration. This law is that we consecrate our time, talents, strength, property, and money for the upbuilding of the kingdom of God on the earth and the establishment of Zion. Until one abides by the laws of obedience, sacrifice, the gospel, and chastity, he cannot abide the law of consecration, which is the law pertaining to the celestial kingdom." (*The Teachings of Ezra Taft Benson*, 121).

Covenants are a source of power for Latter-day Saints to live their lives in harmony with eternal laws. Covenants remind us of the potential blessings that we may receive if we live righteously. Ordinances represent our signature that we are willing to abide by the provisions of the covenant. Ordinances involve a physical sign or action on our part that implants in our minds the sacred promises of the covenant. These commitments are two-way promises made by mortals with One who has the ability to fulfill His part of the covenant. Our safety then, lies in keeping covenants.

Application: List covenants you 'signed' to accept by an ordinance. What blessings are associated with each covenant?

JANUARY 4

Gordon B. Hinckley: "We live in a world that is filled with filth and sleaze, a world that reeks of evil. It is all around us. It is on the television screen. It is at the movies. It is in the popular literature. It is on the Internet. You can't afford to watch it, my dear friends. You cannot afford to let that filthy poison touch you. Stay away from it. Avoid it. You can't rent videos and watch them as they portray degrading things. You young men who hold the priesthood of God cannot mix this filth with the holy priesthood" ("A Prophet's Counsel and Prayer for Youth," *Ensign*, Jan 2001, 2).

Though this address by President Hinckley was directed to the youth of the Church, pornography is not limited to just young men. It infects men and women of all ages and is hugely destructive to marital relationships. Recent surveys of attorneys who specialize in divorce requests indicate that over half of the cases they handle involve one partner being heavily involved in viewing pornographic websites! The best instructor, teacher, and source of information on sexual intimacy is your spouse! He or she is the only one to please. We learn best from each other what is stimulating, arousing, and pleasurable. Pornography does nothing to enhance marital relationships or promote realistic, loving marital encounters. Rather, it is a multi-billion commercial enterprise with huge production budgets and paid actors who promote material calculated to addict and appeal to baser human desires.

Application: As a wife, clearly explain to your husband why pornography is repulsive to right-thinking women.

JANUARY 5

Jeffrey R. Holland: "Life is too short to be spent nursing animosities or keeping a box score of offenses against us—you know, no runs, no hits, all errors" ("The Peaceable Things of the Kingdom," *Ensign*, Nov. 1996, 83).

A wife is her husband's greatest treasure, his sweetheart who willingly accepted his offer of engagement and marriage. The key question for married men to answer is this: Are you still treating your companion with the dignity, charity, and kindness you did while dating her? A wife should view her husband as her companion, confidante, friend, sweetheart, and equal partner. There can be no hint of arrogance or superiority on the part of either one. Remember, you 'faked' each other into marriage by being on your best behavior! Your charming behavior at that time actually proves that you really can be charitable when you want to be! Now married, the two of you will spend the rest of your lives convincing each other that your decision to marry was your best choice ever! Of course, by now you have learned that you actually married a stranger. You had no idea when you were dating how your life would turn out, how many children you would have, where you would live or be employed. But in spite of the twists and turns of life, you are growing in your capacity to be compatible companions and lovers!

Application: Share a positive personal attribute of your spouse that attracted you to each other.

JANUARY 6

Robert L. Simpson: "Every couple, whether in the first or the twenty-first year of marriage, should discover the value of pillow-talk time at the end of the day" ("A Lasting Marriage," *Ensign*, May 1982, 21).

One of the joys in which happily married couples engage, is sharing their innermost feelings and thoughts with their spouse-therapist. In marriage, we plumb the heart and mind of a kindred spirit and come to know well each other's heart. The end of the day is not a time to rehash problems or frustrations, but rather a time to rejoice that another day is safely tucked away. Because you *do* marry your therapist, pillow talk is a therapeutic aspect of your relationship. When you exchange your deepest feelings, you confirm in your heart that you married the right spouse for you. Happily married couples view bedtime as a retreat from children as well as the world —physically and emotionally. Pillow talk keeps open the channels of communication.

Application: Spend at least five to ten minutes in 'pillow talk' tonight before bedtime.

JANUARY 7

Gordon B. Hinckley: "How wonderful a thing is a child. How beautiful is a newborn babe. There is no greater miracle than the creation of human life" ("Walking in the Light of the Lord," *Ensign*, Nov. 1998, 99).

Is it not amazing to think that you two were able to create a physical body for one of Father's spirit sons or daughters? The miracle of birth is one of the thrilling miracles of life. To rear one of the Father's beloved spirit children, whether yours by birth or adoption, is a sacred privilege and gives the most profound reasons to be your best self. Every new addition you invite into your home expands the meaning of 'family.' You two will never be the same as the inevitable sacrifices that come with parenthood add greatly to your maturity. Remember that you represent the most frequent model your children will see of a happy, or a sad marriage, so do your best!

Application: Share an insight of how your children impact your lives for good. If no children yet, how do you see your lives changing with the birth of a child?

JANUARY 8

Boyd K. Packer: "The distance between the Church and a world set on a course we cannot follow will steadily increase....Across the world, those who now come by the tens of thousands will inevitably come as a flood to where the family is safe. Here they will worship the Father in the name of Christ, by the gift of the Holy Ghost, and know that the gospel is the great plan of happiness, of redemption...." ("The Father and the Family," *Ensign*, May 1994, 21).

Here is a modern prophecy that if Latter-day Saints will establish strong and stable marriages, the 'honest-in-heart' of the world will be attracted to the Lord's Church because of our position on marriage and family life. If divorce were eliminated among Church members, would we not dramatically stand out in today's world? 'Till death do us part,' living together as unmarried couples, 'same gender attraction couples' who demand the marriage label, shock people of goodwill who understand Biblical teachings. Imagine the impact Latter-day Saints could have on the world if those outside the Church could collectively say: "I have never met a Mormon who divorced." Or, if they could say: "I don't know how Mormons have such big families, but their kids are great. You hire one of them and they get the job done right. They are the nicest, most mannerly kids I know."

Application: What impact could we, as Latter-day Saints, have on the world if we fully lived our religion? How impressive would it be if our marriages remained intact?

JANUARY 9

Joseph F. Smith: "The lawful association of the sexes is ordained of God, not only as the sole means of race perpetuation, but for the development of the higher faculties and nobler traits of human nature, which the love-inspired companionship of man and woman alone can insure" ("Unchastity the Dominant Evil of the Age," *Improvement Era*, 1917, 739).

When a couple marries, intimacy is authorized for the two of them for the first time in their existence! What a unique way God has given married couples to enrich marriage. The Lord commands this union in His ceremony and its purpose is not simply for procreation, but is also a profound way in which marital bonds are strengthened and marriage enlivened. In this union a couple renews their commitments to each other and to the marital enterprise. This embrace allows a couple to express their love for each other and instills within their hearts a desire to excel as a husband and a wife. This union renews their unique emotional and spiritual connections. Latter-day Saints view the act of love as a powerful way to weld two souls together in an unbreakable union.

Application: Latter-day Saints are taught to be chaste, to reserve sexual intimacies for marriage. How is this relationship enriching your marriage?

JANUARY 10

Boyd K. Packer: "The ultimate end of all activity in the Church is that a man and his wife and their children can be happy at home" ("Cleanse the Inner Vessel," *Ensign*, Nov. 2010, 77.)

What are the purposes of scripture study, family prayer, family home evening, Young Men/Young Women programs, Seminary, Institute, and serving missions, etc.? They help individuals develop spiritually, mentally, physically, and socially so that at an appropriate time they can attract a mate, consummate a marriage, and begin a family. Following their marriage, Church service and callings, activities, and programs strengthen marriages. Wise parents hold family home evenings to help their children develop social skills and character traits by participating in lesson preparation and presentation, leading music/songs/hymns, and acquiring scriptural knowledge. Wise parents use Church programs to assist them in their primary responsibility to rear spiritually mature adults.

Application: What can parents do specifically to prepare their children to be active Church members, to serve missions, and to marry in the temple?

JANUARY 11

Gordon B. Hinckley: "I am offended by the sophistry that the only lot of the Latter-day Saint woman is to be barefoot and pregnant. It's a clever phrase, but it's false....Of course we believe in children. The Lord has told us to multiply and replenish the earth that we might have joy in our posterity, and there is no greater joy than the joy that comes of happy children in good families. But he did not designate the number, nor has the Church. That is a sacred matter left to the couple and the Lord." ("Make Marriage a

Partnership" Couples Counseled at Fireside" *Ensign*, Apr. 1984, 75-76).

How sad that we live in a day when children are not always valued or welcomed into a home. For many, abortion has become a form of birth control. There have been millions of abortions since a Supreme Court edict in 1973! But, what parents will not attest to the joy that accompanies the reception of a child regardless of whether it comes by natural birth or adoption? President Hinckley explained: "Though it was never easy to be parents, to be involved in the growth and development of a child from youth to maturity is surely one of life's grand privileges and most satisfying accomplishments" ("Cornerstones of a Happy Marriage," 6).

Application: What lessons is parenting teaching you that you did not anticipate? If not yet parents, what blessings do you appreciate now that your received from your own parents?

JANUARY 12

Harold B. Lee: "If [couples] would resolve from the moment of their marriage, that from that time forth they would resolve and do everything in their power to please each other…their home would indeed be a happy home." (*Conference Report*, Apr. 1947, 49).

At the time of marriage it is hard to imagine either spouse voicing a cross word or flashing an angry temper. However, in our mortal simulator, where we learn how to become an effective spouse, we occasionally say or do things that are offensive. A resolve to please each other is an important key to happiness. When a spouse manifests genuine love and care, the companion feels obligated to respond in kind. Healthy and happy marriages develop as each one keeps the other in mind throughout the day. Sharing positive verbal and non-verbal messages greatly enriches marriages. Positive expressions of love and appreciation are freely given in the lives of happily married couples.

Application: Explain how positive comments from your companion motivate you to want to be a better companion?

JANUARY 13

Spencer W. Kimball: "One comes to realize very soon after marriage that the spouse has weaknesses not previously revealed or discovered....The habits of the years now show themselves; the spouse may be stingy or prodigal, lazy or industrious, devout or irreligious; he may be kind and cooperative or petulant and cross, demanding or giving, egotistical or self-effacing" ("Oneness in Marriage," *Ensign*, Mar. 1977, 3).

A good friend said: "A major cause of marital unhappiness is the unwillingness and/or inability of one partner in a marriage relationship to behave in the manner that is expected by the spouse" (Charles Beckert). When a couple dates each other sufficiently long and then concludes to marry, a major reason that marital difficulties surface is due to one spouse being unable or unwilling to act or behave as the spouse would prefer. Every person comes into marriage with expectations about how specific marital roles *should be* enacted by the other. When the partner fails to meet a specific behavioral expectation of the spouse, a 'role discrepancy' occurs that impacts the marriage in a negative way. When roles are carried out as expected by a spouse, harmony prevails.

Application: Marital roles include spouse, kinship—in-laws, sexual, parent, therapist, housekeeping, provider, recreation, and religious. Which of these roles do you appreciate most about your spouse because he or she is meeting your expectations?

JANUARY 14

"By divine design, fathers are to preside over their families in love and righteousness and are responsible to provide the necessities of life and the protection of their families" ("The Family: A Proclamation to the World, Ensign," *Ensign*, November 1995, 102).

The Lord has wisely balanced priesthood authority for men with motherhood for women. Mothers greatly influence children in their formative years. Dad has the divine mandate to preside—not rule— over his family by virtue of a divine commission to insure that his family is involved in righteous undertakings. Fathers give blessings, call families together for worship, scripture study, family prayer, and family councils. When fathers preside in righteousness and kindness, wives and children are thankful that he is their family patriarch.

Application: As a wife, what do you appreciate most about your husband as a father? If no children yet, what attributes are important if fathers are to be good dads?

JANUARY 15

"Fathers and mothers are obligated to help one another as equal partners" ("The Family: A Proclamation to the World," *Ensign*, November 1995, 102).

'Equal partners' means that both companions have an equal responsibility to contribute to the success of the family enterprise. A couple has equal responsibility in rearing healthy, stable children who learn important lessons in the home such as money management, care of personal property, maintaining the family premises, and to foster each child's spiritual, mental, social, and physical welfare. Mothers and fathers have equal responsibility to rear children who function well at home and away from home. Each child is in need of loving parents at all stages and ages of his or her youth. Parents are wise to counsel together about each child's progress at home, at school, and in the community. When both spouses take parenting responsibilities seriously, children are more likely to adopt the values and character traits of their parents.

Application: In what ways do you function as equal partners? Actually, we can't be equal because we possess different talents and skills, so what does it mean to be equal partners?

JANUARY 16

Spencer W. Kimball: "If it is unnatural, you just don't do it. That is all, and all the family life should be kept clean and worthy and on a very high plane. There are some people who have said that behind the bedroom doors anything goes. That is not true and the Lord would not condone it" (*Teachings of Spencer W. Kimball*, 312).

There are individuals who assert that whatever sexual behavior a married couple chooses in the privacy of their own bedroom must be 'acceptable' to the Lord because they are married. President Kimball refutes that idea and indicates that there are sexual practices and aberrations that are inappropriate in a marriage relationship. He states emphatically that the Lord would not approve of such practices. Marriage is a relationship that requires a tender and kind sensitivity for the feelings of a spouse. We would not want to do anything that would offend our sweetheart in this sacred and cherished relationship.

Application: What does President Kimball mean by 'it is not true' that 'anything goes' in the bedroom? What sexual conduct in the bedroom might be inappropriate?

JANUARY 17

Joseph Smith: "Except a man and his wife enter into an everlasting covenant and be married for eternity, while in this probation, by the power and authority of the Holy Priesthood, they will cease to increase when they die; that is, they will not have any children after the resurrection" *(Teachings of the Prophet Joseph Smith, 300-301).*

Latter-day Saints are unique among Christian churches in the belief that families can be together forever. The Prophet taught the doctrine of everlasting marriage and received sealing keys to perform marriage ordinances from Elijah, in the Kirtland Temple, April 3, 1836. This priesthood key allows the binding or sealing of a couple together forever. Jesus Christ provided a resurrection whereby each person retains gender and the ability to generate life. It would be a major tragedy to come to earth, obtain a body of element, marry, establish a family, spend mortality 'wasting and wearing out our lives' only to find out at death that we revert back to our previous single spirit state. What a waste that would be! Thanks be to God for restoring the doctrine of eternal marriage (see D&C 131:1-4).

Application: Read 2 Nephi 9:8-13. Jacob reasons (vss. 8-9) that without a Savior, there would be no resurrection. Reverting back to a spirit existence as a single individual would be similar to the curse Satan received; thus Jacob's statement that we would become 'angels to a devil.' In what ways does the concept of eternal marriage affect the way you treat each other?

JANUARY 18

Bruce R. McConkie: "If righteous men have power through the gospel and its crowning ordinance of celestial marriage to become kings and priests to rule in exaltation forever, it follows that the women by their side (without whom they cannot attain exaltation) will be queens, and priestesses. (Rev. 1:6; 5:10). Exaltation grows out of the eternal union of a man and his wife. Of those whose marriage endures in eternity, the Lord says, 'Then shall they be gods.' (D&C 132:20); that is, each of them, the man and the woman, will be a god. As such they will rule over their dominions forever" (*Mormon Doctrine*, 613).

Similar to other ordinances, we enter marriage covenants in a simple, dignified way, without pomp or ceremony. That fact should not mask the grand and eternal nature of what these ordinances signify. We need to see beyond the routine and mundane aspects of life and realize that our marriage represents a coming together of two future god-like individuals. Wives will one day qualify as a 'god' as will husbands. Exaltation is unattainable alone. The highest of glories is inhabited by righteous husbands and wives who have honored their covenants.

Application: What are the functions of a king and a queen in a kingdom? Of a priest and a priestess?

JANUARY 19

Spencer W. Kimball: ". . . lasting happiness is possible and marriage can be more an exultant ecstasy than the human mind can conceive. This is within the reach of every couple, every person. "Soul mates" are fiction and an illusion; and while every young man and young woman will seek with all diligence and prayerfulness to find a mate with whom life can be most compatible and beautiful, yet it is certain that *almost* any good man and any good woman can have happiness and a successful marriage if both are willing to pay the price" ("Oneness in Marriage, *Ensign*, March 1977, 4; italics added).

When a righteous man meets and dates a righteous woman and they marry, a new unit of the Church is organized. It is then their responsibility, as husband and wife, to become soul mates even though they did not make that choice in the premortal realm. As they share their very souls with each other, as they establish home as a place where they apply gospel principles in their daily living, where they attend religious services, worship in temples, and enjoy the intimate closeness of marriage, they become soul mates, eternal sweethearts.

Application: In what ways are you two turning into soul mates? How would you describe 'exultant ecstasy?'

JANUARY 20

First Presidency and Quorum of Twelve Apostles: "Successful marriages and families are established and maintained on principles of faith...." ("The Family: A Proclamation to the World," *Ensign*, Nov. 1995, 102).

"Marriage requires faith—-faith in oneself, faith in one's marriage partner, and faith in the Lord." (James E. Faust, "Challenges Facing the Family," Worldwide Leadership Training, Jan. 10, 2004, 1). We normally think of faith as pertaining solely to the Lord Jesus Christ. But, consider the importance of having faith in each other, in a spouse who desires similar spiritual and material goals as you. How difficult would it be to have faith in an inactive spouse or non-LDS spouse, or in one not pulling their share of the marital load, who was uninterested in spiritual matters or whose employment was more important than family time? Faith in each other as eternal companions is an important element in truly happy marriages.

Application: How do you exercise faith in each other? In your potential as eternal companions?

JANUARY 21

First Presidency and Quorum of Twelve Apostles: "Successful marriages and families are established and maintained on principles of...prayer" ("The Family: A Proclamation to the World," *Ensign*, Nov. 1995, 102).

There are typically three prayers offered in our homes: individual, couple, and family. Individual prayer is evidence of a personal testimony that God lives. Couple prayer offers couples an opportunity to kneel together to express gratitude and seek inspiration and counsel from Heavenly Father. As a husband listens to his sweetheart's divine pleas he not only is thankful for his companion, but he learns of her worries and concerns in which he may play a role in resolving. Couple prayer is a morning and evening experience wherein a couple calls down blessings from of heaven on their family. Such prayer provides assurance that both seek similar goals. Family prayer is an opportunity for children to learn to address and petition their Father in Heaven. Surely the old adage is true: 'The couple that prays together stays together.' And can it be said: The family that prays together builds a tradition that blesses the next generation.

Application: Evaluate your prayers together. What time of day are they offered? Any suggestions on improving prayers at home?

JANUARY 22

First Presidency and Quorum of Twelve Apostles: "Successful marriages and families are established and maintained on principles of...repentance." ("The Family: A Proclamation to the World," *Ensign*, Nov. 1995, 102).

We generally think of repentance as involving a church authority and the Atonement of Jesus Christ. Actually, in marriage, most repentance involves a simple "I'm sorry." "I can/will do better." When a person apologizes for an inappropriate action or lack of sensitivity, the charitable spouse, sensing it is a genuine apology, does not 'rub salt in the wound,' but is gracious and accepts the apology without an accompanying sermon. When repentance is sincere and a spouse extends forgiveness, healing takes place. It is the selfish, the proud, who cannot bring themselves to apologize, to reconcile and make things right. Such individuals are unwilling to admit fault. Sincere repentance is the healing balm of marriage.

Application: Do you find it easy to apologize with each other? Can you recall a time when either of you actually apologized to the other for an offense?

JANUARY 23

First Presidency and Quorum of Twelve Apostles: Successful marriages and families are established and maintained on principles of...forgiveness" ("The Family: A Proclamation to the World," *Ensign*, Nov. 1995, 102).

If couples were more forgiving of each other there would be far fewer unhappy marriages and fewer divorces. When a spouse seeks forgiveness, hopefully the offended spouse extends forgiveness for 'to forgive is divine.' Repentance is the more difficult side of the repentance/forgiveness equation and when a spouse makes genuine restitution or clears an offense, it is incumbent on the offended spouse to forgive. A variety of abuses may require more than a simple apology. For example, physical, emotional, drug, alcohol abuses, and certainly the sin of adultery may require more than an apology. However, in most cases, a simple, sincere apology leads to forgiveness. As to how often, the Lord's answer to Peter's query concerning forgiveness: 'Until seventy times seven.'

Application: Do you find that forgiveness comes easily and naturally to both of you? Does either one of you hold grudges?

JANUARY 24

First Presidency and Quorum of Twelve Apostles: "Successful marriages and families are established and maintained on principles of…respect" ("The Family: A Proclamation to the World," *Ensign*, Nov. 1995, 102).

Respect is an essential ingredient for a healthy marriage. Often we see men who think that because they hold the priesthood, family members ought to salute every morning for the privilege to live under their roof! However, husband and wife are 'equal partners' which means that as you carry out marital roles, neither of you is more important or superior. Husbands are wise to exchange information concerning the day's events. A wife who spends the day with children is anxious to hear of her husband's day. Where the wife works out of the home, he needs to catch up on the events of her day. Remember that you married your therapist and that requires you to listen and learn. Respect is obviously a regard for each other's ideas and opinions. Where one spouse dominates or smothers a spouse, that marriage suffers.

Application: In what ways would you say you show respect for each other?

JANUARY 25

Bruce R. McConkie: "A child is an adult spirit in a newly born body. . . [We] lived and dwelt with him for ages and eons before [our] mortal birth. [We] are adults before birth; [we] are adults at death ("The Salvation of Little Children," *Ensign*, Apr., 1977, 3).

What an exciting idea! We were adult spirits when the Council in Heaven was held. We were capable of making important decisions as to whether to sustain Jehovah or accept Lucifer's crazy proposal. We waited a long time to come to the earth to obtain a physical body which then allows us to marry and become parents ourselves.

Children who die before reaching adulthood have to grow their physical body to its adult stature after resurrection which requires parents again to rear them. Thus worthy parents that lost a child will be allowed to rear their child to its adult stature after the Millennium commences. We have been children twice in our existence: (1) as a spirit child of heavenly parents; and (2) as a child born to mortal parents.

Application: Discuss the responsibility of being parents with the privilege of rearing the spirit children of Heavenly Parents!

JANUARY 26

First Presidency and Quorum of Twelve Apostles: "Successful marriages and families are established and maintained on principles of...compassion" ("The Family: A Proclamation to the World," *Ensign*, November 1995, 102).

Compassion is a 'sympathetic consciousness of another's distress with a desire to alleviate it' (Internet Dictionary.) You married your therapist. As you observe each other and evaluate various stressors in your lives, commit to being an active therapist. A husband who comes in the door and senses that his wife has had a rough day with her responsibilities, who then pitches in to help with home and children, blesses both wife and children. A wife who is quick to apply therapy to a stressed spouse is a blessing to her husband. Couples sensitive to each other's stress levels admit to greater satisfaction in marriage. This union is such an intimate companionship and demands your best mutual therapy. A husband understands compassion best when he observes his wife give him the greatest gift of all, fatherhood.

Application: Share a time when either of you showed compassion to the other one and how much it was appreciated.

JANUARY 27

First Presidency and Quorum of Twelve Apostles: "Successful marriages and families are established and maintained on principles of…work" ("The Family: A Proclamation to the World," *Ensign*, Nov. 1995, 102).

Every couple experiences financial pressures. Bills must be paid, mortgage payments come monthly, the careless use of credit or debit cards can result in serious debt, children require orthodontics; expenses are a normal part of life. Work is how we acquire money to meet our obligations. Acquiring a work ethic at home is an important blessing for young men and women before they serve missions, marry, and come to grips with the need to labor. Children need to learn at home to do 'hard things.' The payoff comes in later successes in schooling, employment, and marriage. Some jobs have little flexibility; some have more room for advancement. Unfortunately, the cost of living often requires (not always—we'd like mom to be home with the little ones) dual careers in today's world. A strong work ethic is essential regardless of whether one works in or out of the home.

Application: How did you acquire a work ethic? In what ways are you helping your children develop a work ethic in your children's character?

JANUARY 28

First Presidency and Quorum of Twelve Apostles: "Successful marriages and families are established and maintained on principles of…wholesome recreational activities" ("The Family: A Proclamation to the World," *Ensign*, Nov. 1995, 102).

"The family that plays together stays together." Dating is not just for use in spouse-hunting. Perhaps dating *after* marriage is even more important than before marriage, for both spouses require frequent breaks from their daily routines. No wonder counsel is given by Church leaders for couples to set aside a weekly 'date night' to enrich the romantic component of marriage and to maintain a healthy friendship. The counsel to 'marry your best friend' holds true and escaping together for a brief diversion is a healthy outlet for any marriage. Couples enrich their companionships through a variety of activities: Exercising, attending plays, concerts, movies, and visiting neighbors or extended family members.

Application: When was your last date? Your last 'mini-honeymoon?' Incidentally, getting away from children benefits them as well. Alternate responsibilities for planning Friday dates.

JANUARY 29

First Presidency and Quorum of Twelve Apostles: "Husband and wife have a solemn responsibility to love and care for each other and for their children" ("The Family: A Proclamation to the World, *Ensign*," Nov. 1995, 102).

The covenant of marriage obligates a husband and wife to serve one another and their children. A husband's first obligation to his wife is her emotional and physical needs. A wise husband learns of her interests and dreams and events and activities that contribute to her happiness/frustrations. The same holds true for wives. The Lord said: 'Therefore, shall a man leave father and mother and cleave unto his wife.' The same commandment pertains to a woman leaving her parents and joining her husband in an equal partnership. Though the command to have children adds responsibility for both, parenting is a source of happiness as well. Our highest priorities: first, marriage, second, children.

Application: How do your show 'love and care' for each other in your marriage? How do your children know that you care about them? How do you stay in touch—email? Phone? Texting?

JANUARY 30

First Presidency and Quorum of Twelve Apostles: "Parents have a sacred duty to rear their children in love and righteousness, to provide for their physical and spiritual needs, to teach them to love and serve one another, to observe the commandments of God and to be law-aiding citizens wherever they live" ("The Family: A Proclamation to the World," *Ensign*, Nov. 1995, 102).

To rear children as a partnership is probably the wish of every wife. Often one spouse gets distracted from the important individuals waiting for them at home. Though each spouse contributes personal strengths to each child, both genders are essential if children are to develop normal, healthy personalities. Children with fathers who openly express their love for them will find little need to act out as teens in testing parental and moral standards. Children with mothers who sacrifice on their behalf are anxious not to disappoint their mothers. As parents portray a solid, stable marriage to their children, such youngsters are more apt to adopt the values of the parents. Loving marriage partners, by setting a wholesome example of marriage for their children, give their offspring the best of all gifts.

Application: Discuss the strengths and weaknesses of each of your children; consider ways to assist each one to develop attributes you both consider important.

JANUARY 31

"When [President Ezra Taft Benson] was asked to an important dinner by a Cabinet officer, [he] said, 'Sorry, I have a date with my daughter Bonnie.' The date was a father-daughter party and scavenger hunt at the Mormon Church. After a supper, at which each girl served her father, everybody joined the scavenger hunt. The first father-daughter team to come back with the stipulated 'treasure' won the evening's prize. Residents of the area around the church were rather startled that night to answer their doorbells and find the broad-shouldered Secretary of Agriculture and a 14-year-old girl asking for such things as a green toothpick, an old shoelace, a 1952 calendar, and last September's issue of a news magazine. The Benson team was so fleet, however, that it won first prize: a chest filled with 'dollars' (chocolate candy). 'He was happier about this,' said a fellow church member, 'than an invitation to the White House.'" (Roul Tunley. "Everybody Picks on Benson," *American Magazine*, June 1954, 108).

When fathers make it clear that they love their daughters and strive to build a close relationship with them, it becomes easy for young women to believe in Heavenly Father.

Application: Dad, take time this week for a 'daddy-daughter' date: Ice cream, a swing on the swings, visit her favorite store, etc. Inform her she can purchase anything up to $_____. If no children yet, list some ideas of what good things your fathers did.

FEBRUARY

FEBRUARY 1

3 Nephi 18:21 "Pray in your families unto the Father, always in my name, that your wives and your children may be blessed"

Family prayer is an essential element of strong family relationships. Sometimes mornings are rushed; perhaps evenings are hectic. However, if you set a regular time for morning and evening prayer (perhaps dinner time if there are evening activities) children will make an effort to be there when they see it is important to you. What could be more valuable than for parents to gather their little ones to petition heaven for blessings needed that day? As children hear your pleas in behalf of others, they gain compassion and concern for others. Then when they are old enough to offer prayer themselves, you'll find them imitating you. A friend said that while he was serving his mission he pictured his family gathered for prayer morning and night and he could 'hear' their pleadings in his behalf. That scene inspired him in his labors.

Application: Are you having individual, companion, and family prayer? If not, please consider ways to include all three in your schedule.

FEBRUARY 2

Carlfred Broderick: "I have encountered good marriages that retained their vitality despite an unsatisfactory sexual life and bad marriages that survived mostly because of a terrific physical relationship; but both are uncommon. For the most part, the quality of the marriage is reflected in the quality of the sexual relationship" (*Couples*, (New York: Simon & Schuster, 1979, 138).

Marital intimacy plays an important role in marriage. This union is a profound expression by which we enrich our relationship and remind ourselves that we are one, that we are united by covenants, and that we will be loyal and true sweethearts. Through this coupling we add to our family by creating physical bodies for choice spirit sons and daughters of God. The quality of intimacy in marriage is a fairly reliable barometer/indicator of the quality of the relationship. Happily married couples enjoy this new-to-mortality-experience while unhappily married couples find this relationship problematic. Who wants to share their very soul with a spouse who is insensitive, critical, grumpy, ornery, and shows little appreciation for our efforts?

Application: Make intimate times a special part of marriage. The Lord designed this marital 'sacrament' as an expression of your love for each other. Apply at your leisure!

FEBRUARY 3

Heber J. Grant: "If there is any one thing that will bring peace and contentment into the human…family, it is to live within our means. And if there is any one thing that is grinding and discouraging and disheartening, it is to have debts…that one cannot meet." (*Teachings of Presidents of the Church*, 122).

Spending resources is a daily activity and amounts to a continual reminder of our financial situation and obligations. When collection agencies call or when payments are late or when there is little money for regular expenses, couples often turn on each other with criticism. Successful money management requires sufficient income, a savings plan, and agreement on expenditures. One of you must take responsibility to pay bills and keep good records. Both of you must understand budget provisions and abide by the part for which you are responsible. A payroll deduction directed to savings is a simple way to save inasmuch as we typically spend all of our take home pay.

Application: Who pays the bills? Is there a good record kept for tax purposes? Both should understand the money management system—do you?.

FEBRUARY 4

Robert D. Hales: "An eternal bond doesn't just happen as a result of sealing covenants we make in the temple…. To receive the blessings of the sealing that our Heavenly Father has given to us, we have to keep the commandments and conduct ourselves in such a way *that our families will want to live with us in the eternities* ("The Eternal Family," *Ensign*, Nov. 1996, 65; emphasis added).

Who would want to live in mortality, much less in eternity, with criticism and negativity? Many couples labor under the false assumption that a temple sealing is all that is needed to guarantee exaltation. Elder Hales explodes that myth and explains that we must actually *like each other* if we expect to qualify for an eternal companionship! Is it reasonable to assume that if you don't like each other in this life that in rejoining each other in the spirit world you two will be madly in love? How silly! Now is the time to create strong marital bonds if we want to spend eternity together.

Application: In which temple were you married? Can you recall what covenants you entered on that occasion?

FEBRUARY 5

First Presidency, 1916: ". . . we are to understand that only resurrected and glorified beings can become parents of spirit offspring. Only such exalted souls have reached maturity in the appointed course of eternal life; and the spirits born to them in the eternal worlds will pass in due sequence through the several stages or estates by which the glorified parents have attained exaltation" (*Messages of the First Presidency*, 5:34).

As the spirit children of heavenly parents, we are now passing through a mortal *apprenticeship* in marriage and family relations. Men come to learn how to be effective husbands and fathers. Women come to learn the ins and outs of being a wife and mother. These are callings we may carry into eternity. These are the same offices our exalted parents once passed through in their own mortal sojourn many light years ago! Marriage and parenting is what the faithful do after this life. For this reason, the Lord explained to Moses that His most important work was "to bring to pass the immortality and eternal life" of His children (Moses 1:39). Eternal life—exaltation—is the ultimate goal of faithful Latter-day Saints.

Application: What is the origin of spirit bodies? How are they created?

FEBRUARY 6

Ezra Taft Benson: *"If you are married, avoid being alone with members of the opposite sex whenever possible.* Many of the tragedies of immorality begin when a man and woman are alone in the office or at church or driving in a car. At first there may be no intent or even thought of sin. But the circumstances provide a fertile seedbed for temptation. One thing leads to another, and very quickly tragedy may result. It is so much easier to avoid such circumstances from the start so that temptation gets no chance for nourishment" ("The Law of Chastity," *Devotional and Fireside Speeches of the Year, 1987-88*, 53).

In a world where suggestive and outright displays of immorality are practically daily fare, it may be difficult to avoid immoral pictures and ideas but we do have control over our thoughts. In some situations we can exercise control (not driving in a car alone with a member of the opposite sex) while other situations may be more difficult to control—colleagues at work. President Benson refers to areas under our control. In some cases, in situations out of our control, we mitigate circumstances by leaving an office door open or inviting a third person to a lunch appointment.

Application: Discuss your work environments. Are they situations that invite morality?

FEBRUARY 7

Bruce R. McConkie: "We have the power to perform a marriage and we can do it so that the man and the woman become husband and wife here and now and—if they keep the covenant there and then made—they will remain husband and wife in the spirit world…." ("Celestial Marriage," Brigham Young University 1977 Devotional Speeches of the Year, 172).

Sometimes Latter-day Saints think they have to wait until the resurrection to be reunited as husband and wife. Elder McConkie teaches the principle that after death, we continue as husband and wife in the spirit world. Though the likelihood of us dying on the same day is unlikely, as soon as we pass from this life we are back to our marital state. Though spirits are unable to create children until the resurrection, with "all spirit" being matter (D&C 131:7), husbands and wives continue their intimate, physical relationship inasmuch as spirits can touch and embrace.

Application: Explore Elder McConkie's teaching that faithful couples continue married after death. What work will you do together in the spirit world after death?

FEBRUARY 8

Boyd K. Packer: "The adversary is jealous toward all who have the power to beget life. *He cannot beget life; he is impotent.* He and those who followed him were cast out [of heaven] and forfeited the right to a mortal body" ("Our Moral Environment," *Ensign*, May 1992, 66, emphasis added).

Little wonder that Satan seeks the destruction of marriages and families inasmuch as he is denied ever becoming a husband or father. He is determined to prevent us from succeeding where he has failed. He continues to thwart the work of God. His influence is evident movies, books, television programs and Internet sites where marriage is often mocked and belittled. Immorality, affairs, and sexual themes are rampant in media productions. However, covenants empower Latter-day Saints to avoid the effect of filth and sleaze. Alma reminds us that adultery is the most serious of all sins after the sin against the Holy Ghost and murder.

Application: Discuss why Satan's attempts are to destroy you, your marriage, and your family. Read Alma 39:5. Of the three, to which sin are mortals most susceptible?

FEBRUARY 9

Spencer W. Kimball: "If we live in such a way that the considerations of eternity press upon us, we will make better decisions…." ("The Things of Eternity—Stand We in Jeopardy?" *Ensign*, Jan. 1977:3).

Latter-day Saints understand a different plan of salvation compared to other Christians. For example, the concept of a premortal life is no longer taught in the Christian tradition and the post-mortal spirit existence too has disappeared. President Kimball continued: "The more clearly we see eternity, the more obvious it becomes that the Lord's work in which we are engaged is one vast and grand work with striking similarities on each side of the veil" (*ibid.*) If our perspective is limited to this world only, if marriage and family life were only possible in this brief mortal span, Latter-day Saints, of all people, would be most miserable. If we were to lose in death all that we gain as companions and children in this life, the Father's plan would be a terrible joke played on mortals.

Application: Share a favorite scripture on the doctrine of a premortal life. Read D&C 138 individually and share your insights on President Joseph F. Smith's vision.

FEBRUARY 10

Ezra Taft Benson: ". . .Avoid flirtations of any kind....Avoid being alone with members of the opposite sex whenever possible. ("The Law of Chastity," *BYU 1987-1988 Devotional and Fireside Speeches;* Provo, Utah: Brigham Young University, 52).

A great urban movement has been the separation of husbands and wives during the day. We no longer spend our hours working on farms. Husbands mingle with attractive singles and married women at work, while women work or associate with single and married men. Temple covenants remind us of promises we made in sacred places that protect and empower us to avoid falling into temptation's trap. One reason we honor the law of chastity is because of the misery and unhappiness we see to those who violate this divine mandate. The Lord commanded: "Thou shalt love thy wife with all thy heart, and shalt cleave unto her and none else" (D&C 42:22). The same holds true for wives. A devastating tragedy has to do with couples who break solemn vows and thereby destroy marital trust.

Application: Remind yourselves of your allegiance to one another. Read D&C 42:22-24.

FEBRUARY 11

Dallin H. Oaks: "How many children should a couple have? All they can care for! Of course, to care for children means more than simply giving them life. Children must be loved, nurtured, taught, fed, clothed, housed, and well started in their capacities to be good parents themselves" ("The Great Plan of Happiness," Nov. 1993 *Ensign*, 75).

The Psalmist wrote: "Children are an heritage of the Lord:…Happy is the man that hath his quiver full of them" (Psalms 127:3, 5). Latter-day Saints anticipate being parents from their youth. Sadly, we live in an age when policies in a few nations only allow for one or two children per family. Too, many modern couples intentionally opt to remain childless. In the Lord's plan, couples bring God's spirit children to the earth for a mortal probation. Parents rear these children on behalf of God. He has already been resurrected and is not able to become a mortal again to parent us. We act in His stead as a parent to His children. How sobering is that challenge?

Application: As you look over your children, do you have any thoughts as to why the Lord assigned them to you? What goals would you like to see them achieve?

FEBRUARY 12

Spencer W. Kimball: "We have heard of men who have said to their wives, "I hold the priesthood and you've got to do what I say." Such a man should be tried for his membership. Certainly he should not be honored in his priesthood. We rule in love and understanding." (*Teachings of Spencer W. Kimball,* 316).

Ever since Eve partook of the prohibited fruit, it seems, men in many cultures used that as an excuse to subject and even abuse women. However, the gospel of Jesus Christ portrays women in the highest light as handmaidens of the Lord. In bringing forth life, they imitate the sacrifice of the Savior through the pain they suffer and the blood they shed to bring forth mortal life. Any husband who mistreats his wife offends the Spirit of the Lord. Righteous husbands realize they married a choice daughter of God, and he is to use his priesthood to bless her and their children.

Application: As a husband, ask your wife how she feels about your leadership in the home. Ask her for one (just one) suggestion that she thinks might be helpful in your role.

FEBRUARY 13

Gordon B. Hinckley: "Let that talk [between husbands and wives] be quiet, for quiet talk is the language of love. It is the language of peace. It is the language of God." (*Teachings Gordon B. Hinckley,* Deseret Book Company, *1997, 324).*

It is easy in marriage, with time, to become so comfortable with each other that we become careless in the way we treat each other. It is important to never allow conversations to reach the point where there is yelling, screaming, or throwing things. You can't imagine heavenly parents speaking evil to or of one another can you? Marriage is our time to respect, to be loyal, and to appreciate each other's contribution to marriage. In mortality we apprentice in a variety of marital roles in an effort to be competent and worthy of the Celestial Kingdom. Only righteous individuals who treat each other with the utmost respect and love will qualify for that level of salvation.

Application: Review your patterns of conversation. Are they filled with the 'language of love?' Share your thoughts on the quality of your conversations.

FEBRUARY 14

Valentines Day! First Presidency and Quorum of Twelve Apostles: "Successful marriages and families are established and maintained on principles of...love" ("The Family: A Proclamation to the World," *Ensign*, Nov. 1995, 102).

Love encompasses romantic as well as an emotional attachment between sweethearts. As married life unfolds, couples deal with a myriad of issues that include finances, shopping, parenting, church callings, extended families, and activities that provide experiences that greatly deepen emotional feelings. Love is expressed in physical, emotional, spiritual, and intellectual ways. Love comes from feeling accepted and appreciated and expands through an intertwining of heart and mind. Love inspires each spouse to try to be a better partner. Men and women may equate love with sex, or with gifts, or through recognition, or by compliments. However you define love, when it does not exist, marriages functions poorly. Love is never static.

Application: Philosophers have tried to define 'love.' Do you have a definition? How would rate your love for each other on a scale of one to ten, and explain your choice.

FEBRUARY 15

Jeffrey R. Holland: "Temper tantrums are not cute even in children; they are despicable in adults, especially adults who are supposed to love each other ("How Do I Love Thee," *Brigham Young University 1999-2000 Speeches,* 161).

Anger is a great destroyer of marriage and family relations! Tempers probably reduce marital happiness more than any other cause. Joseph Smith revised Ephesians 4.26 to read: "Can ye be angry, and not sin?" Anger is a tool of the adversary, and when we express anger, the Spirit of the Lord is lost. The Savior told the Nephites: "He that hath the spirit of contention is not of me, but is of the devil, who is the father of contention, and he stirreth up the hearts of men to contend with anger, one with another" (3 Nephi 11:29). Sometimes tempers pass to the next generation by poor modeling. If temper or anger has been 'inherited,' be a 'transitional character,' one who prevents negative patterns from moving on to the next generation.

Application: How would you describe your temperament? What have you learned about the relationship between temper, anger, and marital happiness?

FEBRUARY 16

David O. McKay: "Promise each other, sincerely and solemnly, never to keep a secret from each other [after marriage], under whatever pretext, and whatever excuse it might be. You must continually, as a married couple, see clearly into each other's bosom" (*Gospel Ideals,* 472).

We marry expecting to share our very heart and soul with each other. Marital trust develops as spouses find it comfortable to exchange personal ideas, thoughts, and feelings with each other. Personal information conveyed by a spouse in confidence and then later shared with others, violates marital trust. Being able to trust each other is an important element of marital happiness, an essential ingredient that enriches and strengthens marital bonds. On the other hand, for a spouse to withhold information or fail to express praise and appreciation undermines marriage.

Application: What is trust? What part does it play in your marriage? Are there topics or subjects that you hesitate to bring to the other's attention for fear of reprisal or punishment?

FEBRUARY 17

Gordon B. Hinckley: "Why do we have this proclamation on the family now? Because the family is under attack. All across the world families are falling apart. The place to begin to improve society is in the home....We are trying to make the world better by making the family stronger" (Tokyo Press Conference, 18 May 1996).

With a for-this-life-only perspective on marriage, no wonder people feel free to come and go, or to remain childless, or to live together without being married. Why bother and go to the expense of children when it can be avoided? Modern birth control methods prevent pregnancy. For the most part, antibiotics cure sexually transmitted diseases; so, why not live together when preventing conception or curing an STD which reduces the responsibility that comes with marriage and children? Couples substitute dogs, cats, and other animals for children. Without the expense that children bring they are free to buy bigger homes, accumulate more luxuries, travel more, and purchase expensive automobiles. Divorce is not necessary; one just moves out if things become uncomfortable.

Application: Read the Proclamation on the Family and compare its principles with the current state of marriage and family practices (see *Ensign*, Nov. 1995, 102).

FEBRUARY 18

Ezra Taft Benson: "No one steps into immortality in an instant. The first seeds of immorality are always sown in the mind. When we allow our thoughts to linger on lewd or immoral things, the first step on the road to immorality has been taken. I especially warn you that often the first step on their road to transgression began with pornographic materials" ("The Law of Chastity," 1987-88 *Devotional and Fireside Speeches of the Year,* 53).

In a world where suggestiveness and outright displays of immorality confront us daily, it may be difficult to avoid suggestive messages. However, we can control our thoughts. In situations where we have control—we do not drive in a car alone with a member of the opposite sex, for example. Other situations may be more difficult to control—trips with a boss or co-worker. President Benson's advice comes from years of experience with people who were careless in their relationships with others which led to broken covenants and divorce. It is important that we be wise in our associations with those of the opposite sex. We want to be friendly, but circumspect.

Application: Are you aware of any tragedy or immoral behavior at your work place or neighborhood? Remind each other of your mutual commitments.

FEBRUARY 19

Robert D. Hales: "The doctrine of the family begins with heavenly parents. Our highest aspiration is to be like them. The Apostle Paul taught that God is the father of our spirits" (see Hebrews 12:9). ("The Eternal Family," *Ensign*, Nov. 1996, 64).

We learned from the Prophet Joseph Smith of our premortal life where we were the literal offspring of heavenly parents. Like all parents, they wanted us to move out of the house in order to learn universal truths in an environment where good and evil can exist, where we could practice our use of agency. This mortal school prepares us for an endless life with other righteous people who learned to 'choose the right.' As the literal offspring of heavenly parents, we have a divine heritage, and in this life we imitate the same model used by heavenly parents. An eternal perspective gives us a long-term view of our potential as sweethearts.

Application: Discuss the differences between being a mortal spouse and parent compared to being an immortal spouse and parent.

FEBRUARY 20

Melvin J. Ballard: "The nature of the offspring is determined by the nature of the substance that flows in the veins of the being. When blood flows in the veins of the being [parent], the offspring will be what blood produces, which is tangible flesh and bone [and blood], but when that which flows in the veins is spirit matter [a resurrected being] a substance more refined and pure and glorious than blood, the offspring of such beings will be "spirit children." (Melvin J. Ballard, *Three Degrees of Glory*, talk Sep. 22, 1922, Ogden Tabernacle. Pamphlet, Deseret Book, 10).

This statement in simple terms explains the origin and nature of spirit bodies. Mortal parents create mortal children because of their blood. Glorified, exalted parents, create 'spirit' children because their immortal bodies are activated by spirit. We refer to children in the premortal life as spirit children only because we have forgotten the nature of spirit matter and the nature of our existence in that pre-earthly sphere.

Application: Read the Savior's visit with the Brother of Jared (Ether 3:6-17). What was the nature of the Savior's body before His birth to Mary. What body did Jesus have when he created the earth?

FEBRUARY 21

First Presidency: "We are to understand that only resurrected and glorified beings can become parents of spirit offspring...and these spirits born to them in the eternal worlds will, in due sequence, pass through the several stages or estates by which the glorified parents have attained exaltation" (30 June 1916, James R. Clark, *Messages of the First Presidency*, 5:34).

Mortal spouses possess blood bodies that they inherit from their earthly parents. When resurrected, however, blood is replaced by spirit element so that resurrected parents create spirit offspring. Yet the Prophet Joseph taught that spirit is matter (D&C 131:7-8). We learn the nature of a spirit body from the account of Jehovah talking with the brother of Jared in Ether 3. Jehovah appeared to this man as an adult male spirit two millennia before His birth to Mary in Bethlehem. From this account we reason that we too were adult spirits before this life and must have been so for a long period of time prior to the Council in Heaven. The reasoning is that we had to be mature adult males and females to make this responsible decision. The premortal Jehovah, as an adult male spirit, visited the brother of Jared. It is from this account that we learn more of our nature in the premortal realm.

Application: Consider your ultimate destiny as a faithful couple. D&C 88:20 indicates that the Celestial Kingdom will be this earth. As a couple we will not go back to live with our Heavenly Parents —what parents want that arrangement!? But surely we will go back to their home for occasional visits!

FEBRUARY 22

Bruce R. McConkie: "I believe that the most important single thing that any Latter-day Saint ever does in this world is to marry the right person, in the right place, by the right authority; and that then—when they have been so sealed by the power and authority that Elijah the prophet restored—the most important remaining thing that any Latter-day Saint can ever do is to so live that the terms and conditions of the covenant thus made will be binding and efficacious now and forever" ("Agency or Inspiration?" *New Era*, January 1975, 38).

Little wonder prophets stress the importance of temple marriages. Perhaps the biggest challenge of being single is to find the 'right' person. But you two have now done that. When you married in the temple, you accomplished two of the three things Elder McConkie mentioned. For Latter-day Saints to marry outside of the temple, to accept a secular wedding in place of one with eternal promises, indicates a lack of understanding Church doctrine. Converts must wait a year before an endowment and sealing. To know that in the House of the Lord we solemnize marriage by priesthood authority, is the greatest blessing available to Church members today.

Application: As a single male and a single female in the premortal life, how long did you have to wait to finally come to earth, find each other, and be sealed forever?

FEBRUARY 23

Ezra Taft Benson: "I recognize that most people fall into sexual sin in a misguided attempt to fulfill basic human needs. We all have a need to feel loved and worthwhile. We all seek to have joy and happiness in our lives. Knowing this, Satan often lures people into immorality by playing on their basic needs. He promises pleasure, happiness, and fulfillment" ("The Law of Chastity," *Brigham Young University 1987-88 Devotional and Fireside Speeches, 52)*.

In this day and age it is becoming more and more difficult to rear a generation untouched by sexual transgression. It will not be until we marry, however, that the command will be given us to participate in this sacred venture. Then we are authorized to 'multiply and replenish' the earth. Until then, we have no right to use our masculine and feminine attributes in anything that resembles sexual relations. It is in this union that we express our deeply held feelings of love and adoration—our oneness—with each other. Sadly we live at a time when immoral behavior is seen as more and more acceptable and Latter-day Saint youth must avoid temptations that confront them at earlier and earlier ages.

Application: Now that you *are* authorized to be intimate, are your expressions satisfactory? Give each other one (only one) suggestion to make this relationship even better.

FEBRUARY 24

Heber C. Kimball: "The Spirit that is on me this morning is the Spirit of the Lord; it is the Holy Ghost, although some of you may not think that the Holy Ghost is ever cheerful. Well, let me tell you, the Holy Ghost is a man; he is one of the sons of our Father and our God; and he is that [spirit] man that stood next to Jesus Christ, just as I stand by brother Brigham" (*Journal of Discourses* 5:179).

Though we use various titles for the Holy Ghost such as Holy Spirit, the Lord's Spirit, Holy Ghost, His Spirit, Thy Spirit, Holy Spirit of Promise, etc., it is helpful to know that the Holy Ghost is a spirit son of God with an important role in the Godhead. We have a heavenly Monitor to help us live righteously throughout our mortal lives. We may believe that no one is aware of our actions when it appears that no human being is present (such as pornography). But the Holy Ghost is aware of our behavior. As mortals we are unable to see spirits, but He sees and knows what we do. Our actions are never hidden to Him. At baptism, the age of accountability, we receive this heavenly gift to be with us at all times. We are therefore never really alone.

Application: Share with each other inspiration or an experience where you felt the Holy Ghost assisted you or influenced you—perhaps even in choosing each other.

FEBRUARY 25

D&C 132:17 "For these angels did not abide my law (of marriage); therefore, they cannot be enlarged, but remain separately and singly without exaltation, in their saved condition, to all eternity; and from henceforth are not gods, but are angels of God forever and ever."

Latter-day scriptures are clear on the requirements for exaltation/ eternal life. To live among the gods in eternity means that we must become like them. We must develop the same character traits— Christ-like traits—as they did. How could we live in the presence of Moses, Enoch, President McKay, President Hinckley, Alma, Mormon, for example, if we have not developed celestial attributes. Mortality is when we develop the very traits that qualify us for exaltation, and marriage is how we implement those principles. Those who cannot live the gospel fully, who cannot subscribe to the principles of eternal life, will find themselves single and alone as this scripture points out.

Application: Temple covenants provide Latter-day Saints with power to rise above telestial and terrestrial levels of behavior. Read D&C 132:14-19, where three examples of marriage are presented— two secular, and the one in which you participated.

FEBRUARY 26

Gordon B. Hinckley: "If you have a temper, now is the time to learn to control it. The more you do so while you are young, the more easily it will happen. Let no member of this Church ever lose control of himself in such an unnecessary and vicious manner. Let him bring to his marriage words of peace and composure" ("Living Worthy of the Girl You Will Someday Marry," *Ensign*, May 1998, 50).

Most people have a dozen rationalizations for why it is appropriate to be angry or mad in a particular situation. This attitude obstructs the path to self-improvement. Assume that it is never okay to express anger, and work towards that goal. Is there anything more corrosive to family happiness and solidarity than to live with someone who is temperamental and frequently displays bouts of anger? A Latter-day Saint husband or wife is 'out of order' if such 'unnecessary and vicious' behavior takes place in the home.

Application: Reflect on your individual temperament. What do you do to insure that temper and anger are not part of your character traits?

FEBRUARY 27

Joseph Fielding Smith, Jr.: "Some will gain celestial bodies with all the powers of exaltation and eternal increase....In the (lower) kingdoms there will be changes in the[ir] bodies and limitations. They *will not have the power of increase, neither the power or nature* to live as husbands and wives, for this *will be denied them and they cannot increase. . .* Some of the functions in the celestial body will not appear in the terrestrial body, neither in the telestial body, and *the power of procreation will be removed.*" (Joseph Fielding Smith, *Doctrines of Salvation*, 2, 287-288).

Can you imagine losing the power to create life in the resurrected state when you married and experienced the power of procreation as a pair of mortals? President Smith says that there will be changes in the bodies of those who receive an inheritance less than the highest of glories. What does he mean to lose the 'power and nature' to live as a married couple? After years of marriage, what would be your feelings if you were permanently separated at death? How would you feel if mortality was the only time in your existence you were capable of marriage and parenthood and you did not live in such a way as to be able to continue your marriage after this life? No wonder the scriptures mention that we would rather have the rocks and hills fall upon us if we fail to live true to our covenants.

Application: Discuss what limitations exist in those who attain a lesser degree of glory. Express your love for each other and commit to live in such a way as to inherit the full blessings to which you are already heirs of as the children of Abraham.

FEBRUARY 28

Orson Pratt: "God...has ordained that the highest order and class of beings that should exist in the eternal worlds should exist in the capacity of husbands and wives, and they alone should have the privilege of propagating their species. Now it is wise no doubt, in the Great Creator to thus limit this great and heavenly principle to those who have arrived or come to the highest state of exaltation. Consequently, He does not entrust this privilege of multiplying spirits with the terrestrial or telestial, or the lower order of beings there, nor with angels. But why not? Because they have not proved themselves worthy of this great privilege" *(Journal of Discourses, 13:186).*

Elder Pratt gives a clear explanation as to why those who do not develop a celestial character will not continue married in the life to come. How scary to think that for many people, the only time in their existence they will be able to marry and possess the power to create life will be during this brief period of mortality! What a disappointment it would be to learn that because of the way they lived and treated each other they forfeited the right to be together again. This doctrine is an important reason why we are a missionary church! The message of the possibility of eternal life, should be sufficient incentive for Latter-day Saints to share the gospel with those unaware of this doctrine.

Application: Why do you think those of a telestial or terrestrial nature are not prepared for an eternal relationship?

FEBRUARY 29 (LEAP YEAR)

Thomas S. Monson: "My wife, Frances, and I have been married 53 years. Our marriage took place in the Salt Lake Temple. He who performed the ceremony, Benjamin Bowring, counseled us: 'May I offer you newlyweds a formula which will ensure that any disagreement you may have will last no longer than one day? Every night kneel by the side of your bed. One night, Brother Monson, you offer the prayer, aloud, on bended knee. The next night you, Sister Monson, offer the prayer, aloud, on bended knee. I can then assure you that any misunderstanding that develops during the day will vanish as you pray. You simply can't pray together and retain any but the best of feelings toward one another'" ("Hallmarks of a Happy Home," *Ensign*, Oct. 2001, 4).

While in the wilderness, the Israelites murmured against Moses and the Lord. The penalty came in the form of fiery serpents that bit many of them and a number of them died. In repenting, they asked Moses what to do and the Lord told Moses to place a 'brazen serpent' up on a pole. For their lives to be spared, all they had to do was to look at the brazen serpent fastened to the pole. Such a simple thing saved their temporal lives. Likewise, a 'simple thing' to save marriages is to pray together night and morning.

Application: Read the Biblical account in Numbers 21:5-9; see also Helaman 8:14-15. Why is couple prayer important to any couple's marriage?

MARCH

MARCH 1

Neil L. Andersen: "The bearing of children can also be a heartbreaking subject for righteous couples who marry and find that they are unable to have the children they so anxiously anticipated or for a husband and wife who plan on having a large family but are blessed with a smaller family" ("Children," *Ensign*, Nov. 2011, 30).

How sad it is for couples in the Church to learn that biologically they will be childless. What couple does not anticipate having their own children? Great strides are being made in the area of fertility research, so there is always hope. There are also priesthood miracles. There are couples who would like more children than they are able to have. Children are an important part of the Latter-day Saint concept of family. Adoption is a viable option through Family Services.

Application: Read President Boyd K. Packer's address "And a Little Child Shall Lead Them," *Ensign*, May 2012. Access online through *lds.org*).

MARCH 2

Boyd K. Packer: "The ultimate end of all activity in the Church is to see a husband and his wife and their children happy at home, protected by the principles and laws of the gospel, sealed safely in the covenants of the everlasting priesthood. Husbands and wives should understand that their first calling—from which they will never be released—is to one another and then to their children" ("And a Little Child Shall Lead Them," *Ensign*, May 2012, 5).

Over the years President Packer has addressed the "ultimate end of all activity in the Church." Church leaders and our doctrine sustains the family unit. Marriage is how we organize a family and as we add children, we move from a dyad to a triad, to a quad, etc. To be happy at home, protected by temple ordinances, and living the principles of the Restoration, allow us to reach our highest goals as couples.

Application: How does the Church 'sustain' you as a married couple?

MARCH 3

Dallin H. Oaks: "The kind of marriage required for exaltation— eternal in duration and godlike in quality—does not contemplate divorce. In the temples of the Lord, couples are married for all eternity" ("Divorce," *Ensign*, May, 2007, 70).

President Gordon B. Hinckley: ". . . among the greatest of tragedies, and I think the most common, is divorce. It has become as a great scourge" ("What God Hath Joined Together," *Ensign*, May 1991, 72). Speaking of divorce, President Spencer W. Kimball said: "The divorce itself does not constitute the entire evil, but the very acceptance of divorce as a cure is also a serious sin of this generation" ("Marriage and Divorce," *1976 Devotional Speeches of the Year,"* BYU University Press, Young House, 7 Sep. 1976, 144-145). How could a couple that once loved each other so much that they wanted to marry in the House of the Lord, turn on each other to such an extent as to want to split up? Of course it does take two people to make a great marriage; one can certainly ruin it. But wo to the person responsible for breaking marriage covenants through sins such as adultery, spouse abuse, apostasy, or a variety of addictions. There are justifiable reasons to break up a marriage, but you do not want to be the one responsible. Divorce should be extremely rare among Latter-day Saints.

Application: Discuss your feelings about divorce. Perhaps you have close family members who have done so. What has been the impact of divorce on couples you know?

MARCH 4

Joseph Fielding Smith, Jr.: "If all mankind would live in strict obedience to the gospel, and *in that love which is begotten by the Spirit of the Lord*, all marriages would be eternal, divorce would be unknown. Divorce is not part of the gospel plan and has been introduced because of the hardness of heart and unbelief of the people....There never could be a divorce in this Church if the husband and wife were keeping the commandments of God" (*Selections from Doctrines of Salvation, Sermons and Writings of Joseph Fielding Smith,* The Church of Jesus Christ of Latter-day Saints, 2001, 181-82).

Does this statement ring true? The gospel should equip a couple to not only remain in love after they marry, their love should mature and grow stronger as they conquer life's challenges. Do couples who are living the gospel ever divorce? Is that possible? Do you think that a couple kneeling in prayer morning and night, calling down the powers of heaven on their marriage and family, ever divorce? It is righteous living, applying gospel principles in our lives, and honoring temple covenants, that marriages have the best chance of success.

Application: What are you doing to 'divorce-proof' your marriage? List four or five things.

MARCH 5

Elder Parley P. Pratt: "It was from Joseph that I learned that the wife of my bosom might be secured to me for time and all eternity; and that the refined sympathies and affections which endeared us to each other emanated from the fountain of divine eternal love. . .and grow and increase in the same to all eternity" (*Autobiography*, 3rd Ed. 297-98).

Joseph Smith restored to the earth the doctrine of eternal marriage. Latter-day Saints remain the only Christian religion or world religion teaching this doctrine. Jesus Christ made it possible for a couple to live together because of the resurrection. If we were to live forever as a male and female, and we were united by a priesthood key that seals us together, why wouldn't it be possible? Couples scaled in a temple ceremony are promised to come forth in the next resurrection with spirit and physical bodies united forever. What more important concept could God have restored through the latter-day Prophet than the doctrine of eternal marriage?

Application: When did you first learn that an eternal marriage was possible? What was the name of the sealer who performed your sealing? What was his counsel to you?

MARCH 6

"O, the comfort—-the inexpressible comfort of feeling safe with a person, having neither to weigh thoughts nor measure words—but pouring them all right out just as they are, chaff and grain together certain that a faithful hand will take and sift them—-keep what is worth keeping, and with the breath of kindness, blow the rest away" *(Dinah M. M. Craik, "Friendship," reprinted in Between Friends (USA: Hallmark).*

One of the important blessings of marriage is the privilege to come to know another person so well that we begin to think alike; we can read each other's hearts and intentions. Emotional intimacy—feelings of love developed as couples communicate their deepest positive thoughts and feelings—is built through acts of friendship. Marriage is strengthened through verbal and nonverbal exchanges. Happily married couples find therapy in friendship, and trust develops as they learn to confide in each other. Sharing genuine thoughts and feelings without ridicule, without negative responses, is how trust is built. Intimate levels of conversation are elements of marital satisfaction. For either spouse to remain aloof or to maintain an air of superiority or to consider themself the more intelligent of the two, displays a controlling or dominating personality. One who disrespects a spouse's ideas as being juvenile, is setting up conditions for a disaster.

Application: To what extent can you comfortably risk personal ideas, thoughts, and feelings freely with each other?

MARCH 7

Spencer W. Kimball: ". . . many of the social restraints which in the past have helped to reinforce and to shore up the family are dissolving and disappearing. The time will come when only those who believe deeply and actively in the family will be able to preserve their families in the midst of the gathering evil around us." ("Families Can Be Eternal," *Ensign*, Nov. 1980:4).

What social restraints have disappeared in recent decades? Could it be the ease in which divorce is available? Or, could it be the number of same-gender advocates clamoring for the marriage label. Other illustrations include individuals avoiding marriage or living together without marriage, a cultural phenomenon that is increasing numerically. President Kimball predicts that conditions in our society will not improve without a return to righteousness. He cautions Latter-day Saints that they "should not be taken in by the specious arguments that the family unit is somehow tied to a particular phase of development a mortal society is going through. . . We know that when things go wrong in the family, things go wrong in every other institution in society" (*ibid.*).

Application: List other social restraints you think have dissolved or disappeared since you left school.

MARCH 8

Gordon B. Hinckley: "The girl who marries you will not wish to be married to a tightwad. Neither will she wish to be married to a spendthrift. She is entitled to know all about family finances. She will be your partner. Unless there is full and complete understanding between you and your wife on these matters, there likely will come misunderstandings and suspicions that will cause trouble that can lead to greater problems" ("Living Worthy of the Girl You Will Someday Marry," *Ensign*, May 1998, 50).

Family counselors agree that finances are a major factor in divorce. Sometimes one partner is excessively tight with money while the other one sinks the relationship through over spending and debt accumulation. Spending can be addictive psychologically as evidenced by the number of shopaholics! Sometimes money can be used as a weapon in petty marital disputes.

Application: Evaluate your present financial practices. Are you carrying balances on any credit cards? Loans? Are you in agreement as to spending limits?

MARCH 9

Boyd K. Packer: "When we speak plainly of divorce, abuse, gender identity, contraception, abortion, parental neglect, we are thought by some to be way out of touch or to be uncaring. Some ask if we know how many we hurt when we speak plainly. Do we know of marriages in trouble, of the many who remain single, of single-parent families, of couples unable to have children, of parents with wayward children, or of those confused about gender? Do we know? Do we care?...Because we *do* know and because we *do* care, we must teach the rules of happiness without dilution, apology, or avoidance. That is our calling" ("The Father and the Family," *Ensign*, May 1994, 20).

When individuals choose to behave contrary to the revelations of God, they suffer the consequences. This is not a sufficient reason for apostles and prophets to be silent or to avoid teaching what God would have us know and do. If we are to be called by the title of 'saints,' Church members must live righteous and pure lives to be worthy of that designation.

Application: What responsibility do prophets and Apostles have to teach the saints true doctrines? What if they fail to teach us what God would have us know? Read D&C 112:30-34. We have an opportunity to hear from our Church leaders every six months, at least, in General Conference. Agree to read one talk per day from the most recent conference addresses.

MARCH 10

D&C 131:7-8 "There is no such thing as immaterial matter. All spirit is matter, but it is more fine or pure, and can only be discerned by purer eyes; we cannot see it but when our bodies are purified we shall see that it is all matter."

Latter-day Saints understand that two kinds of matter exist in the universe—spirit and element. Spirit matter is assumed by many to be intangible, vaporous, ethereal, ghost-like, or non-material. Joseph Smith refuted that position and revealed that the permanent, immortal part of us, our spirit identity, is a spirit body created by immortal parents. Our mortal body was created by earthly parents through physical generation. This present body dies and returns to dust, to earthy material. Elsewhere our spirit was born as an infant spirit and grew to its adult stature as we learn from the account of Jehovah and the brother of Jared in Ether, chapter 3. In time, a council was held whereby adult spirits were given the opportunity to come to the earth and obtain another body, one of physical element. These two bodies allow us to marry and generate physical bodies for other spirit brothers and sisters. This combination of bodies constitutes the 'soul' of man.

Application: Review the nature of a spirit body from Ether 3:16-17. Read D&C 88:14-16 to see the Lord's definition of the soul.

MARCH 11

Brigham Young: "When people are married, instead of trying to get rid of each other, reflect that you have made your choice, and strive to honor and keep it, do not manifest that you have acted unwisely and say that you have made a bad choice, nor let anybody know that you think you have. You made your choice, stick to it, and strive to comfort and assist each other" (*Deseret News*, 29 May 1861, 98). Also Gordon B. Hinckley, "Great Shall Be the Peace of Thy Children," *Ensign*, Nov. 2000, 53).

What a wonderful adventure we experience as we grow up in our flesh bodies. They mature to the point where we begin to date and look for someone with whom we can build a lasting friendship that culminates in marriage. Temple worship instructs us on our identity and prepares us to be sealed together by one holding divine authority! How sad and disappointing it must be to Heavenly Father when His children marry, only to see them decide to divorce. That is not His plan and it is not what we came to earth to do. Little wonder that Church leaders plead with us to be fiercely loyal to each other, and to abide by our temple covenants. There are termites in this secular world that are determined to undermine our happiness.

Application: Marriage tests our very souls. Living with one of a different gender and family background challenges every couple. What tests have you two faced so far and passed?

MARCH 12

Ezra Taft Benson: "The world worships the learning of man. They trust in the arm of flesh (see D&C 1:19). To them, men's reasoning is greater than God's revelations. The precepts of man have gone so far in subverting our educational system that in many cases a higher degree today, in the so-called social sciences, can be tantamount to a major investment in error! Very few men build firmly enough on the rock of revelation to go through this kind of indoctrination and come out untainted." (*The Teachings of Ezra Taft Benson*, 319).

We live in a secular environment, a world that is becoming less and less religious, and a world that has little or no understanding of any divine plan for them. For this reason Joseph Smith was called to restore true doctrines which are the important elements of the plan for all of God's children. Latter-day Saints are encouraged to pursue education in order to earn income and provide a decent standard of living for that is the world in which we live. However, in our educational pursuits, we must not be overwhelmed by the philosophies of men. Jacob gave us this maxim: "To be learned is good," he said, and then added this caveat: "If they hearken unto the counsels of God" (Jacob 2:29). The counsels of God come to us officially twice a year in the April and October General Conferences and are published in the monthly *Ensign* magazine or are available on-line at *lds.org*.

Application: Subscribe to the *Ensign*. Why do you think the Church builds seminary and institute facilities next to practically all high schools and colleges?

MARCH 13

Neal A. Maxwell: "Do not expect the world's solutions to the world's problems to be very effective. Such solutions often resemble what C. S. Lewis wrote about — those who go dashing back and forth with fire extinguishers in times of flood. Only the gospel is constantly relevant, and the substitute things won't work." ("Remember How Merciful the Lord Hath Been," *Ensign*, May 2004, 45; Screwtape Letters, 1959, 117-18).

Joseph Smith restored doctrines and principles lost during the 'great apostasy.' Through the Restoration we were given divine counsel that provides solutions that are unknown in the secular world. We have to be educated if we are to sustain ourselves financially. But true doctrine is not taught in our public schools, and that is as it should be. If it were taught there, whose doctrines would it be? We learn secular information in schools and gospel principles at home and in the Church on the Sabbath. Our nation honors the principle of separation of church and state.

Application: Why is a secular education essential? Contrast secular teachings on marriage and family, for example, with gospel principles.

MARCH 14

James E. Faust: "Divorce can be justified only in the most rare of circumstances, because it often tears people's lives apart and shears family happiness. Frequently in a divorce the parties lose much more than they gain. The traumatic experience one goes through in divorce seems little understood and not well enough appreciated; and certainly there needs to be much more sympathy and understanding for those who have experienced this great tragedy and whose lives cannot be reversed....In my experience there is another reason which seems not so obvious but which precedes and laces through all of the others. It is the lack of a constant enrichment in marriage. It is an absence of that something extra which makes it precious, special, and wonderful, when it is also drudgery, difficult, and dull" ("The Enriching of Marriage," *Ensign*, Nov. 1977, 9-10).

Surely you have seen the effect of having the novelty of something wear off, perhaps a toy or even a used car. The honeymoon can last a lifetime or it can be shortened if we are not genuinely striving to become Christlike in our character. You've heard the phrase, "life's too short." Well, your new maxim should be: 'Married life is too short to _____ (fill in the blank).' We have a relatively tiny amount of time in this life to work out the kinks in marriage as we prepare for a glorious life together in eternity. Don't waste mortality in petty, prideful actions.

Application: Most individuals are creative daters. Recall the fun and joy of anticipating your partner's response when you sprung a little surprise? Spring one today/this week!

MARCH 15

Boyd K. Packer: "To suffer some anxiety, some depression, some disappointment, even some failure is normal. Teach our members that if they have a good, miserable day once in a while, or several in a row, to stand steady and face them. Things will straighten out. There is great purpose in our struggle in life" ("Solving Emotional Problems in the Lord's Own Way," *Ensign*, May 1978, 91).

Mortality teaches us lessons that we are not sure we want to learn! We see the damage that comes to individuals who choose unwisely. We see the blessings that come to those who choose to live righteously. The Father said that it was His plan to "bring to pass the immortality and eternal life of man" (Moses 1:39). The Atonement compensates for the negative effects we all experience because of the Fall of Adam and Eve. We must not let challenges that come to us in the form of anxiety, depression, disappointment and occasional failure throw us off course permanently. Actually these disappointments minister to our education and prepare us for eternity. As children of God, we can surmount any trial if our faith is placed in the Lord Jesus Christ and we live the principles of life and salvation.

Application: Life is certainly not without its problems and challenges. Marriage requires personal sacrifices and efforts that the 'natural man' does not want to make. Share a challenge you faced that turned out to strengthen you physically and/or spiritually.

MARCH 16

Harold B. Lee: "Teach those who are having problems to go to the father of the ward, their bishop, for counsel. No psychiatrist in the world, no marriage counselor, can give to those *who are faithful members of the Church* the counsel from one any better than the bishop of the ward. Now, you bishops don't hesitate to say marriage is the law of God, and is ordained by him and man and wife are not without each other in the Lord, as the apostle Paul declared" ("President Lee's Priesthood Address," *Ensign*, January 1974, 99).

In each unit of the Church, the Lord provides a bishop or branch president who is ordained, set apart, and blessed with the gifts of the Spirit. Bishops go directly to the heart of marital problems by asking couples such simple questions as: "Are you praying individually and as a couple?" "Are you attending the temple?" "Do you read scriptures and other good literature?" "Do you pay your tithing?" "Are you holding family home evening?" Marital problems are generally spiritual in nature because mistreating each other results in the loss of the Spirit of the Lord. Without that divine influence they lose humility and have difficulty resolving issues. Bishops help people repent and return to treating each other as do happily married couples—living gospel principles. Except where mental health issues such as schizophrenia, depression, drug or pornography addictions persist, a bishop is a married couple's best friend and the first line of defense when outside assistance is needed. Bishops refer couples with mental health issues to professional counselors.

Application: What advantages does a bishop having in assisting Latter-day Saint couples with marital problems? In what situations would couples require outside assistance?

MARCH 17

Boyd K. Packer: "Some worry endlessly over missions that were missed, or marriages that did not turn out, or babies that did not arrive, or children that seem lost, or dreams unfulfilled, or because age limits what they can do. I do not think it pleases the Lord when we worry because we think we never do enough or that what we do is never good enough. "Some needlessly carry a heavy burden...." ("The Least of These," *Ensign*, Nov. 2004, 87).

Despite prophets announcing the need for young men to serve missions, only one-third to one-half actually serve full-time missions. Yet, with the world 'ripening in iniquity' as it is, every young man who is mentally and physically qualified to serve, is needed if we are to change the direction of the larger culture. However, when a mission is missed, or a divorce was necessary, or a baby comes as a stillborn, or any number of events take place, righteous living and the Atonement of Jesus Christ compensates for missed opportunities or misfortunes. Here President Packer recommends that individuals in these situations stop obsessing about them. The past is now history, and it is time to stop the personal emotional beatings and move on with life. The Atonement compensates for immature and unwise decisions, and humility with the resolve to learn from past mistakes, can compensate for lost opportunities.

Application: Discuss how the Atonement and humility can compensate for poor decisions and choices?

MARCH 18

Spencer W. Kimball: "The marriage that is based upon selfishness is almost certain to fail....If one is forever seeking the interests, comforts, and happiness of the other, the love found in courtship and cemented in marriage will grow into mighty proportions. Many couples permit their marriages to become stale and their love to grow cold like old bread or worn-out jokes or cold gravy ("Oneness in Marriage," *Ensign*, March 1977, 4-5).

We often think of the Nephites whose downfall was attributable to selfishness and pride. But what did they have to create proud hearts? Was it a necklace from the Zarahemla factory? A new burlap dress? A new spoke on their chariot wheel? Had the Book of Mormon people possessed automobiles, airplanes, watches, GPSs, computers, toilets, toilet paper, washers, dryers, and pianos, would technology have made them more righteous? Or, do you think they would they have fallen apart more quickly? President Kimball identifies selfishness as the primary cause of divorce.

Application: In what way does selfishness destroy marriages? What is the best antidote to selfishness?

MARCH 19

Ezra Taft Benson: "Pride....is manifest in so many ways, such as faultfinding, gossiping, backbiting, murmuring, living beyond our means, envying, coveting, withholding gratitude and praise that might lift another, and being unforgiving and jealous. . . Another face of pride is contention. Arguments, fights, unrighteous dominion, generation gaps, divorces, spouse abuse, riots, and disturbances all fall into this category of pride." ("Beware of Pride," *Ensign*, May 1989, 5).

President Benson details the serious consequences of pride in the lives of individuals, couples, and nations. He suggests that divorce is a casualty of pride. We all are guilty of prideful behavior at times. President Benson points out the damage that comes through pride in our lives. Does pride always have to be negative? President Dieter Uchtdorf reviewed President Benson's address and suggested ways in which pride can be positive.

Application: Read President Dieter F. Uchtdorf's address: "Pride and the Priesthood," *Ensign*, Nov 2010, 55–58 or access it online at *lds.org*).

MARCH 20

Ezra Taft Benson: "The family has serious problems. Divorce is epidemic. The incidence of delinquency is on the rise. The answer is not more marriage counselors or social workers. The answer lies in a husband and wife taking their marriage covenant seriously, realizing that they both have a responsibility to make their marriage a happy one ("The Ten Commandments," *New Era* 8 [July 1978]: 38; *The Teachings of Ezra Taft Benson*, 532-533).

How sad to live at a time when marriage is mocked by some, when it is portrayed as something far less than what God intended. Is there a movie where a couple meets, marries, and lives happily with their children? That would be unusual! Scriptwriters think there has to be an affair with a neighbor, a co-worker, or a murder to keep viewer interest. If the couple *is* married, it has to be a comedy with the husband such a klutz that everyone in the family is embarrassed. In real life, Latter-day Saint couples who take marriage covenants with God seriously and keep their promises to each other, find marriage their real joy in life.

Application: How does taking covenants seriously strengthen marriage? Next time you participate in marriage or family sealings in the temple, review the covenants you entered.

MARCH 21

Ezra Taft Benson: "We have some divorces in the Church, entirely too many, especially of those who have been married in the temple. I interview some of these couples who are having these problems and I find, almost without exception, they have not been living the gospel. They haven't had family prayer. They haven't had family home evening. They haven't been going to sacrament meeting and Sunday School with their families together. They haven't been living the gospel" (*The Teachings of Ezra Taft Benson*, 340.)

It is clear to bishops and LDS counselors that couples struggling in marriage are simply not living gospel principles. They are not praying as a couple, they are not attending the temple or reading scriptures and other Church literature individually or as a couple. In other words, they are not doing the simple things that bring or maintain the Spirit of the Lord in their relationship. Inasmuch as marriage is the crowning ordinance of the Father's plan, nothing is more tragic than to see couples break their union and possibly jeopardize eternal blessings through the spiritual injuries that come from divorce. Divorce destabilizes the social order.

Application: List several activities that help you retain the Spirit of the Lord in your marriage.

MARCH 22

Gordon B. Hinckley: "Why all of these broken homes? What happens to marriages that begin with sincere love and a desire to be loyal and faithful and true one to another? There is no simple answer. I acknowledge that. But it appears to me that there are some obvious reasons that account for a very high percentage of these problems. I say this out of experience in dealing with such tragedies. I find *selfishness* to be the root cause of most [marital problems]" ("What God Hath Joined Together," *Ensign*, May 1991, 74).

Have you been to a wedding ceremony or reception where the couple looked so happy that you were sure that you were witnessing a great love affair in the making? What *does* happen to couples who begin so promisingly only to later come to the point where they are no longer 'in love?' It is especially troubling when a couple that marries in the temple concludes, sometimes within the first year or two, that they 'made a mistake,' and divorce. President Hinckley explains that the real problem that leads to broken homes are typically matters of selfishness. Each spouse must do all he or she can to safeguard marriage, and the best deterrent to divorce appears to be in avoiding selfishness.

Application: Have you been surprised by any couples you know that divorced—much to your surprise? What is your explanation for their decision?

MARCH 23

Gordon B. Hinckley: "There may be now and again a legitimate cause for divorce. I am not one to say that it is never justified. But I say without hesitation that this plague among us, which seems to be growing everywhere, is not of God, but rather is the work of the adversary of righteousness and peace and truth" ("What God Hath Joined Together," *Ensign*, May 1991, 74).

Divorce devastates families and does untold damage to children who are often shifted back and forth between still feuding parents. No wonder President Hinckley calls divorce a plague that grips the land. It does not appear that these tragic statistics will be reversed anytime soon. Because of the magnitude of divorce and its negative impact on individuals, many couples in our culture are opting to live together without the commitment or responsibilities that come with a 'real' marriage. Perhaps they think that by their choices, they will avoid any hurt or pain that accompanies divorce. However, this is not a marriage. Our missionaries spend time working to convince couples to marry before they can become members.

Application: What would you say are legitimate reasons to divorce?

MARCH 24

Mosiah 5:2 "Yea, we believe all the words which thou hast spoken unto us; and also, we know of their surety and truth, because of the Spirit of the Lord Omnipotent, which has wrought a mighty change in us, or in our hearts, that we have no more disposition to do evil, but to do good continually."

This statement by King Benjamin correlates with President Boyd K. Packer's statement that "true doctrine, understood, changes behavior quicker than will the study of behavior change behavior" ("Do Not Fear," *Ensign*, May 2004, 73). Here the Nephite assembly acknowledges that the doctrines King Benjamin taught them—the coming Messiah's life, death, and atonement—were true. These teachings wrought a 'mighty change' in their hearts and eliminated any 'disposition to do evil.' As the Nephites came to understand the doctrines King Benjamin taught them, their behavior changed to conform to their new beliefs.

Application: Are you married to a spouse who has 'no more disposition to do evil' but only wants to 'do good continually'? Could divorce come to a couple with such attributes?

MARCH 25

JST Ephesians 4:6 "Can ye be angry, and not sin? Let not the sun go down upon your wrath."

Joseph Smith, under inspiration, revised this New Testament verse to teach the principle that anger is sin! This is especially true in marriage where two covenant sweethearts have made eternal commitments. However, we live in a world where anger is thought by many to be a normal reaction to life's frustrations. Some believe in the need for an occasional venting just to 'clear the air.' Such a philosophy is silly. For two temple-married people to spout angry words at each other is un-Christlike behavior. Anger simply destroys marriages and families. Can you imagine heavenly parents using anger with each other? How nonsensical to even contemplate. Little wonder the Lord wanted this verse changed to align with celestial principles. Couples have many topics to discuss together, but rancor is inexcusable.

Application: Discuss temperament in your family background. What is your experience with people who displayed anger as you were growing up?

MARCH 26

Spencer W. Kimball: "If you study divorces...you will find there are one, two, three, four reasons. *Generally sex is the first.* They did not get along sexually. They may not say that in the court. They may not even tell that to their attorneys, but that is the reason. Husband and wife...are authorized, in fact they are commanded to have proper sex when they are properly married for time and eternity (*The Teachings of Spencer W. Kimball*, 312).

Jeffrey R. Holland, in a devotional address, said: "Perhaps no challenge is greater for your generation. As someone recently wrote, 'It is as if America is down on all fours sniffing, and what she smells is a glandular stench.' There is too much sexual transgression in our society. There are too many exploitive movies seen and prurient videos watched and smutty magazines read. There is too much obscene language used, by men and women" ("Nailing our Colors to the Mast," *1985 BYU Speeches of the Year*, 10). Sexual relations are confined to marriage because of their intrinsic power to enrich and renew marital vows. This union is an important form of 'therapy,' for couples who deal with life—children, money issues, school, and employment. Outside of marriage, sexual relations represent a selfish misuse of another's body to gratify personal lust. Fornication and adultery are serious offenses because they involve people who are not under either a civil commitment or a gospel covenant. Such behavior is condemned by the Lord and can be a factor in the forfeiture of one's Church membership.

Application: Discuss how sexual relations strengthen your marital bonds. Discuss damages you have observed in couples that violated marital trust.

MARCH 27

Joseph Fielding Smith, Jr.: "If a man or a woman who has been sealed in the temple for time and eternity should sin and lose the right to receive the exaltation in the celestial kingdom, he or she could not retard the progress of the injured companion who had been faithful. Everyone will be judged according to his works, and there would be no justice in condemning the innocent for the sins of the guilty" (*Doctrines of Salvation*, 2:177).

A healthy, stable marriage is the result of a couple's righteous living of gospel principles. Occasionally couples seek a divorce because one partner violates the marriage covenant to such an extent that a divorce becomes necessary to preserve the spiritual and emotional climate of the home, or to protect children from further abuse.

However, the innocent one, the spouse who kept his or her covenants, will not be held accountable for the actions of a wayward spouse. In time all the blessings of the gospel will be theirs whether here or in the next life. The wickedness of one spouse cannot destroy the blessings of the innocent spouse. Blessings may be delayed, but will not be lost.

Application: Reassure each other of your desire to be loyal and true to each other and to avoid the damage that results from abuse, sins, or abandonment.

MARCH 28

Brigham Young: "There is not a person here today but what is a son or a daughter of that Being. In the spirit world their spirits were first begotten and brought forth, and they lived there with their parents for ages before they came here. . . If you do not believe it, cease to call Him Father; and when you pray, pray to some other character." (*Journal of Discourses,* 4:216).

Latter-day Saints understand their divine parentage. To know that we have a heavenly father who loves us, and who no doubt worries about us as any parent does when a child leaves home with agency and can therefore make choices contrary to the desires or counsel of the parent. We are not aware that evil existed in the premortal sphere until Satan rebelled. His punishment was to be cast out of the family to this earth where we again confront him. His punishment of being cast out is used by God to further our education by allowing him to tempt us and to thoroughly try us. In this way we learn from the consequences of good and evil choices. Mortal parents have the same goal. They want their children to leave home, but they do not want their children corrupted by evil; yet they must learn the truth that 'wickedness never was happiness," a lesson best learned outside the presence of celestial beings.

Application: As a parent, do you worry about how your children will use their agency after they leave your presence? What are you doing now to prevent any disappointment in their choices?

MARCH 29

Joseph Smith: "All your losses will be made up to you in the resurrection, provided you continue faithful. By the vision of the Almighty I have seen it" *(Teachings of the Prophet Joseph Smith,* 296).

As mortals, we lament that fact that death cheats many of longevity, of marriage, and of parenthood. Gratefully the Savior restores blessings that are lost through no fault of our own and those of which we sincerely repent. Such blessings will be restored either in this life or the next. Women who are childless will yet rear children of their own; singles will yet marry and experience parenthood. Divorcees who then keep baptism and temple covenants will yet have the opportunity to marry again and enjoy the blessings of a righteous companion. Children who die in their youth will yet be reared to adulthood by their parents during the millennial era. The Atonement compensates for a variety of mortal limitations and tragedies and though some blessings may be delayed, given time, they will not be lost.

Application: When will a couple who are childless in mortality bear their own biological children? How is divorce compensated for in the long run? Make time to read Elder McConkie's article: "The Salvation of Little Children," *Ensign,* April, 1977, 3-7; or online at *lds.org.*

MARCH 30

M. Russell Ballard: "A family can live with Him only after a man and a woman are sealed in marriage for eternity by the power of the holy priesthood ("Equality through Diversity," *Ensign*, Nov. 1993, 90).

We learn from latter-day scripture that to attain the highest degree of glory and live in the presence of other exalted beings, we must receive certain ordinances and enter into certain covenants. Individuals are baptized, confirmed, and men must receive the higher priesthood. In the temple, we experience initiatory, endowment, and sealing ordinances. In this life we develop the celestial attributes that must become part of our character as we apply the principles of the restored gospel as marriage partners. Marriage has a way of testing our very souls in order that we might learn the lessons that best prepare us to live in the highest of the glories.

Application: Priesthood is the power possessed by eternal beings. When you covenant with God, an eternal being, you know that He has the power to fulfill His promises if you do your part. What is the outcome if you covenant with another mortal?

MARCH 31

Spencer W. Kimball: "The hour has come for understanding hearts, for self-appraisal, and for good common sense, reasoning, and planning" ("Oneness in Marriage," *Ensign*, Mar. 1977, 3).

After the honeymoon and reception, couples find the realities of living together on a daily basis more complex than they anticipated during the heady days of courtship. Every married couple experiences occasional bouts of misunderstanding, differing opinions, and misinterpretations of words and/or actions— especially in a relationship as proximate as marriage. The issue is not whether couples will have differences or not, but how their love allows them to resolve difficulties quickly. Incidentally, few couples agree on everything. Each individual has preferences concerning colors, styles, tastes, food, and entertainment; preferences that don't always match those of the spouse. Too, neither of you came from the 'true family' (where everything was done correctly!). Most decisions have several viable options. As you yield to your spouse's preferences, he or she will soon reciprocate by bending to your decisions when its importance to you is evident.

Application: Differences in personality and taste add spice to marriage. Share a difference that was resolved because of an 'understanding heart" or through just plain 'common sense.'

APRIL

APRIL 1

Carlos E. Asay: "Endowed members of the Church wear the garment as a reminder of the sacred covenants they have made with the Lord and also as a protection against temptations and evil. *How it is worn is an outward expression of an inward commitment to follow the Savior"* (First Presidency Letter, 3 July 1974, as quoted in "The Temple Garment: "An Outward Expression of an Inward Commitment," *Ensign*, Aug. 1997, 22.)

The garment we wear from our temple worship serves as a reminder of covenants entered into with the Lord in His house. Elder Asay said: "I like to think of the garment as the Lord's way of letting us take part of the temple with us when we leave" (*ibid.*) As we dress each day it would be well if we stopped just long enough to remind ourselves of the specific covenants we made in sacred precincts. It is through faithful observance of covenants with Deity that we receive the blessings of the Lord. Sometimes we hear of people removing the garment, thereby placing themselves in a position where Satan is capable of tempting them—not a fair fight!

Application: Discuss how covenants protect you against the wiles of Satan? Was there an adjustment for you as you began wearing garments?

APRIL 2

Father, Consider Your Ways: "A father is the presiding authority in his family. On this earth your initial experience of being a father of a family gives you opportunities to learn to govern with love and patience, and with your wife to teach each of your children correct principles, to prepare them to become proper fathers and mothers. When you do this according to the pattern given us by the Lord, and you endure to the end, your family will be added upon eternally. A righteous family is an eternal unit" ("A Message from The Church of Jesus Christ of Latter-day Saints," by the Quorum of the Twelve Apostles, pamphlet, 1973).

It is important to have a wise balance as a father. Overly dominating fathers or absentee fathers are not the equal of a righteous *and* active father can have on his family. Fathers are to be teachers of two primary lessons: (1) gospel principles, and (2) principles of life that prepare children to live outside the home. Family life specialists are in agreement that the lack of effective fathering is one of the more serious issues that afflict modern families.

Application: Father, ask your wife and children for a little feedback on your role as a father and try out one of their ideas or suggestions.

APRIL 3

Bruce R. McConkie: "We come into the Church and a legal administrator places his hands upon our head and says, 'Receive the Holy Ghost.' This gives us the gift of the Holy Ghost, which is the right to the constant companionship of that member of the Godhead, based on faithfulness" (Agency or Inspiration? *New Era*, Jan. 1975, 39).

Perhaps the most important single key to a great marriage is to live so that each spouse enjoys the Holy Ghost as a constant influence.

Missionaries learn the value of this member of the Godhead as they pray and work together as a companionship. They learn that without the Spirit's influence they are simply going through the motions. Bishops do their best counseling when they encourage members to gain or re-gain the Spirit of the Lord in their lives so as to calmly and peaceably resolve marital issues. Retaining the Spirit comes through spiritual activities—scripture reading, couple prayer, regular temple attendance, paying tithing, etc. Such acts insure a continuance of this divine influence. Surely you have learned by now that the Spirit of the Lord is very sensitive to the way you treat each other.

Application: What activities insure the influence of the Holy Ghost in your individual lives and as a companionship? Remember that the weekly sacramental service contains a promise to always "have His Spirit to be with us."

APRIL 4

Marvin J. Ashton: "True love is a process. True love requires personal action. Love must be continuing to be real. Love takes time. Too often expediency, infatuation, stimulation, persuasion, or lust are mistaken for love. How hollow, how empty if our love is no deeper than the arousal of momentary feeling or the expression in words of what is no more lasting than the time it takes to speak them....Love of God takes time. Love of family takes time. Love of country takes time. Love of neighbor takes time. Love of companion takes time. Love in courtship takes time. Love of self takes time" ("Love Takes Time," *Ensign*, Nov. 1975, 108, 110).

What wise counsel. Today, what passes for physical attraction is labeled 'love' by many. Love is much deeper and more fulfilling than mere infatuation, and requires time and experiences together as a couple. Love can inspire the sacrifice of one's own preferences in favor of that of a spouse or child. Love is an anxious concern for the welfare of another. It is an emotion that can be stronger than death itself. Love is constant, kind, and is the highest form of charity. Couples learn to love each other at the most profound depths as they treat one another with respect due one's eternal companion.

Application: Describe the growth of your love from your first meeting, or marriage, to the present. What are the basic elements of your love for each other?

APRIL 5

Spencer W. Kimball: "While sitting here, I have made up my mind that when I go home from this conference this night there are many, many areas in my life that I can perfect. I have made a mental list of them, and I expect to go to work as soon as we get through with conference" ("Spoken from Their Hearts," *Ensign*, November 1975, 111).

Every six months we are privileged to listen to apostles and prophets in the Church's General Conference. There speakers discourse on a myriad of topics, but due to the importance of marriage and families in the plan of salvation, there are usually a number of addresses that bear on that theme. Now, as a married couple, listen carefully to instructions that strengthen you as a pair. With the number of temples being added in the Church, marriage is always going to be a major topic of instruction in these conferences.

Application: Read D&C 21:4-6. What is the obligation of Latter-day Saints to listen to and follow the living prophet? What does the word 'church' refer to in verse 4? Who is 'the church?'

APRIL 6

D&C 21:4-5 "Wherefore, meaning the church, thou shalt give heed unto all his words and commandments which he shall give unto you as he receiveth them, walking in all holiness before me; For his word ye shall receive, as if from my own mouth, in all patience and faith."

The actual Church is its membership and its organization. The Lord counsels its members to give heed to the words of the living prophet. How silly it would be to ignore his counsel and teachings. The Church was organized on this date almost two centuries ago. We hear from our prophet at least twice a year in General Conference and frequently in the *Ensign*. We receive counsel and wisdom from the Lord's anointed. President Dieter F. Uchtdorf reminded us that "Answers to your specific prayers may come directly from a particular talk or from a specific phrase. At other times answers may come in a seemingly unrelated word, phrase, or song. A heart filled with gratitude for the blessings of life and an earnest desire to hear and follow the words of counsel will prepare the way for personal revelation" ("General Conference—No Ordinary Blessing," *Ensign*, Sept. 2011, 4).

Application: As you listen to General Conference, look for themes and counsel on strengthening your marriage. Arrange your study schedule to read the May and November issues of the *Ensign* magazine or conference addresses on-line at *lds.org*.

APRIL 7

Jeffrey R. Holland: ". . . may I stress that human intimacy is reserved for a married couple because it is the ultimate symbol of total union, a totality and a union ordained and defined by God" ("Personal Purity," *Ensign*, November 1998, 76).

When we marry, we consummate marriage through sexual relations. In doing so, we share ourselves emotionally and physically in a private, intimate, and sacred way. This union is a powerful commitment and promise of complete fidelity. The command to 'multiply and replenish the earth,' authorizes this marital act only with each other—none other. This act of marriage is confined to the pair. Unfortunately we live in a world where sexual relations between unmarried people are prominently portrayed in almost every media presentation. However, such behavior has no divine approval or authority. In marriage, this relationship brings a sense of security and wholeness to each husband and wife.

Application: Rejoice as a married couple in the privilege of renewing your marriage vows—to be one, and to renew commitments to one another by this wonderful association. Discuss how intimacy was an adjustment for both of you as newlyweds?

APRIL 8

Gordon B. Hinckley: "I think the nurture and upbringing of children is more than a part-time responsibility. I recognize that some women must work, but I fear that there are far too many who do so only to get the means for a little more luxury and a few fancier toys" ("Live Up to Your Inheritance," *Ensign*, Nov. 1983, 83).

When sealed in a temple marriage, couples are promised that the spirits assigned to them will be among the best spirit children the Father is sending to the earth in this final dispensation. It is a promise associated with the blessings of Abraham. Special spirits were foreordained to come to the earth at this critical time in the world's history. Therefore church leaders past and present have stressed over and over the importance of parents rearing these special children with the greatest of care. The Proclamation mandates that father is responsible to provide financial and spiritual resources for the family, while mother has the primary responsibility to tenderly care for their little ones in early childhood by rearing them in the nurture and admonition of the Lord. Fathers must be fathers when they arrive home from the field, farm, factory, or office. Who can place a value on the worth of mothers in rearing children?

Application: The ideal of a mother at home with young children is scoffed at by many. Share your thoughts concerning the value of a mother at home versus her value in contributing to the family income. Did your parents work out of the home?

APRIL 9

Gordon B. Hinckley: "To the mothers of this Church , . . I want to say that as the years pass, you will become increasingly grateful for that which you did in molding the lives of your children in the direction of righteousness and goodness, integrity and faith. That is most likely to happen if you can spend adequate time with them ("Women of the Church," *Ensign*, Nov. 1996, 69).

As couples mature and reflect on how their children turned out, that reflection is a source of pride and joy, or it brings varying degrees of pain for parents depending on how the lives of their children turned out. As we observe couples where a child strayed or suffered a divorce, or who had difficulty finding adequate employment, or a boy who declined missionary service—regret often swells in the bosoms of these parents. It is then that sleepless nights and emotional distress can haunt parents. Spending quality time with children when they are young is important to their success and enables grandparents to enjoy their later years. It is also important for children to see their parents express love for each other, for when children see that their parents cherish one another, they are more apt to adopt the values and beliefs of their parents.

Application: How do you display your love for each other so that your children have no question as to your feelings for one another?

APRIL 10

Elder Boyd K. Packer: "To willfully destroy a marriage, either your own or that of another couple, is to offend our God. Such a thing will not be lightly considered in the judgments of the Almighty and in the eternal scheme of things will not easily be forgiven" ("Marriage," *Ensign*, May 1981, 14).

Of all the people on planet earth, you were successful in finding each other! What were the odds? You dated, married, and invited children to join you—essential steps in organizing an eternal family. These decisions carry with them a trust to safeguard covenants and procreative powers by being completely loyal to each other. Unfortunately, we live in a world where marriages are sometimes thrown aside in favor of lustful and evil practices. Divorce stalks the land. Our Father in Heaven loves His children and we honor Him when we honor our covenants. The rewards for faithful observance of and commitment to marriage principles are worth every effort on your part. The heavens rejoice over valiant sons and daughters who cherish each other and establish a companionship worthy of an eternal inheritance.

Application: Have you observed tragedies among family members or friends where loyalty and fidelity were flaunted? What were the long-term results?

APRIL 11

Marlin K. Jensen: "After I had performed the sealing ceremony and the couple had exchanged rings and embraces, I asked them to share their feelings about each other and the Lord. The new bride spoke first. Her brief remarks expressed both gratitude and emotion as she told how from her very youngest years she had desired to keep herself virtuous and had hoped to find a companion who shared her values and righteous aspirations. She confirmed the goodness of her new husband by witnessing that he was all she had hoped for and more" (A union of Love and Understanding," *Ensign*, Oct. 1994, 49).

How wonderful it is to have chastity be an important value among our youth. Today, well over half of the young people in our land have experienced sexual relations by the time they reach twenty years of age. It refreshing to know that to marry in the temple requires complete chastity on the part of both individuals prior to marriage and complete fidelity during their lives. Coming into marriage with the knowledge that you and your fiancé are clean and wholesome, as symbolized by temple clothing, you are now ready to discover the intricacies of marital intimacy.

Application: Discuss the blessings of chastity prior to and during marriage. Why was chastity an important value to you as you anticipated marriage?

APRIL 12

Harold B. Lee: "The greatest work you will ever do will be within the walls of your own home" (*Strengthening the Home*, 1973, 7).

After President David O. McKay's emphasis on "no other success in life can compensate for failure in the home," perhaps this statement by President Lee is second in familiarity. Though we may succeed in a variety of endeavors—business, church, finances, popularity, educational attainment—if our relationships at home suffer, true happiness is elusive. So what if an engineer can design a building or computer programmers can create technological marvels, if there is little joy in the reunion of husband and wife at the end of the work day, or if children go out the backdoor when one or both parents come in the front door, our priorities are skewed. When a husband and wife love each other and they love each child and that love is reciprocated within the walls of that home, success is achieved.

Application: Review work schedules. Interview your children to see if a happy family is living 'within the walls of your own home!' As a father or mother, ask a child privately what they like or don't like about your spouse as a parent and then exchange feedback.

APRIL 13

Gordon B. Hinckley: "Companionship in marriage is prone to become commonplace and even dull. I know of no more certain way to keep it on a lofty and inspiring plane than for a man occasionally to reflect upon the fact that the helpmeet who stands at his side is a daughter of God, engaged with Him in the great creative process of bringing to pass His eternal purposes. I know of no more effective way for a woman to keep ever radiant the love for her husband than for her to look for and emphasize the godly qualities that are a part of every son of our Father and that can be evoked when there is respect and admiration and encouragement. The very processes of such actions will cultivate a constantly rewarding appreciation for one another" ("Except the Lord Build the House," *Ensign*, June 1971, 71-72).

Many people in our culture have a hard time believing that a couple could live with each other for an entire lifetime. How could they stand each other for eternity?! But in a gospel perspective we look at a much longer time frame than just mortality! Elder Hinckley provides both spouses with a simple formula that will keep any marriage alive and prospering. Staying positive and being complimentary with each other is a powerful incentive to treat each other with "respect and admiration and encouragement."

Application: What do you do to keep your marriage from becoming 'dull?' Can you think of additional ways to add a little spice to your relationship? Offer one suggestion.

APRIL 14

Richard G. Scott: "Righteous love is the foundation of a successful marriage. It is the primary cause of contented, well-developed children. Who can justly measure the righteous influence of a mother's love? What enduring fruits result from the seeds of truth that a mother carefully plants and lovingly cultivates in the fertile soil of a child's trusting mind and heart? As a mother you have been given divine instincts to help you sense your child's special talents and unique capacities. With your husband you can nurture, strengthen, and cause those traits to flower" ("The Eternal Blessings of Marriage," *Ensign*, May 2011, 96).

Though women do not hold the priesthood, they are blessed as mothers with gifts and talents that equal or surpass their husbands in discernment and sensitivity. Mothers, without priesthood, have great power in influencing the rising generation through teaching, praying, loving, and care giving. What husband does not consider him blessed to have a wife who not only cares for him, but in observing her dedication to her children, falls more deeply in love with her for her service and sacrifice?

Application: Husband, in what ways have you watched your wife function as a mother in impressive ways? Help your wife understand her value to you as the mother of your children. Share one trait with her in which you see her blessing your children.

APRIL 15

Carlos E. Asay: "Don't forget that the word *garment* is used symbolically in the scriptures and gives expanded meaning to other words such as *white, clean, pure, righteous, modesty, covering, ceremonial, holy, priesthood, beautiful, perfection, salvation, undefiled, worthy, white raiment, shield, protection, spotless, blameless, armor, covenants, promises, blessings, respect, eternal* *life,* and so forth. All of these words occupy special places in the vocabularies of people sincerely essaying to become Saints" ("The Temple Garment, An Outward Expression of an Inward Commitment," *Ensign,* Aug. 1997, 22.)

The temple garment is a daily reminder of our divine nature, of our covenants, and of our desire to live as latter-day saints. "The temple garment given to Latter-day Saints . . ." Elder Asay went on to say, "is given to remind wearers of the continuing need for repentance, the need to honor binding covenants made in the house of the Lord, and the need to cherish and share virtue in our daily living so that promised blessings may be claimed" (*ibid.,* 21). This clothing reminds us of the sacred nature of our bodies and is a protection against the wiles of the Adversary.

Application: The next time you attend the temple, listen carefully for specific instructions and blessings associated with temple clothing.

APRIL 16

Spencer W. Kimball: "In true marriage there must be a union of minds as well as of hearts. Emotions must not wholly determine decisions, but the mind and the heart, strengthened by fasting and prayer and serious consideration, will give one a maximum chance of marital happiness. It brings with it sacrifice, sharing, and a demand for great selflessness" ("Oneness in Marriage," *Ensign,* Mar. 1977, 3).

In the Church we stress the importance of marriage and family relations to such an extent that perhaps it is easy for young people to believe that marriage will be an easy transition. They understand the need for a temple marriage in their heads and they conclude that all that is needed to succeed is to find a good returned missionary or an individual who grew up active in the Church. However, in every union, temple or secular, marriage has a way of testing our natures. In marriage we learn more clearly the nature of specific strengths and weaknesses that we possess. We marry one of a different gender, one from a different family background with contrary ideas on a whole host of opinions on child-rearing practices, money management, homemaking, etc. In marriage we learn to do 'hard things,' the very things that build character, and mold us into functional human beings.

Application: Looking back, how much 'heart' and how much 'mind' was involved in getting you together?

APRIL 17

Joseph Fielding Smith, Jr.: "We have no scriptural justification, however, for the belief that we had the privilege of choosing our parents and our life companions in the spirit world…Most likely we came where those in authority decided to send us. Our agency may not have been exercised to the extent of making choice of parents and posterity" (*Way to Perfection*, 44).

It is thought by many that we chose each other in the premortal realm to be companions here in the flesh. Those who have great marriages are sure of it! Those who end up in a divorce do not agree! Here Elder Smith suggests that we most likely did not make that decision in the premortal realm. However, as our love for each other grows, it does seem as though we knew each other before. No doubt we lived a very long time as adult spirits before our 'turn on earth,' and as members of the House of Israel we must have known each other there or at least had an acquaintance. Elder Smith likens our coming to the earth to a mission call; we are sent where we are needed and most likely a choice of a companion or parents was not open to us.

Application: Have you considered the possibility that you knew each other in the premortal life? What are your feelings and thoughts concerning President Smith's statement?

APRIL 18

Boyd K. Packer: "The knowledge that we are the children of God is a refining, even an exalting truth. On the other hand, no idea has been more destructive of happiness, no philosophy has produced more sorrow, more heartbreak, more suffering and mischief, no idea has contributed more to the erosion of the family than the idea that we are not the offspring of god, but only advanced animals. There flows from that idea the not too subtle perception that we are compelled to yield to every carnal urge, are subject to physical but not to moral law" ("The Fountain of Life," *Things of the Soul*, 111).

If we were simply advanced animals, then it would be easy to justify animal-like behavior on our part. But we are not animals; not even 'advanced' animals. We are the offspring of Heavenly Parents who themselves, at one time in the distant past, passed through experiences similar to our own. We love animals, we enjoy them and they will live in every degree of glory in eternity. But we are not of their species; we belong the species of the gods. This doctrine gives meaning to what we do in this life and because of our heritage provides the confidence we need to accomplish any righteous goal.

Application: List the types of behavior that would follow from the idea that we are simply 'advanced animals.' What behavior could be justified by such a belief?

APRIL 19

Bruce R. McConkie: "It is not, never has been, and never will be the design and purpose of the Lord—however much we seek him in prayer—to answer all our problems and concerns without struggle and effort on our part....We are being tested to see how we will respond in various situations, how we will decide issues, what course we will pursue while we are here walking, not by sight, but by faith" ("Why the Lord Ordained Prayer," *Ensign*, Jan. 1976, 11).

Mortality is a sober test by which we learn to develop celestial character traits. We are on earth with a telestial body that by itself provides a number of challenges as to whether or not our spirit can master its physical counterpart. We are learning the differences between good and evil through the use of our agency and the consequences that follow choice. How we handle mortal tests is a prelude as to how we will use agency after we are resurrected and death is banished. The quality of life we merit in the hereafter depends to a great extent on choices that we make here. Prayer is our way to receive counsel from our Heavenly Father. The Prophet Joseph Smith taught the principle that at one time our Heavenly Father passed through mortality and therefore He clearly understands our challenges and succors us in this mortal curriculum and gives us confidence that He can assist us through any earthly issue we confront.

Application: We have stressed the point that a great marriage requires daily individual and couple prayer. Do not substitute family prayer for couple prayer. If you have not been having individual and couple prayers, please get back to that tradition.

APRIL 20

Dallin H. Oaks: "We should study things out in our minds, using the reasoning powers our Creator has placed within us. Then we should pray for guidance and act upon it if we receive it. If we do not receive guidance, we should act upon our best judgment" ("Our Strengths Can Become our Downfall," *Ensign*, Oct. 1994, 13-14).

We are the offspring of eternal beings. We have been endowed with an intellect that allows us to think for ourselves and to make choices. God expects us to use our mental faculties to make wise choices among competing alternatives. Though God answers sincere prayer, there are some things we ought to be able to figure out on our own with our own intellectual powers. As Elder Oaks suggests, we petition Father for help, but in some cases, as with any wise parent, He lets us wrestle with issues in order to learn the blessings and consequences inherent in our choices. Obviously, where we lack insight or experience in important matters, we receive inspiration. But we are equipped mentally and physically to solve many of our own problems. In marriage the solution to most marital problems are resolved by putting our heads together and making joint decisions.

Application: Most marital problems are resolved when two soft-hearted people discuss issues and determine the best course of action. What kinds of problem-solving and decision-making skills do you possess?

APRIL 21

Boyd K. Packer: "To willfully destroy a marriage, either your own or that of another couple, is to offend our God. Such a thing will not be lightly considered in the judgments of the Almighty and in the eternal scheme of things will not easily be forgiven" ("Marriage," *Ensign*, May 1981, 14).

Unfortunately we live in a day when immorality, adultery, and gross sexual sins are played out before us on television and other media sources. For example, are there many movies where the two unmarried stars do not end up in bed before the movie ends? We watch actors, athletes, and entertainers marry or live together for a brief period but soon tire of that relationship and move on to someone new. Latter-day Saints are sickened at the way marriage and family matters are treated in the public square. In the gospel context, there is nothing more serious than breaking marriage vows or covenants. In a day of rampant sexual themes that bombard us from all sides, we must learn to have control over our environment.

Application: How would the conversation go if one had to explain at the judgment bar how they broke their covenants by claiming they 'fell in love' with someone else?

APRIL 22

Joseph Fielding Smith, Jr.: "If a man and his wife were earnestly and faithfully observing all the ordinances and principles of the gospel, there could not arise any cause for divorce" (Conference Report, Apr. 1965, 11).

No one cares more about your success in marriage and family relations than our Heavenly Parents. They must weep over decisions made by sons and daughters who break temple covenants. A few simple keys to remain happily married are to live righteously and to obey the commandments of a loving Heavenly Father who has our best interest at heart and who will do all that He can to help us succeed. Remember Nephi's response to his father, Lehi, in 1 Nephi 3:7, wherein Nephi testified that no commandment is given to mankind but what divine help is available to fulfill the command. Inasmuch as marriage is the crowning ordinance of the gospel, God will help you succeed as a couple if you will keep your commitments. Yes, we all face tests of character, but they are designed to see if we are worthy to live with those who have already proven that they can be trusted to live celestial principles regardless of the environment.

Application: Discuss the feelings you had for each other on your wedding day. Can you remember the counsel you were given by the sealer, and have you been faithful to his counsel?

APRIL 23

Orson Pratt: "The more righteous a people become the more they are qualified for loving others and rendering them happy. A wicked

89

man can have but little love for his wife; while a righteous man, being filled with the love of god, is sure to manifest this heavenly attribute in every thought and feeling of his heart, and in every word and deed" ("Celestial Marriage," *The Seer*, Oct. 1853, 156).

The Holy Ghost is given to each member of the Church at the time of confirmation following baptism. What a wonderful gift we receive to have a member of the Godhead 'assigned' to us as individuals. We do not want to lose His influence. We retain that assistance from the third member of the godhead by the way we live and honor covenants. To maintain the right to inspiration and revelation from this source, the Lord commanded: "Let thy bowels also be full of charity towards all men. . . and let virtue garnish thy thoughts unceasingly;...[then] "the Holy Ghost shall be thy constant companion"....(D&C 121:45, 46). Marriage is an internship. Love is a fruit of the Spirit. When couples live righteously, each feels the influence and peace of the Spirit "in every thought and feeling of his heart."

Application: Would you agree that the more righteous we become, the more lovable we become? Read and discuss the counsel of the Lord in D&C 121:39-46.

APRIL 24

Richard G. Scott: "Satan promotes counterfeit love, which is lust. It is driven by a hunger to appease personal appetite....You know how to be clean and live a righteous life. We trust you to do it" ("Making the Right Decisions," *Ensign*, May 1991, 35).

Even in marriage, men and women can be selfish in the area of intimate relations. President Spencer W. Kimball counseled: "It is not love if it manipulates; it is selfishness; it is irresponsibility. If sex relations merely become a release or a technique and the partner becomes exchangeable, then sex returns to the compulsive animal level." (Love Versus Lust, Provo, Utah: Brigham Young University Publications, 1975, 15).

In a Latter-day Saint marriage happiness is more likely to be achieved when both partners are in agreement as to the frequency and appropriateness of sexual arousal methods that uplift and enrich the relationship. Intimacy is not the place to 'force' a sexual practice on your spouse that is repulsive and offensive.

Application: Share your thoughts and feelings about how intimacy contributes to your marital happiness. Any suggestions or ways to improve this time together?

APRIL 25

Joe J. Christensen: "Be quick to say, 'I'm sorry.' As hard as it is to form the words, be swift to say, 'I apologize, and please forgive me,' even though you are not the one who is totally at fault. True love is developed by those who are willing to readily admit personal mistakes and offenses" ("Marriage and the Great Plan of Happiness," *Ensign*, May 1995, 65).

Why is it so hard to apologize, to genuinely admit when we are at fault? Prophets call it pride and selfishness which prevents the humility necessary to admit we are wrong. Why is it so difficult to take responsibility for our behavior and willingly change and improve? One reason people resort to secular counseling is the inability on the part of one or the other to apologize, to repent, to change behavior, or to take responsibility for their actions. Why must it always be the same spouse who initiates 'making-up?' Why don't we quickly apologize when we err? That is the course that humble people take. Most marital issues are resolved through a sincere, genuine apology with 'real intent' not to repeat the same action or behavior.

Application: When was the last time you actually apologized about something to each other? Be the first to take responsibility when you err or make a mistake.

APRIL 26

Neal A. Maxwell: "Perfect love is perfectly patient." (*All these Things Shall Give Thee Experience*, 69).

When two people live in such close proximity as they do in marriage, it is only natural that there will be misunderstandings and challenges to their unity. It is then that the attribute of patience, a Christ-like virtue, must come to bear. How easy it is to miscommunicate about times and places to meet, or to experience unforeseen circumstances or delays. For some reason even these minor issues can test even the best of lovers. However, when we consider our weaknesses, our own mortality, when we realize that we are mistake-prone too, that we married a sweetheart whose motives are pure, that neither one is purposely trying to frustrate the other, then occasional flare-ups and misunderstandings can be quite humorous. Remember this equation: Crisis plus time = humor. Of course cell phones and texting help couples eliminate potential misunderstandings.

Application: What would you say is 'perfect patience?' Is it an issue in your marriage? Can you laugh about past misunderstandings or miscommunications or did they evolve into a crisis?

APRIL 27

Marvin J. Ashton: "True love is a process. True love requires personal action. Love must be continuing to be real. Love takes time" ("Love Takes Time," *Ensign*, Nov. 1975, 108).

Have you learned that no matter how long you dated each other, you still ended up marrying a stranger? How can we really know that much about the other before we marry? We only see each other for a few hours a day when dating and anyone can be decent for a few hours! Besides, while dating we are usually on our best behavior. Marriage, it turns out, is a profound commitment that we have a great deal to learn from each other now that we have a permanent relationship! Now we learn the intricacies of marriage, about the influence of in-laws, about parenting practices, and about our ability to build a strong, healthy marriage relationship. It isn't until after the honeymoon that we settle into the 'work' of marriage when we revert back to our 'real self.' Hopefully that version is the genuine one that we grew to love.

Application: How long did you know each other before marriage? What do you recall doing that impressed each other? How well do you feel you really know each other by now?

APRIL 28

John A. Widtsoe: "True love of man for woman always includes love of God from whom all good things issue" (*Evidences and Reconciliations*, 297).

You have heard the idea that love of God must come before love of spouse. The point is that if both partners are committed to live the gospel, they will be more committed to each other, for marriage is the ultimate religious commitment. What spouse would not want their companion to have God as his or her first priority? If our sweethearts are true to their covenants, there is a high likelihood that they will be true to us. When we know that personal righteousness is the highest of a spouse's priorities, we are more apt to build trust and fall more deeply in love. When a husband and wife feel allegiance to the doctrines, covenants, and ordinances of the gospel, there is less likelihood of contention disrupting their happiness.

Application: In couple prayer today, express appreciation for your spouse's priority of putting God and the gospel first. Explore the idea that righteousness builds trust.

APRIL 29

Russell M. Nelson: "Without a strong commitment to the Lord, an individual is more prone to have a low level of commitment to a spouse. Weak commitments to eternal covenants lead to losses of eternal consequence" ("Endure and Be Lifted Up," *Ensign*, May 1997, 72).

One reason missions are valuable for men is that later on when must lead a family, they are already experienced in praying individually, with a companion (couple prayer) and with investigators (family prayer). They are proficient in reading and studying scripture, in giving priesthood blessings, in teaching others, in cooking, in cleaning, in organizing time, and in understanding covenants. Where a wife served a mission—more common now—both should have developed spiritual patterns that sanctify their marriage and prepare them to teach and lead their children. If neither served a mission, compensation comes in scripture and the study of gospel literature, in Sabbath meeting attendance, in temple worship and individual, companion, and family prayer.

Application: How is a mission the best way to prepare for marriage?

APRIL 30

David O. McKay: (quoting George Q. Morris) "My mother once said that if you meet a girl in whose presence you feel a desire to achieve, who inspires you to do your best, and to make the most of yourself, such a young woman is worthy of your love and is awakening love in your heart' ("As Youth Contemplates an Eternal Partnership," *Improvement Era*, March 1938, 139).

Think back to how much you wanted to impress each other after your initial meeting. At that stage of the relationship men open doors, both are on their best manners, and both like to surprise the other with clever poetry or gifts. We do our best to appear romantic, humorous, and fun-loving. If we continued that behavior throughout marriage, there would be fewer marital problems! The fact that we can be nice to each other as dating partners proves that we actually do have the skills to treat each other in Christlike ways. In marriage we continue to inspire each other to be our best selves. Positive encouragement is more helpful than nagging, carping, or being critical—something we would never have done when we were dating.

Application: How did dating affect your desire to want to be your best self; to awaken love in your heart?

May

May 1

Gordon B. Hinckley: "Too many who come to marriage have been coddled and spoiled and somehow led to feel that everything must be precisely right at all times, that life is a series of entertainments, that appetites are to be satisfied without regard to principle. How tragic the consequences of such hollow and unreasonable thinking!" ("What God hath Joined Together," *Ensign*, May 1991, 73).

Success in marriage requires mature individuals who are mentally, socially, physically, emotionally, and spiritually competent. Children who enter marriage from a background of having most things given to them or where they were not required to work, who had few responsibilities, who had money doled out, find marriage difficult. How much better off are children who learn to complete chores, who learn to play musical instruments, who participate in athletics, who earn money for their own clothing, who wisely manage leisure time activities, and who learn to be independent. Sometimes parents who grew up during difficult economic times, overcompensate children in an attempt to spare them the lessons that hard work teaches. Where else can children learn the value of hard work and personal effort if it is not at the feet of their parents?

Application: In your family, what chores were you given? From your employment experience, how important is a work ethic to success? What do you do to help your children develop the ability to work?

MAY 2

Howard W. Hunter: "Keep yourselves above any domineering or unworthy behavior in the tender, intimate relationship between husband and wife. Because marriage is ordained of God, the intimate relationship between husbands and wives is good and honorable in the eyes of God "("Being a Righteous Husband and Father," *Ensign*, Nov. 1994, 51).

The tender union of a husband and wife is designed to strengthen their emotional bonds. However, selfishness can manifest itself when one spouse thinks it is a marital 'right' to be exercised at his or her discretion. In marriage, charity must always be the ruling virtue. There are times when a wife or husband may have a health issue or a concern that requires a delay in their relations. Too, it is difficult for both partners to enjoy intimacy when there are unresolved issues. Husbands and wives should be patient and considerate of each other as they consider the pressures that each is under—work, health, small children—and be flexible enough to re-schedule when timing is awkward or inappropriate.

Application: Discuss your satisfaction with the frequency of your intimate relations.

MAY 3

Bruce R. McConkie. "Mortal persons who overcome all things and gain an ultimate exaltation will live eternally in the family unit and have spirit children, thus becoming Eternal Fathers and Eternal Mothers. (D&C 132:19-32.) Indeed, the formal pronouncement of the Church, issued by the First Presidency and the Council of the Twelve, states: 'So far as the stages of eternal progression and attainment have been made known through divine revelation, we are to understand that only resurrected and glorified beings can become parents of spirit offspring.'" (*Man: His Origin and Destiny*, 129; *Mormon Doctrine*, 517).

The most important roles the two of you play in your mortal and immortal lives will be those of husband and wife, father and mother. Your time as a fireman, salesperson, manager, teacher, or lawyer, for example, will be minuscule compared to the duration you will fill these roles. We take little of what we learn in our jobs here with us to the next life. Our real, long-term goal is to so live as to qualify for the Celestial Kingdom and then assist each member of our earthly family to be worthy to join us there. We will all be adults at that time. As resurrected beings, we will start a new family, this time creating spirit children and we will be to them there as our Heavenly Parents were to us in our premortal lives. Those who attain to lesser kingdoms of glory will not live in the family unit.

Application: Write a brief obituary from the point of view of your spouse and children. How do they view you as a spouse and as a parent?

MAY 4

Parley P. Pratt: ". . . our natural affections are planted in us by the Spirit of God, for a wise purpose; and they are the very main-springs of life and happiness—they are the cement of all virtuous and heavenly society—they are the essence of charity, or love; and therefore never fail, but endure forever" (*Writings of Parley Parker Pratt*, First ed., 1952, 52).

Purity is a treasured virtue. In marriage we share our very souls with each other as 'best friends.' Those couples who have built a healthy marriage relationship enjoy sharing their physical and emotional endowments with each other in a frequency that meets the needs of both. Sexual relations are an important part of marriage and a profound expression that refreshes and renews a couple's commitments and strengthens mutual feelings of love. How blessed are couples who possess a 'natural affection' for each other.

Application: As you witness events in our culture, many want to consider same sex marriage as a civil right. What is your view? Be grateful and express appreciation that you both possess 'natural affection' for each other.

MAY 5

Spencer W. Kimball: "Couples do well to immediately find their own home, separate and apart from that of the in-laws on either side. The home may be very modest and unpretentious, but still it is an independent domicile" ("Oneness in Marriage," *Ensign*, March 1977, 5).

In-laws greatly bless their married children. They make great sacrifices to insure that their children get off to the very best start. They feed you, occasionally help out financially, baby-sit and watch their grandchildren, but it is wise counsel that you not live with them. Each couple must find their own way, depending on each other for success rather than being dependent on relatives on either side. Many marriages have been derailed through interfering in-laws. Though parents have your best interest at heart, even innocently they sometimes involve themselves in your lives in such a way as to hinder your own goals. Occasionally in-laws compete with each other to win a couple over to their side of the family or to create a dependency. Remain loving and appreciative, but independent in domicile and decision-making.

Application: If either one of you or both live close to in-laws, determine a reasonable visiting schedule. Make sure both of you are comfortable with time spent with family members.

MAY 6

Boyd K. Packer: "The simple rule has been to take care of one's self. This couplet of truth has been something of a model: 'Eat it up, wear it out, make it do, or do without'...The principle of self-reliance or personal independence is fundamental to the happy life. In too many places, in too many ways, we are getting away from it" ("Solving Emotional Problems in the Lord's Own Way," *Ensign*, May 1978, 91).

In recent years we have seen government policies passed that regulate much of what we can and cannot do in many areas of life. Are we rearing an 'entitlement generation' that looks to the government to care for us from cradle to grave? Often parents are guilty of similar behavior in failing to allow their newly married children to work things out on their own. Would it be so bad if a new couple had to live without two cars for a few years? Will they survive in a modest apartment? Self-reliance is an important principle of the gospel whereby we work together to make our own way in life.

Application: As parents and in-laws, are you overly involved in the lives of your children? As newlyweds or mature couples, how dependent are you on your parents or in-laws?

MAY 7

Joseph B. Wirthlin: "We live in a day when Lucifer's influence is greater than we ever have known in our lifetimes. In terms of the sin, evil, and wickedness upon the earth, we could liken our time to the days of Noah before the flood" ("Our Lord and Savior," *Ensign*, Nov. 1993, 5).

A common phase describing the progress of people or civilizations in the Book of Mormon is that of 'ripening in iniquity' (see 1 Nephi 17:35). Consider its meaning. A cycle is similar to a clock whereby the hands circle clockwise. There are cycles in politics. For a while Democrats prevail, then Republicans, and then a return to the Democrats. But ripening is neither of these; it is unidirectional in that the process only moves in one direction. As examples, tomatoes and bananas ripen from green to their full splendor. The process does not reverse itself with the fruit returning to its green, unripe state. As it pertains to nations, when people grow wicked over time and do not repent, they eventually suffer divine judgments. Wickedness destroyed the Antediluvians, Jaredites, and Nephites. In Noah's day, society grew to the point where "every man was...evil continually" (see Moses 8:22).

Application: In what ways have the media, morality, marriage, and drugs 'ripened in iniquity' in your lifetime?

MAY 8

Gordon B. Hinckley: "Perhaps our greatest concern is with families. The family is falling apart all over the world. The old ties that bound together father and mother and children are breaking everywhere. We must face this in our own midst" ("What God Hath Joined Together," *Ensign*, May 1981, 74).

Satan, or Lucifer as he was known in the premortal realm, knows his days are numbered before he is cast out to an eternity with no glory. One of his major targets has to do with married couples and their children—families—especially those organized in the temple; those who live for the promise of eternal life. With the restoration of the Gospel and priesthood authority wherein men and women are sealed together forever as husband and wife, Satan is doing all he can to prevent a temple marriage in the first place. If he fails in that effort, his attempts are aimed at destroying them after they are set up as a family unit. Thus we see President Hinckley's concern about the quality of family life within the Church. Latter-day Saints are not without their own challenges to marital stability—divorce rate, and marital satisfaction—quality of marriage.

Application: In what ways do you see families 'falling apart all over the world?'

MAY 9

Spencer W. Kimball: "No indecent exposure or pornography or other aberrations to defile the mind and spirit. No fondling of bodies, one's own or that of others, and no sex between persons except in proper marriage relationships. This is positively prohibited by our Creator in all places, at all times, and we reaffirm it. *Even in marriage there can be some excesses and distortions.* No amount of rationalization to the contrary can satisfy a disappointed Father in Heaven" ("Guidelines to Carry Forth the Work of God in Cleanliness," *Ensign*, May 1974, 7, italics added).

Our bodies house our individual spirits, entities created by heavenly parents. We now have the ability, as mortals, to organize a physical body through procreation. We are given the authority to bring spirits from the premortal life to earth when we marry. To defile or misuse this power is a serious violation of divine law. President Kimball teaches the principle that there are some sexual practices in marriage that can be 'excesses and distortions.'

Application. Before marriage: Complete chastity. During marriage: Complete fidelity. What did President Kimball mean by: "No amount of rationalization to the contrary can satisfy a disappointed Father in Heaven?' What might be disappointing to Heavenly Father?

MAY 10

Gordon B. Hinckley: "To men within the sound of my voice, wherever you may be, I say, if you are guilty of demeaning behavior toward your wife, if you are prone to dictate and exercise authority over her, if you are selfish and brutal in your actions in the home, then stop it! Repent! Repent now while you have the opportunity to do so" (Cornerstones of a Happy Home," Satellite Broadcast, 29 Jan. 1984).

Is it possible for individuals who grow up in the Church, who understand the elements of the plan of salvation and who seal their love by priesthood authority in the House of the Lord, to reach the point where they become abusive and demeaning? President Hinckley, with the responsibility and authority to seal or cancel a sealing, pleads with husbands to treat their wives as priesthood holders ought. In our society, the man extends the offer of marriage. Ironically, it is these same husbands who often become the chief offenders. He cautions those who are guilty to cease such behavior; to repent of selfish motives lest the stage is reached where they lose both spouse and children.

Application: As a husband or wife, how do you repent if there were any demeaning behavior by either one of you? List three or four ways in which you bless each other.

MAY 11

Marvin J. Ashton: "Let us each remember: First: Not to confuse wants with needs. Second: Avoid spoiling our children; Third: Live modestly and avoid debt. Fourth: Be generous in giving to others" ("Finances," Booklet from Welfare Session, 1975 general conference").

Elder Ashton gave a classic address on the importance of financial management in marriage. He outlined principles that every couple ought to review and implement. Many family life educators are of the opinion that effective money management is the most important factor in maintaining a happy marriage. Most partners come to marriage with different views and experiences in this area and it is important to establish a workable plan in which they budget and put aside some savings. When couples fail to manage finances judiciously, it places a major strain on the relationship. Bills must be paid, savings accrued, and each couple should have a bookkeeping system that is simple enough for both partners to understand and take over in case of an emergency.

Application: Evaluate your money management system. Do both of you understand its workings? For more excellent ideas, read "One for the Money," *Ensign*, Sep. 2007, 36–39.

MAY 12

Ezra Taft Benson: "Wholesome recreation is part of our religion, and a change of pace is necessary, and even its anticipation can lift the spirit" ("Do Not Despair," *Ensign*, Nov. 1974, 66).

One of nine suggestions in the 1995 Proclamation on the Family is to strengthen marriages and families through 'wholesome recreational activities.' The stress of daily life, work, children and finances, dictate that individuals need time to renew and re-charge and to have a break from mundane, daily schedules. Whether it involves walking together, having lunch or dinner out, or visiting friends or family, vary your activities and plan for regular breaks. The Lord decreed the Sabbath as a break from typical work schedules. Times of renewal should involve both partners. On a 'mini-honeymoon,' for example, it is important that both partners spend their time together. It would not be wise to have one spouse play golf, for example, while the spouse sits alone in the hotel room.

Application: What constitutes 'wholesome recreation' for you two? Church leaders suggest a weekly date. Take turns planning wholesome recreation activities.

MAY 13

Marlin K. Jensen. "I hope that we will vow never to be satisfied with a mediocre marriage. Not long ago a friend told me that one of his young children had asked, 'Do you think Grandpa ever kissed Grandma?' I certainly hope my wife and I are sufficiently in love and demonstrative about it that our grandchildren will not have to wonder. We can never afford to let our relationships become merely mutual toleration or accommodation" (A Union of Love and Understanding," *Ensign*, Oct. 1994, 51).

When a couple is introduced as having been married 30, 40, or 50 years, the audience claps as if they have been married for a long time. For Latter-day Saints, these decades are just the beginning of an eternal companionship. When you consider that marriage in the temple seals a couple together for eternity, a hard concept to grasp, a few decades of mortality is simply a time for couples to make whatever adjustments they need to continue their relationship into eternity. Being grandparents does not end intimacy, happiness, nor concern for each family member. In fact, in the later years, love for these couples should be in full bloom.

Application: From your observations, are your parents and grandparents, still 'in love?' Which ones would you judge to have the 'most loving' relationships?

MAY 14

James E. Faust: "How should those who bear the priesthood treat their wives and the other women in their family? Our wives need to be cherished. They need to hear their husbands call them blessed, and the children need to hear their fathers generously praise their mothers" ("Keeping Covenants and Honoring the Priesthood," *Ensign*, Nov. 1993, 38).

Husbands who work away from home are typically thought to be under greater stress from their employment. In some cases it may be true; but typically it is the wife and mother with little ones under her feet who bears the greater stress. It is the mother who needs a break and anticipates help when her husband arrives home. Men often relax in the car on the way home with the radio or CDs. His work often provides variety and personal stimulus via interaction with colleagues and clients. However, there is little time out for mom to relax. She does not punch a clock! Sensitive husbands are aware of their wives' housekeeping and child care responsibilities and are anxious to pitch in on their arrival. The best way for a husband to immediately enrich his marriage is to jump in and help —at the least ask—with meal preparation or fatherly functions. If the wife is the last one to come home, wouldn't it be nice if dinner were waiting her upon arrival?

Application: Husband, ask your wife if your homecoming is a happy time for her and the children. No one wants a grumpy husband or wife to walk through the door!

MAY 15

James E. Faust: "There are no simple, easy answers to the challenging and complex questions of happiness in marriage. There are also many supposed reasons for divorce. Among them are the serious problems of selfishness, immaturity, lack of commitment, inadequate communication, unfaithfulness; and all of the rest, which are obvious and well known" ("The Enriching of Marriage," *Ensign* Nov. 1977, 10).

President Faust spoke frequently in General Conference concerning marriage and parenting issues. In this case, as a member of the Seventy, he listed a number of factors that contribute to divorce. Selfishness, immaturity, lack of commitment, inadequate communication and unfaithfulness are certainly 'marriage killers.' Their opposites, on the other hand, are marriage helpers: Humility, maturity, commitment, covenants, adequate communication and faithfulness, enrich marriages. When apologies are offered and accepted, marriage moves from tolerable to satisfying. We all perform at less than our potential at times, and a humility that allows for acknowledging mistakes and making appropriate changes contributes to a well-functioning marriage. Children are quick to forgive when a parent offers an apology.

Application: Repentance is not an apology to 'get my spouse off my back,' but a genuine desire to make things better. As you read Elder Faust's list of reasons for divorce, ask yourself if you are blameless?

MAY 16

Gordon B. Hinckley: "Who can calculate the wounds inflicted, their depth and pain, by harsh and mean words spoken in anger?… In every marriage there are, of course, occasional differences. But I find no justification for tempers that explode on the slightest provocation" ("Our Solemn responsibilities," *Ensign* Nov. 1991: 50-51).

Anger destroys tender feelings. We seem to live in an angry generation, where tempers flare and harsh words cause deep wounds. A temper is a detriment to marriage and to effective parenting practices. Prophets have spoken often concerning the damage that anger and temper have on spouses and children. Exploding tempers can do long-term damage that may carry on for years. Do not excuse outbursts of temper as simply "blowing off steam" or "clearing the air." It is not always men who are at fault. Some women have developed anger that has a destructive effect on husbands and children. Temper and anger are out of place in the life of a latter day 'saint.'

Application: How has your temperament changed since marriage? Remember that children tend to model parental temperament.

MAY 17

Howard W. Hunter: "You [husbands] should express regularly to your wife and children your reverence and respect for her. Indeed one of the greatest things a father can do for his children is to love their mother" ("Being a Righteous Husband and Father," *Ensign*, Nov. 1994, 50).

Of course the other side of this statement also holds true: 'One of the greatest things a mother can do for her children is to love their father.' Every human being has a need to feel loved, appreciated, cherished, accepted, valued, and worthwhile. It is in the home that such messages ought to be conveyed on a daily basis. No one cares to live in a home where what they do is taken for granted or goes unappreciated. Regular compliments and genuine affection seen and heard by all in the home will do far more than any family night lesson on love and respect for parents. It is incumbent on a husband and wife to be positive and to express gratitude for the efforts of both spouse and children. Children thrive on positives. Fathers can do much to bless sons and daughters, and mothers play a key role in influencing their sons' attitudes toward women. Complimenting and expressing thanks for the efforts of others in our behalf should be frequent and natural.

Application: Find something each day to compliment each other and each child.

MAY 18

Marlin K. Jensen: "Recently, I visited with a widower as he stood bravely at the side of his wife's casket, surrounded by several handsome and stalwart sons. This man and his wife had been married for fifty-three years, during the last six of which she had been seriously ill with a terminal kidney disease. He had provided the 24-hour care she required until his own health was in jeopardy. I expressed my admiration for him and the great love and care he had given his wife. I felt compelled to ask, 'How did you do it?' It was easy, he replied, when he remembered that fifty-three years earlier, he had knelt at an altar in the temple and made a covenant with the Lord and with his bride. 'I wanted to keep it,' he said" ("A Union of Love and Understanding," *Ensign*, Oct. 1994, 51).

We are deluged daily with advertisements and media messages emphasizing short term pleasures, some useful for making life more convenient, some appealing to baser instincts that distract from that which is good. Our marriage relationship can be a source of joy to us eons after the bright wrapping and enticing tastes of mortal experiences have faded and gone. It is the constant, unfailing loyalty, the care and attention we give to our relationship and to the underlying covenants that undergird marriage that are of everlasting value.

Application: Today, give your spouse the gift of time. Make yourself available for an hour to talk, to listen, to help around the house, to shop, or just relax together.

MAY 19

Gordon B. Hinckley: "How beautiful is the marriage of a young man and a young woman who begin their lives together kneeling at the altar in the house of the Lord, pledging their love and loyalty one to another for time and all eternity" ("Our Solemn Responsibilities," *Ensign*, Nov. 1991, 52).

The temple represents sacred spaces on the earth's surface. Where there is a temple, it is a place that has been consecrated and dedicated as the House of the Lord. As God's children, we have been commanded to build temples for a number of reasons, but primarily they are places for God to come to visit His children (D&C 109:5). They are places where we perform ordinances for the living and the 'dead.' In marriage, the temple sealer stands in place of Elohim, our Father, who, by proxy is present to witness the union of two of His children. When we kneel at the altar we make solemn covenants with God and are then sealed in an unbreakable union by priesthood authority. We pledge our love to each other for a very long time! We are blessed to live in a day when temples are so readily available to the Church membership.

Application: On your next visit to the temple, do couple sealings and listen carefully to the blessings that are promised in the sealing.

MAY 20

The First Presidency and Quorum of the Twelve: "We bear testimony, as His duly ordained Apostles—that Jesus is the Living Christ, the immortal Son of God. He is the great King Immanuel, who stands today on the right hand of His Father. He is the light, the life, and the hope of the world. His way is the path that leads to happiness in this life and eternal life in the world to come. God be thanked for the matchless gift of His divine Son" (The Living Christ: The Testimony of the Apostles," *Ensign*, Apr. 2000, 2).

Typically Latter-day Saints express appreciation for Jesus Christ's mission because of His Atonement and its cleansing power in our lives. However, a major contribution Christ made in behalf of married couples has to do with their resurrection and the promise of eternal life. Were it not for the resurrection, at death our physical body would return to the grave. Were it not for the Savior, our spirit would revert back to its former existence, incapable of procreation for spirits cannot generate life. Therefore had it not been for the Savior, marriage and family life would end at death. Married Latter-day Saints are grateful to the Savior for this part of His mission of redemption and restoration in their behalf.

Application: Share your understanding of how resurrection preserves your marriage and family life beyond this life.

MAY 21

Howard W. Hunter: "Be faithful in your marriage covenants in thought, word, and deed. Pornography, flirtations, and unwholesome fantasies erode one's character and strike at the foundation of a happy marriage" (Being a Righteous Husband and Father," *Ensign*, Nov. 1994, 50).

It must be disappointing for our Father in Heaven to see the extent of divorce and unhappiness among His married children. Loyalty and charity are important components of happy marriages. The point of a temple marriage is to organize an eternal family. It has been estimated that 80-90% of all divorces result from sexual sins, affairs, or seduction by pornography. To create a stable marriage requires working together toward the same goals. Pornography easily erodes 'one's character and strike[s] at the foundation of a happy marriage." When we are faithful in honoring our marriage covenants, we qualify for blessings that pertain to our post-earth life.

Application: Evaluate your viewing of media habits. Unwisely we can bring the filth and sleaze of our day right into our living spaces. Commit to each other to avoid unwholesome media presentations.

MAY 22

Gordon B. Hinckley: "My brethren, you who have had conferred upon you the priesthood of God, you know, as I know, that there is no enduring happiness, that there is no lasting peace in the heart, no tranquility in the home, without the companionship of a good woman. Our wives are not our inferiors" (Our Solemn Responsibilities," *Ensign*, Nov. 1991, 51).

What righteous husband does not appreciate the contribution of his sweetheart to his happiness and to the wellbeing of his children? Wives typically have a built-in temperament to sacrifice for others. It is part of their divine nature. Joseph Smith, from Liberty Jail, reminded men that "the rights of the Priesthood are inseparably connected with the powers of heaven, and that the powers of heaven cannot be controlled nor handled only upon the principles of righteousness." He continued: "We have learned by sad experience that it is the nature and disposition of almost all men, as soon as they get a little authority, as they suppose, they will immediately begin to exercise unrighteous dominion. Hence many are called, but few are chosen" (D&C 121:36, 39-40). Nowhere does this counsel apply more than in our homes.

Application: Wife, give your husband credit for the good things he does to enrich your life and that of your children. Share a specific thing you appreciate about him or something he does to make life enjoyable for you.

MAY 23

David O. McKay: "No other success can compensate for failure in the home" (*Improvement Era*, June 1964, 445).

Though not original with President McKay, he used this quote a number of times to emphasize that no matter how much worldly or secular fame we may achieve, if there is contention and fighting in the home, we have missed the point of marriage. Our priorities are out of whack. If a wife and husband are at odds, or where children are neglected, there has been failure in this most critical area. Don't get out of balance or lose perspective due to the immediate rewards and recognition of the workplace. It is when we receive acclaim and love from those who live under our roof that true happiness exists. When husbands love their wives and wives reciprocate that love in full measure, happiness exists in that home.

Application: How do you define success in your marriage and family life?

MAY 24

Joe J. Christensen: "Many Church leaders as well as professional counselors have indicated that they have never seen a marriage in serious difficulty in which the couple was still praying together daily. When problems arise and marriages are threatened, praying together as a couple may be the most important remedy" (Marriage and the Great Plan of Happiness," *Ensign,* May 1995, 64).

There is something wonderful and inspiring to see a couple kneeling together in prayer as the day begins and as it ends. Morning prayer is important because of the need for the Lord's Spirit to accompany us throughout the day. In the evening we have a chance to 'report in' and thank God for the blessings of that day. You two completed another day safely. When you call down the blessings of heaven on your marriage and children by kneeling in humble prayer, there is little chance that an issue that surfaces during the day, the kind that irritates most of us, will remain.

Application: How do you decide who offers prayer?

MAY 25

Howard W. Hunter: "Keep yourselves above any domineering or unworthy behavior in the tender, intimate relationship between husband and wife. Because marriage is ordained of God, the intimate relationship between husband and wives is good and honorable in the eyes of God" ("Being a Righteous Husband and Father," *Ensign*, Nov. 1994, 51).

The Lord authorizes sexual intercourse for married couples. The union is a profound way in which couples fulfill the command to 'Be fruitful, and multiply, and replenish the earth' (Genesis 1:28). When we marry, it is presumed that marital intimacy will be an on-going and enjoyable part of marriage as long health and desire exists. Certainly every couple learns that sexual relations only bless them when the marriage is a happy one, where each spouse is doing their best, and where love and affection are on-going. Sexual relations represent a simple way by which couples renew their love and commitment to each other and to the marital enterprise.

Application: Does any 'domineering or unworthy behavior' exist in your relationship? What might constitute 'unworthy behavior?'

MAY 26

George Albert Smith: "We should not lose our tempers and abuse one another....Nobody ever abused anybody else when he had the spirit of the Lord. It is always when we have some other spirit" (in *Conference Report*, Oct. 1950, 8; or as quoted in Howard W. Hunter, "Being a Righteous Husband and Father," *Ensign*, Nov. 1994, 51).

Temper and anger are detrimental to a happy marriage. They have no place in the home of a Latter-day Saint. People often offer excuses for bad tempers or angry outbursts, but the Lord instructed the Nephites: "For verily, verily I say unto you, he that hath the spirit of contention is not of me, but is of the devil, who is the father of contention, and he stirreth up the hearts of men to contend with anger, one with another. Behold, this is not my doctrine, to stir up the hearts of men with anger, one against another; but this is my doctrine, that such things should be done away (3 Nephi 11:29-30.)

Anyone who minimizes or excuses anger displays or who flashes temper toward spouse or children is out of order and in need of swift repentance. To display anger and temper with the very ones we invited to spend eternity with us, seems rather silly and surely is offensive to God. We resolve difficult issues as disciples of the Savior would, not by imitating Lucifer.

Application: When was the last time you 'lost' your temper? Over what issue? What did you do to repair any damages?

MAY 27

Marlin K. Jensen: "As designed by our Heavenly Father, marriage consists of our first entering into a covenant relationship with Christ and then with each other. He and his teachings must be the focal point of our togetherness. As we become more like him and grow closer to him, we will naturally become more loving and grow closer to each other" ("A Union of Love and Understanding," *Ensign*, Oct. 1994, 51).

We have before us literally thousands of books, pamphlets and seminars on achieving marital bliss. We also have before us the scriptures and teachings of modern day prophets and apostles. The former are fine and can be helpful. The latter, if used consistently, are a sure way to invite the Spirit of the Lord into marriage and thereby foster healing, charity, kindness, and joy. True happiness comes from living covenants that give us power to resist the temptations of the day and concentrate on each other's happiness. We function better and enjoy a much greater chance of success in our relationship when we have divine assistance and inspiration in carrying out marital roles.

Application: While reading scripture, look for ideas relevant to marriage and family matters. For example, read 1 Nephi 3:7 and relate its message to marriage.

MAY 28

Ephesians 5:28, 31 "So ought men to love their wives as their own bodies. He that loveth his wife loveth himself…For this cause shall a man leave his father and mother, and shall be joined unto his wife, and they two shall be one flesh."

The Apostle Paul was clear that a husband ought to love his wife as himself. Though we don't usually think of loving ourselves, consider how much time and effort we give to caring for our own welfare with food, clothing, housing, transportation, and comforts. We live in 'our own skin' and our primary interest is in our welfare. However, marriage opens up the privilege to have that same care for others, especially a spouse and children. Through these relationships, we glimpse our potential as an eternal couple and family. In the next life, our children will be adults and not little children as they are here. We will all be adult family members having passed through mortality together. How grateful do you think children will be when they had righteous parents that loved them and cared deeply for them? How sad it will be for parents who neglected the very souls that Heavenly Father entrusted to their care.

Application: After your children are asleep, observe your 'creations.' Recommit to being the best parents you can, for you have been given choice sons and daughters of God.

MAY 29

Howard W. Hunter: ". . . remember that priesthood is a righteous authority only. Earn the respect and confidence of your children through your loving relationship with them. A righteous father protects his children with his time and presence in their social, educational, and spiritual activities and responsibilities. Tender expressions of love and affection toward children are as much the responsibility of the father as the mother. Tell your children you love them" ("Being a Righteous Husband and Father," Ensign, Nov. 1994, 51).

Sometimes men are accused of not being very feeling-oriented, affectionate, or sensitive. The excuse often given is that the world does not encourage men to verbalize their feelings and certainly they are taught not to cry. They must be 'tough' to compete in the world. However, children need anything but a gruff, tough father. They need a dad who will get down on the floor and play and wrestle with them, one who provides encouragement and who deeply loves them. They need a dad who is not afraid or ashamed to verbalize his feelings of love. Perhaps this is the most important contribution a father makes to his children.

Application: Ask your wife for feedback on your affection levels with her and the children.

MAY 30

Gordon B. Hinckley. "God-sanctioned marriage between a man and a woman has been the basis of civilization for thousands of years. There is no justification to redefine what marriage is. Such is not our right, and those who try will find themselves answerable to God" ("Why We Do Some of the Things We Do," *Ensign*, Nov. 1999, 54).

President Hinckley also says: "Some portray legalization of so-called same-sex marriage as a civil right." Then he clarifies the Lord's position: "This is not a matter of civil rights; it is a matter of morality" (*ibid.*) There are voices pressuring the Church to change its position on a number of social matters, but Latter-day Saints are duty-bound to uphold divinely revealed principles as taught by living prophets. If marriage is to be eternal, and generating life is limited to only male and females in the next life, how could there be a substitute plan? President Hinckley wisely added this caution: "I wish to say that our opposition to attempts to legalize same-sex marriage should never be interpreted as justification for hatred, intolerance, or abuse of those who profess homosexual tendencies" (*ibid.*)

Application: Are you aware of individuals with same-sex attraction? How are we to treat them? What would be your counsel to them based on President Hinckley's comments?

MAY 31

Joe J. Christensen: "Avoid 'ceaseless pinpricking.' Don't be too critical of each other's faults. Recognize that none of us is perfect. We all have a long way to go to become as Christlike as our leaders have urged us to become. 'Ceaseless pinpricking'…can deflate almost any marriage." Generally, each of us is painfully aware of our weaknesses, and we don't need frequent reminders" ("Marriage and the Great Plan of Happiness," *Ensign*, May, 1995, 64).

Pinpricking hurts, but is not life threatening. But its jabs are painful. There is nothing worse than a spouse who consistently criticizes his or her companion. Some of us would rather 'pinprick' over issues instead of resolving the underlining matter. Constant criticism destroys trust and prevents open communication of thoughts and feelings so vital to healthy relationships. We all do much better with encouragement than criticism. Human beings function better when their actions are recognized and appreciated. Ceaseless pinpricking breaks the heart and spirit of loved ones.

Application: Discuss how positives help you function better. Where a need exists to address a subject or topic that needs your attention, deal with it directly; don't resort to 'pinpricking.'

JUNE

JUNE 1

Joe J. Christensen: "Be a true partner in home and family responsibilities. Don't be like the husband who sits around home expecting to be waited on, feeling that earning the living is his chore and that his wife alone is responsible for the house and taking care of the children. The task of caring for home and family is more than one person's responsibility" ("Marriage and the Great Plan of Happiness," *Ensign*, May 1995, 66).

Are current husbands doing a better job of helping around the house than husbands of an earlier generation? What is more frustrating to a wife than to have a husband who does no dishes, who does not pick up after himself, who leaves clothes on the floor, and who fails in keeping the entire home orderly. Wives, on the other hand, appreciate husbands who cheerfully help with cooking, cleaning, and laundry, and who enthusiastically jump into fatherhood activities. This sacrifice of time and energy on a husband's part is far more meaningful than the occasional flowers or jewelry. Men who allow their wives a break from home to attend Relief Society meetings, to shop, or to have lunch with a friend, will find a happy wife returning home to a dad who actually learned more about his children while she was away!

Application: Husband, be a good father; give your wife a break from home responsibilities and routines on a regular basis.

JUNE 2

Spencer W. Kimball: "When a husband and wife go together frequently to the holy temple, kneel in prayer together in their home with their family, go hand in hand to their religious meeting, keep their lives wholly chaste, mentally, and physically, and both are working together for the up-building of the kingdom of God, then happiness is at its pinnacle" ("Marriage and Divorce," 1976, 24).

President Kimball lays out a simple list of spiritual activities that strengthens any marriage. Establishing a routine similar to that which he outlines has the effect of maintaining the Spirit of the Lord in a marriage relationship. Remaining mentally chaste, which precedes physical chastity, is essential in the lives of every husband and wife. We live in a day when there is an abundance of titillating literature, immoral media presentations, an easily accessible Internet, and movie and TV trailers that just have to show a provocative scene. Sadly, these satanic traps catch too many individuals who end up destroying their marriage by foolish decisions. In a day when wickedness is rampant, every individual must safeguard his or her mind and heart by monitoring outside influences that warp their sense of right and wrong. This list of simple activities will go a long way in bringing 'happiness.'

Application: Are you consistent in doing these simple activities? If not, why not include them in your schedule and see if they make a difference.

JUNE 3

Gordon B. Hinckley: "How wonderful a thing is marriage under the plan of our Eternal Father, a plan provided in His divine wisdom for the happiness and security of His children and the continuity of the race" ("What God Hath Joined Together," *Ensign*, May 1991, 71).

Mutual attraction leads to marriage. If both married partners seek the welfare and comfort of the other, happiness is more certain. Who ever thought the day would come when marriage would be maligned, when parenting would be avoided, and when the simple things God has revealed to bring joy and true happiness would be undermined or ignored? Heavenly Father established a plan of salvation for His children so that they might enjoy the same blessings He enjoys—marriage and the thrill of creating life. How blessed we are to live in a day when God has revealed the ultimate goal of marriage—exaltation. To members of the Church who live the gospel, who are involved in activities that enrich and strengthen marriage, a happy life is not difficult to achieve. To those who remain inactive or travel the secular path, there are no guarantees.

Application: Discuss reasons Latter-day Saints you know struggle in marriage.

JUNE 4

Brigham Young: "It is for the husband to learn how to gather around his family the comforts of life, how to control his passions and temper, and how to command the respect, not only of his family but of all his brethren, sisters, and friends. It is the calling of the wife and mother to know what to do with everything that is brought into the house, laboring to make her home desirable to her husband and children, her own creating, securing her husband's love and confidence, and tying her offspring to herself, with a love that is stronger than death, for an everlasting inheritance." (*Discourses of Brigham Young*, 1951 ed., 198).

Men and women bring different strengths to marriage. This statement by President Young may seem outdated in this day and age but to active Latter-Day Saints, it makes complete sense. The Proclamation on the Family clearly outlines the primary responsibilities of husbands and wives as well as fathers and mothers. When we fulfill these divine roles in harmony with the counsel of the Lord's prophets, home life functions more smoothly. Many couples have reduced family sizes so that mother can quickly return to 'work.' However, even teenagers need a mother at home as much or perhaps more than do the little ones. Of course, the cost of living hinders the ability of wives to be home. In some families where a husband has a health issue, or he works a job with little chance of advancement, a wife is forced into the work force. If this is true in your home, it is important that you both agree as to its necessity.

Application: As a husband, if your wife can be with your children during the day, express appreciation to her because she no doubt has a tougher job than you do! As a wife, if you can be a full-time mom, express appreciation to your husband for his ability to provide.

JUNE 5

N. Eldon Tanner: "Let us consider first the purpose of the Creation of the earth. The scriptures make it clear that it was for no other purpose than to provide a place for the sons and daughters of God to dwell in mortality and prove themselves worthy, through keeping the commandments, to return to the presence of God from whence they came" ("The Eternal Nature of Marriage," Gospel Classics, *Ensign*, Sep. 2011, 50).

All parents desire that their children leave home at an appropriate time! Not too early and not too late! Why? Leaving home is an essential part of maturation. Children learn gospel principles at home, but to implement them, children must leave the nest and learn to fly on their own. The greater tests to agency come outside the home. When Satan would not sustain the Father's plan or Jehovah as the Savior and Redeemer, he was expelled from the family and cast out to this earth. Elohim said to Jehovah following the Fall: "Behold, the man is become as one of us to know good and evil" (Moses 4:28). Without the knowledge of good and evil, men and women are not free to exercise agency responsibly. They must be able to see the consequences that follow choices. In this life, evil exists, and we are able to see the great harm that comes from making that choice; we also see the blessings that come to individuals who make righteous choices.

Application: Why is knowledge of good and evil a necessary part of our mortal education? How fully, do you think, we understood the consequences of evil in the premortal life setting?

JUNE 6

Robert D. Hales: "Temple marriage describes the place you go to have a marriage performed. *Celestial marriage* is what you create by being true to the sacred covenants you make during the temple marriage ceremony" ("A Little Heaven on Earth," *Ensign*, Sep. 2011, 45.)

For Latter-day Saints, it is not sufficient just to marry or even to marry in the right place. Our task is to build a relationship that creates in each husband and wife a desire to never be apart again. Mortality provides us with an apprenticeship in marriage. It is where we first choose a sweetheart, then we combine masculine and feminine traits in a wonderful synthesis. It is in the process of 'falling in love' with a compatible spirit, that hearts and souls are joined in an unbreakable union and constitute the elements of happiness. As we add a few of the Father's children to our kingdom, we learn parenthood principles too, for that is our great work in eternity (see Moses 1:39).

Application: Sometimes we confuse temple marriage with celestial marriage. Discuss this interesting distinction made by Elder Hales.

JUNE 7

Julie B. Beck: ". . . the Lord wanted His daughters to increase faith and personal righteousness, strengthen families and homes, and seek out and help those in need" ("Relief Society History: A Look at the Lord's Vision for His daughters," *Ensign*, Sep. 2011, 40.)

What righteous husband does not rejoice in the wife of his youth, of middle age, and of old age? Women possess the endowments of gentleness, kindness, and service to others in the home, ward, and community. When a righteous wife's spiritual nature becomes transparent, her husband is filled with joy and gratitude that he had the good sense to invite her to join him in marriage in a temple ceremony. What would man be without a woman? A righteous woman is the crowning blessing to her husband. When a man honors his priesthood and he unites with a woman who honors her motherly creativity, the ideal combination of male and female attributes become activated through marriage.

Application: Now that you are married, you realize that each of you 'took a gamble.' Thankfully you both had sense enough to follow through on divine promptings and now you are rejoicing in your union. Express gratitude to each other and in prayer.

JUNE 8

Robert D. Hales: "If we live the laws pertaining to celestial marriage, we will, with our spouse and with our family, be able to have a little heaven on earth. And when we live those laws, we are practicing the same laws that are practiced in heaven. We are practicing how to live with the Father and the Son and with our families in the eternities to come. That to me is the message to the world of The Church of Jesus Christ of Latter-day Saints" ("A Little Heaven on Earth," *Ensign*, Sep. 2011, 45).

The crowning ordinance of the gospel is performed in sacred precincts where, away from the world, a man and woman pledge their very souls to one another in a union that extends far beyond this telestial sphere. Here we imitate heavenly parents in marriage and parenthood. In the highest degree of glory within the Celestial Kingdom, couples live as resurrected beings capable of creating 'spirit' offspring. Earth life is our time to apprentice in the very roles we may carry into eternity. Mortality may be a short time on the eternal timeline, but oh what great effect it has on how and where we spend eternity. Of all the things we do in this life, one of our primary goals is to learn how to build a wonderful marriage. Those who gain exaltation learn through marriage and parenting children to exercise Christ-like traits with each other. The world speaks of 'til death do us part' while Latter-day Saints talk of 'eternal lives.' To live together as an eternal partnership may not excite the secular mind, but to Church members, it is the ultimate goal.

Application: Read the entire address of Elder Hales in the *Ensign,* or online at *lds.org*.

JUNE 9

Ezra Taft Benson: "In latter-day revelation the Lord speaks again of this obligation (of husbands). He said, 'Thou shalt love thy wife with all thy heart, and shalt cleave unto her and none else' (D&C 42:22). To my knowledge there in only one other thing in all scripture that we are commanded to love with all our hearts, and that is God Himself. Think what that means! This kind of love can be shown for your wives in so many ways. First and foremost, nothing except God Himself takes priority over your wife in your life—not work, not recreation, not hobbies. Your wife is your precious, eternal helpmate—your companion....Love means being sensitive to her feelings and needs. She wants to be noticed and treasured. She wants to be told that you view her as lovely and attractive and important to you. Love means putting her welfare and self-esteem as a high priority in your life" ("To the Fathers in Israel," *Ensign*, Nov. 1987, 50).

In this classic address to fathers in the Church, President Benson provides wise counsel, insight, and firm admonitions to men as to how to treat their wives. When a husband cherishes his sweetheart in ways that the President mentions here, wives blossom into magnificent companions as wives and mothers who in turn, reciprocate by blessing husbands and children.

Application: Write a 'love note' to each other.

JUNE 10

Spencer W. Kimball: "The principle of self-reliance stands behind the Church's emphasis on personal and family preparedness....We hope that you are conscious of proper diet and health habits, that you may be fit physically and able to respond to the many challenges of life" ("Becoming the Pure in Heart," *Ensign*, May 1978, 79-80).

As families we are responsible to be self-reliant. We are encouraged to be self-sufficient by putting aside food, water, and materials when hard times come. Purchasing additional food, being aware of fluctuating food prices, building your own family 'store' of supplies, is your responsibility. It is wise to store food that you will actually eat. We live in a day when dehydrated food lasts many years and freeze dried fruits and vegetables can be stored safely up to 25 years! Rotating food supplies is the smart way to prevent waste and spoilage. In addition to proper nutrition, regular exercise to remain physically fit should be part of your routines.

Application: Look over your food supplies? Could you survive a job loss or other tragedy? Add to family food supplies on a regular basis. Do you have an exercise program?

JUNE 11

Ephesians 4:23 "Husbands, love your wives, even as Christ also loved the church, and gave himself for it." **Titus 2:4:** That they may teach the young women to be sober, to love their husbands, [and] to love their children."

The Savior is the Head of the Church and as its Founder the saints of His day were His greatest concern. He established Apostles and Seventies as church officers and organized the Church as a blessing to its members. To say that husbands should love their wives as the Savior loved the Church was Paul's way of saying that a husband's greatest interest must be to see that his wife is cared for, loved, cherished, and her needs attended to. Of course wives can reciprocate as loving, sensitive companions who display love for their husbands by carrying out their roles as wives and mothers in a way that, in turn, blesses husband and children. The 'Proclamation on the Family' indicates that men have the mandate to provide material blessings and spiritual guidance while the wife's greatest contribution will be through her motherhood skills.

Application: In what ways would you say that the Savior 'loved the Church?' How do you translate Paul's statement into the love of spouse and children?

JUNE 12

Howard W. Hunter: "Take seriously your responsibility to teach the gospel to your family through regular family home evenings, family prayer, devotional and scripture-reading time, and other teaching moments. Give special emphasis to preparation for missionary service and temple marriage" ("Being a Righteous Husband and Father," *Ensign*, Nov. 1994, 51).

This address by President Hunter was the only talk he ever gave in a General Conference priesthood meeting as the president of the Church; it is a classic! Although the talk was directed to husbands, wives ought to understand his counsel in order to know how to assist her husband to be more a more effective husband

and father. Men are responsible to see that simple gospel rituals take place. The President further counseled: "We urge you to do all in your power to allow your wife to remain in the home, caring for the children while you provide for the family the best you can" (*ibid*). This idea of a wife being home as a mother is not a popular theme in today's society as you hear in the political harangue, but this simple principle, if followed, would bless the rising generation more than almost any other single thing that could be done for children.

Application: Find time to read this entire classic address. Access it through *lds.org*.

JUNE 13

Ephesians 6:11 "Put on the whole armor of God, that ye may be able to stand against the wiles of the devil."

We have pointed out numerous times that Satan's great damnation is to remain a single, male spirit forever. Limited for all time to a spirit body, he will never enjoy the power of procreation as do you. Absent that power, you can now more fully understand why he labors night and day to destroy marriages and families. His goal is to have everyone end up impotent as he is. Such a condition would constitute 'hell' for Latter-day Saints. After being married and enjoying the blessings of parenthood, to return to an existence of singleness would be a tragedy of the worst magnitude. To never be able to experience the warm and tender companionship marriage offers would be a severe penalty indeed. The 'armor' we put on, of course, is spiritual armor, the kind that deflects major sins from ruining our divine potential.

Application: Remind yourselves why Satan hates you and *your* marriage. Name three things Satan is forever denied.

JUNE 14

Joseph Smith: "Except a man and his wife enter into an everlasting covenant and be married for eternity, while in this probation, by the power and authority of the Holy Priesthood, they will cease to increase when they die; that is, they will not have any children *after the resurrection*. But those who are married by the power and authority of the priesthood in this life and continue without committing the sin against the Holy Ghost, will continue to increase and have children in the Celestial glory" (D.H.C. 5:391-2; italics added).

This quote by our founding Prophet is not found in the *Doctrine & Covenants*. Its ideas are found in D&C 131:1-4. But the teaching here is clearer in some ways. Couples that marry in the temple may live so as to qualify for innumerable blessings, foremost of which is the continuation of their relationship in the spirit world following death, and again as they reach the highest degree of glory. Only Latter-day Saints even converse about eternal marriage, about eternal lives. The apostasy relative to marriage continues to take its toll on the world's theology. It is to Joseph Smith that we express our appreciation for the restoration of gospel doctrines, principles, and priesthood authority that came through his hands. Angels restored priesthood authority to him that culminates in the uniting of a man and woman in an endless association. There is a caution, however: Unless we treat each other well, honor our covenants, and cherish each other and each child, we cannot expect to live as an eternal family.

Application: Read D&C 131:1-4 and then re-read the Prophet's statement above. Discuss its value to you.

JUNE 15

Brigham Young: "There are multitudes of pure and holy spirits waiting to take tabernacles…. It is the duty of every righteous man and woman to prepare tabernacles for all the spirits they can" (*Discourses of Brigham Young*, 197).

Our ability to produce a physical body through our male and female procreative powers is one of the more amazing miracles of this life. To think that through an act of love we conceive a child, and then give birth to a real, live, breathing soul. Some couples with physical limitations are unable to share in that blessing. But for those who are able, the blessings of Abraham sealed upon us at the time of a temple marriage, assures us that the spirits assigned to be our children are among the most valiant of the Father's premortal family. These spirits are needed now, in this last dispensation, to perform a work to which they have been foreordained. The Law of Chastity is given us to insure that the Father's children come to earth under the umbrella of a family with a loving father and mother to care for His children in His behalf. What a profound responsibility is entrusted to couples privileged to rear these infants to their adult stature.

Application: Discuss the miracle of conception and birth. What kind of parents are you turning out to be? Is there more 'sacrifice' involved in parenting than you anticipated? If no children yet, what kind of parents will you two be?

JUNE 16

Ezra Taft Benson: "What does it mean to love someone with all our hearts? (D&C 42:22.) It means with all our emotional feelings and our devotion. Surely when you love your wife with all your heart, you cannot demean her, criticize her, find fault with her, abuse her by words, sullen behavior, or actions" ("What Manner of Men Ought We to Be?" *Ensign*, Nov. 1983, 43).

Marriage and parenthood allow a man and a woman to love someone other than themselves with such devotion that their greatest desire is to spend eternity together. As parents we assist the Creator by helping to bring to pass the eternal life of each family member. At the time we marry, we are sure that we are 'in love.' It is true, but love, at that point, is in its elementary stage. Love blossoms as we come to care more about our spouse's welfare than we do about our own. There must be no ill-treatment of a spouse or child. Should it happen on occasion because we are not yet perfected, sincere repentance must be forthcoming. We are in the process of building a kingdom, an everlasting kingdom. We are laboring to fashion a marriage worthy of 'time and all eternity.' What disgraceful behavior and desecration of priesthood takes place when a husband mistreats his companion.

Application: Discuss how your love feelings for each other have blossomed since you married. How would you contrast what you thought was 'love' with your present feelings?

JUNE 17

John Taylor: "Husbands, do you love your wives and treat them right? They are given to you as part of yourself, and you ought to treat them with all kindness, with mercy and long suffering, and not be bitter, or harsh, or in any way desirous to display your (priesthood) authority. Then, you wives, treat your husbands right, and try to make them happy and comfortable. Endeavor to make your homes a little heaven, and try to cherish the good Spirit of God" (*Journal of Discourses* 2:118-119).

When a man has found his eternal companion, he has found his other half. When a woman finds a righteous man who loves and honors her, she has found a husband worthy of her greatest efforts to love him. She joins her femininity with his manhood. It is only through marriage that the two of you can attain exaltation in the long run. Take every opportunity to enrich your relationship, to make it a special companionship. You never know what may be growing inside of your body, or what accident or illness is just a street corner or doctor's appointment away that may cut short your time here together. Yes, you are sealed together by priesthood authority, so you have that assurance, but make each day count!

Application: Plan a fun surprise today. Perhaps a love note, a letter of appreciation, a treat, or flowers are simply ideas.

JUNE 18

Marvin J. Ashton: "True love is a process. True love requires personal action. Love must be continuing to be real. Love takes time. Too often expediency, infatuation, stimulation, persuasion, or lust are mistaken for love. How hollow, how empty if our love is no deeper than the arousal of momentary feeling or the expression in words of what is no more lasting than the time it takes to speak them....Love of God takes time. Love of family takes time. Love of country takes time. Love of neighbor takes time. Love of companion takes time. Love in courtship takes time. Love of self takes time" ("Love Takes Time," *Ensign*, Nov. 1975, 108, 110).

This is wise counsel from Elder Ashton. What passes for physical attraction, for infatuation, is labeled as 'love' by many. Love is deeper, more fulfilling, more enriching, and it takes time and experience to develop the kind of 'love' that inspires a sacrifice of personal preferences in behalf of another. Love is manifested as an anxious concern for the welfare and comfort of another. Love is an emotional attachment that can be stronger than death itself. Love is constant, kind, and tender. The couple that learns to love each other at the deepest levels, though they find it hard to express in words, are consistent in the way they treat each other.

Application: What would you say are the basic elements of love? How would you describe your love for each other to someone else?

JUNE 19

D. Todd Christofferson: "Attitudes toward human sexuality threaten the moral authority of women on several fronts. Abortion for personal or social convenience strikes at the heart of a woman's most sacred powers and destroys her moral authority. The same is true of sexual immorality and of revealing dress that not only debases women but reinforces the lie that a woman's sexuality is what defines her worth" ("The Moral Force of Women," *Ensign*, Nov. 2013, 31).

Historically women have been the gatekeepers of moral behavior in society. However, in today's world, with skimpy costumes, vulvar videos, sexual immorality on college campuses, and accessibility to pornography as near as a cellphone, women are too often portrayed as to their sexual attraction rather than as daughters of God, future wives and mothers. Perhaps chastity cannot be completely understood until a man watches his wife go through the pain and sacrifice of childbirth as she brings forth newborn life bearing the DNA of both companions. This is surely proof of the ultimate end of procreation and the meaning of chastity. It is at that point that men and women mature more fully in their understanding and appreciation for complete abstinence before marriage and total fidelity from then on.

Application: Satan tries to convince this generation that the important element of personality is one's sexual attractiveness. Prophets, however, teach that the true measure of manhood and womanhood lies in the purity of soul. Express appreciation to each other for being worthy to marry in the Lord's House and commit now to always remain faithful to the Law of Chastity.

JUNE 20

George Albert Smith: "You are fortunate men if you have been blessed with a good wife, a daughter of God, to stand by your side. And I want to say to you that God loves her just as much as he loves you. If you would have his blessings, you will treat her with love and kindness and tenderness and helpfulness. She will then be able to carry on under the responsibilities that come to her to bring children into the world and nurture and care for them and teach them the plan of life and salvation. And so I plead with you brethren, let your homes be the abiding place of love, and the authority that you bear should magnify that love in your soul and in the lives of your wives and your children" (*Conference Report*, October 1945, 22).

Every husband looks forward to marrying a sweetheart who will return his love and appreciate his contribution to the family, a wife who is committed to marriage and motherhood. A wife who gives herself in marriage to her husband physically, emotionally, mentally, and spiritually, raises her husband to his tallest spiritual stature. An honorable husband and father reciprocates her love for him and is anxious to assist her in her heavy responsibilities. His love for her in turn lifts her spirit as she realizes she is married to a husband who takes seriously his roles as husband and father.

Application: What have you two done 'fun' lately? What do you do to lift each other's spirits after a tough day? On any day?

JUNE 21

J. Ballard Washburn: "Thus we see that in marriage, a husband and wife enter into an order of the priesthood called the new and everlasting covenant of marriage. This covenant includes a willingness to have children and to teach them the gospel. Many problems of the world today are brought about when parents do not accept the responsibilities of this covenant" ("The Temple is a Family Affair," *Ensign*, May 1995, 12).

When you married in the temple you were authorized to 'multiply and replenish the earth.' Adding to your family, assuming health is not an issue, is a principal reason for marriage and the source of life's greatest joys. What greater manifestation of love is there than to unite together in an embrace that expresses so well your love and appreciation for each other? Children will certainly change your lives forever as you welcome a special spirit into your home. Unfortunately, we live in a day when couples are more interested in finding an effective method of birth control than they are interested in becoming parents.

Application: Notice the differences in each of your children. Discuss their personality differences even though they have the same parents—you!

JUNE 22

Elder Bruce C. Hafen: "Every marriage is tested repeatedly by three kinds of wolves. The first wolf is natural adversity....Second, the wolf of their own imperfections will test them....The third wolf is the excessive individualism that has spawned today's contractual attitudes" ("Covenant Marriage," *Ensign*, Nov. 1996, 26-27).

Mortality brings with it a train of accidents, diseases, genetic challenges, and tests of all kinds that fit in the category of 'natural adversities.' Our own weaknesses often contribute to a measure of misery and unhappiness. The emphasis in Western culture on individuals 'doing their own thing,' militates against the cooperation and unity that a happy marriage requires. In marriage we must move from "I" and "me" to "we" and "us." It is the command to be one in marriage that requires each spouse to subjugate personal desires for the good of the relationship and the family. The three wolves mentioned by Elder Hafen can disturb any marriage. Some of these tests are beyond our control; others result from our own misuse of agency. The gospel assists us in coping with the consequences of all three 'wolves.'

Application: Discuss how well you two function as a couple. What personal strengths did you bring to marriage that allow you to cooperate and work well together?

JUNE 23

D&C 82:10 "I, the Lord, am bound when ye do what I say, but when ye do not what I say, ye have no promise."

There is a difference between promises, commitments and covenants. Promises and commitments are between mortals. Covenants are made with the God of Heaven, with a Father who cares deeply about each of His children. We learn from scriptural and sacred sources that God presides over a *universe,* not merely a galaxy or a solar system. He instituted laws that bring us happiness when we obey them. As we come to understand His love for us and His desire for us to accomplish good in our lives, how foolish it would be for us to not obey His every command. For us to avoid binding ourselves to Him by covenant would be a form of insanity on our part! To act contrary to the laws God has given us, is not wise. To illustrate, when you marry in the temple, you have a divine assurance that you *will be* married forever. Is it within God's power to fulfill that covenant? Of course! We call it priesthood. On the other hand, were you to marry out of the temple, such an act would be contrary to God's law of marriage and as such would end up being temporary.

Application: What short and long-term blessings are yours if you honor God's laws? What consequences do we suffer when we disobey His laws?

JUNE 24

Gordon B. Hinckley: "I have in my office a file of letters received from women who cry out over the treatment they receive from their husbands in their homes. They tell of the activity of some of these men in Church responsibilities. They even speak of men holding temple recommends. And they speak of abuse, both subtle and open. They tell of husbands who lose their tempers and shout at their wives and children. They tell of men who *demand offensive intimate relations*. They tell of men who demean them and put them down and of fathers who seem to know little of the meaning of patience and forbearance with reference to their children" ("Keeping the Temple Holy," *Ensign*, May 1990, 52).

There is no place in a Latter-day Saint home for either husband or wife to become careless in the way they treat each other. President Hinckley accuses some men of treating their wife in ways that are abusive in the area of intimacy, and in being a father, and in their temperament. Possessing a recommend, exhibiting an impressive knowledge of scripture, or having an unusual ability to teach and speak in Church, do not compensate for rude behavior to a spouse. Inasmuch as we are in the process of learning how to function as husbands and wives, as fathers and mothers, the home is our laboratory where we learn to correlate gospel principles and behavior. It is in the home that we treat each other at least as good as we treat our neighbors and friends!

Application: Is there any abusive behavior in your relationship? Is there any sarcasm, cutting remarks, or harshness? Only you two know the answers. Resolve to always treat each other with love and respect.

JUNE 25

M. Russell Ballard: "Don't be afraid of marriage. I have been much more effective and much more able to accomplish things in my life with Barbara at my side than I ever would have been alone. Did we have hard times? Oh, yes. But they were some of the best times because we drew together, we prayed together, we worked together, we saw our way from one point of our lives on until today" ("Preparing for the Future," *Ensign*, Sept. 2011, 28).

We live in a day when the cost of living deters young men from assuming the responsibilities of marriage and family. Of course young married couples struggle, if not in adjusting to each other, in the area of limited resources. Of course challenges come with bearing and caring for children. They have a tendency to interrupt and interfere with *our* time and *our* interests. Of course there are more responsibilities with children than when you two were trying to convince each other that 'two can live as cheaply as one.' Then you were free to come and go at your leisure. Now you are 'tied down.' But you found each other out of myriad possibilities and now you are to make the best of your selection by becoming your best selves. Your ultimate purpose now is to build an excellent marriage companionship and unite yourselves together with such love that your children will call you blessed.

Application: Review current challenges you face: Income, education, Church callings, parenting issues, in-laws, etc. These 'opportunities,' believe it or not, build character that will yet prove valuable in your lives.

JUNE 26

Gordon B. Hinckley: "Surely no one reading the scriptures, both ancient and modern, can doubt the divine concept of marriage. The sweetest feelings of life, the most generous and satisfying impulses of the human heart, find expression in a marriage that stands pure and unsullied above the evil of the world" ("What God Hath Joined Together," *Ensign*, May 1991, 71).

The decline of traditional marriage in recent years is a departure from thousands of years of marriage history. We are stunned to see a worldwide phenomenon of people living together without marriage. It has always been an American tradition to look forward to marriage and becoming parents. Marriage appears burdensome to many. They want sexual relations without the responsibility of parenthood! Perhaps the one concept in an urban society to blame for this phenomenon is the notion that marriage is only for this brief lifetime, for 'as long as you both shall live.' With the idea that marriage is limited in time, individuals justify seeking the pleasures of the flesh without any real commitment to each other. Latter-day Saints understand that the doctrine of eternal marriage is part of the restoration of the gospel and priesthood to the earth in this final dispensation. Marriage is a requirement to live in the highest order of heaven. Such doctrine places marriage as a sacred trust between a man and woman.

Application: Discuss the state of marriage as you view it in our culture. What percent of couples would you say live together without being married? Search for the answer online.

JUNE 27

Spencer W. Kimball: "Two people coming from different backgrounds learn soon after the ceremony is performed that stark reality must be faced. There is no longer a life of fantasy or of make-believe; we must come out of the clouds and put our feet firmly on the earth. Responsibility must be assumed and new duties must be accepted. Some personal freedoms must be relinquished, and many adjustments, unselfish adjustments, must be made" ("Oneness in Marriage, *Ensign*, Mar. 1977, 3).

It is obvious in reading President Kimball's marriage addresses that he spent considerable time counseling married couples. All couples, of course, face adjustments as a married partnership. How could you fully envision as a single what adjustments you would face in marriage? There are issues that married couples find accentuate their different perspectives, upbringings, and backgrounds. Coming from two different families with varied ideas on how to do things may not be so apparent in the dating stage because we are so in love with love at that point that we don't make close observations. But marriage brings to bear reality. Successful marriage, it must be said, requires mature individuals. Ironically, much of that needed maturity can only be gained by being married!

Application: Discuss differences in family backgrounds that have surfaced. How have any differences required adjustments that you never contemplated in your premarital innocence?

JUNE 28

Harold B. Lee: "If young people 'would resolve from the moment of their marriage, that from that time forth they would resolve and do everything in their power to please each other in things that are right, even to the sacrifice of their own pleasures, their own appetites, their own desires, the problem of adjustment in married life would take care of itself, and their home would indeed be a happy home. Great love is built on great sacrifice, and that home where the principle of sacrifice for the welfare of each other is daily express is that home where there abides a great love" (*Conference Report*, April 1947, 49).

Prophets have recently stated that selfishness and pride are the major contributors to marital unhappiness. Living in an age of prosperity and technology, there are many distractions to lure us away from our primary objectives. Marriage involves sacrifices of time, hobbies, personal interests, leisure, and television. One of the most valuable training grounds for marriage available to the youth of the Church is missionary service where sacrifice is a daily occurrence. Living with a number of different companions who come from different family backgrounds while surviving without electronic 'toys,' men and women spend their days in the Lord's service. They are more concerned at this time of their lives in bringing joy and happiness to others rather than themselves. What better preparation for marriage is there? An effective returned missionary, because of his or her experience, should make an effective spouse.

Application: What sacrifices in marriage have you found that you were not expecting? In what ways does a mission prepare someone for marriage?

JUNE 29

Spencer W. Kimball. "One comes to realize very soon after marriage that the spouse has weaknesses not previously revealed or discovered. The virtues which were constantly magnified during courtship now grow relatively smaller, and the weaknesses which seemed so small and insignificant during courtship now grow to sizable proportions. The hour has come for understanding hearts, for self-appraisal, and for good common sense, reasoning, and planning" ("Oneness in Marriage," *Ensign*, March 1977, 3).

As we look into each other's eyes across the altar, what do we see? We see the 'perfect specimen.' However, marriage brings into focus things that were not clear to us while dating. In our singleness, we managed our own money, we spent it as we pleased, we ate when and whatever we wanted, we kept our rooms the way we wanted, and we made decisions we thought only impacted us. Now, marriage brings with it someone with different ideas about how life should be lived and carried out. Adjusting to the wishes and preferences of another in the initial stages of marriage may grate against our souls as we are 'forced' to learn and tolerate their opinions and ideas that are contrary to our own. At such times, humility and a willingness to be unselfish and learn the skill of compromise are essential! A successful marriage requires that both parties possess 'understandings hearts," and "good common sense, reasoning, and planning."

Application: Name the biggest adjustment you made in getting married. How difficult was it to adjust and how have your feelings for each other improved as you learned to make adjustments?

JUNE 30

Gordon B. Hinckley: "Of course, one is expected to be a full-tithe payer. The payment of tithing is simply a faithful response to a commandment of the Lord. It is a mark of obedience to the divine will. Furthermore, long observation has shown that the faithful and honest payment of tithing is an indicator of faithfulness in other matters" ("Keeping the Temple Holy," *Ensign*, May 1990, 51).

Tithing is one principle that we can obey precisely and with a grateful heart, or we can do so grudgingly. The manner in which we obey this commandment impacts our children too. Being united as a couple in the payment of tithing, and other contributions, and the attitude in which we pay them, is an important issue to the Lord. Tithing is the Lord's law of finance, and couples will, over the years, learn more fully the value of this law. The Lord doesn't need our funds, but we pay tithing out of obedience and thereby reap the blessings the Lord promised the obedient. You can be sure that along the way tithing may test your faith and resources, but you will also live to enjoy the blessings that come from living this law.

Application: Do you remember the first tithing you paid? Discuss your experience with tithing as a child, teenager, adult, and now married. Commit to each other to always qualify for a temple recommend.

JULY

JULY 1

Joseph F. Smith: "The lawful association of the sexes is ordained of God, not only as the sole means of race perpetuation, but for the development of the higher faculties and nobler traits of human nature, which the love-inspired companionship of man and woman alone can insure ("Unchastity the Dominant Evil of the Age," (*Improvement Era*, June 1917, 739).

Latter-day Saints view proper sexual relations as a sacred and private union of a lawfully married couple. This coupling was designed by the Lord to enrich marriage and create a stronger bond between spouses. Though sexual intimacy is often treated as crass and as the topic of humor for comedians, to Church members this relationship represents a recommitment to marriage. Its frequency in marriage says something about the stability and health of the marriage. Happily married people enjoy their private moments together while unhappily married couples find ways to avoid this part of their relationship. When couples like *and* love each other, intimacy further enriches their companionship; when a couple struggles, the frequency of this union drops off dramatically.

Application: Share your feelings about the intimate side of marriage. Is this an enriching time in your marriage? In what ways is this therapeutic to both of you?

JULY 2

Jeffrey R. Holland: "In seeking true peace, some of us need to improve what has to be improved, confess what needs to be confessed, forgive what has to be forgiven, and forget what should be forgotten in order that serenity can come to us. If there is a commandment we are breaking, and as a result it is breaking us and hurting those who love us, let us call down the power of the Lord Jesus Christ to help us, to free us, to lead us through repentance to that peace "which passeth all understanding" (The Peaceable Things of the Kingdom," *Ensign*, Nov. 1996, 83).

Marriage has a way of disturbing our quest for peace! While dating, we couldn't imagine any difficulty or problem that could create ill-will or angry feelings. However, the divorce rate reflects the fact that many couples are not prepared for the sacrifices that marriage entails. The 'honeymoon glow' evaporated for them somewhere along the way. Most of us do well in the beginning of an endeavor, but as time passes, we become more familiar with each other's weaknesses. It is then that the application of gospel principles grows more urgent. Along with personal weaknesses, our bodies lose their bloom as wrinkles, creaking joints, sore muscles, thinning hair, and bodily infirmities jolt us into the reality that we are mortal beings. It is then that true love, developed over many years, minimizes the impact of such superficial annoyances. As the adage says, 'old age ain't for sissies.' It turns out that happiness, after all, is not about bodies, looks, money, or prestige; happiness comes from the care and daily involvement of each one in the life of the other. By now we should be easy to entreat, and apologies should come with greater ease and with greater frequency. It is at that point that charity and a soft heart allows us to repent, to forgive, to improve, and to gain that peace "which passeth all understanding."

Application: Are you finding that the longer you are married, the easier it is to apologize, to not take yourselves so seriously? Which one of you is first to initiate the 'repentance' process?

JULY 3

Gordon B. Hinckley: "Avoid profanity. It is all around you.... Young people seem to pride themselves on using filthy and obscene language as well as indulging in profanity, taking the name of our Lord in vain. It becomes a vicious habit which, if indulged in while you are young, will find expression throughout your life. Who would wish to be married to a man whose speech is laden with filth and profanity?" ("Living Worthy of the Girl You Will Someday Marry," *Ensign*, May 1998, 50).

The use of profanity can easily become habitual. Like any habit, profanity can be fertilized or starved by its use or non-use. The phrase, 'O My G - -' has become a common expression in sit-coms, interviews with prominent people, movie scripts, and most public programming. To Latter-day Saints, profanity manifests a shallowness of personality and character and should be eschewed by all right-thinking people. The atmosphere and environment of the home should be a refuge from this "noise pollution." Our children are exposed to profanity with some regularity at school, at athletic contests, etc. To 'take the name of God in vain,' is the most serious form of profanity and is so offensive that it must never pass through our minds or lips.

Application: Do you recall the first time you heard someone swear? Do you recall how it shocked you? Take time to discuss this topic with your children.

JULY 4

L. Tom Perry: "We want our nation to hear again the words 'And this is our motto—In God We Trust.' We hope that our own members and all citizens throughout the nation will bow down on their knees on July 4 and thank God for his blessings and confess his goodnesses to them and all mankind. We hope it will be a time of recommitment to serving the God of this land" ("The Church and the U.S. Bicentennial," *Ensign*, June 1976, 9).

Four civilizations have inhabited this 'promised land' we call America. Four times the Lord has established a humble people upon this soil only to see the first three destroyed through eventual wickedness: The Antediluvians, those before the flood of Noah's day, the Jaredites, and the Lehite/Mulekite civilizations preceded this modern nation. The Lord led the present inhabitants—Gentiles—to this land as the fourth group, and established His Church among them. In setting this nation on its feet, God inspired men to compose a Constitution for its governance and then called forth a prophet for the latter-days—Joseph Smith. Unfortunately, recent prophets have pointed out that shadows are appearing among us that bear a striking similarity to the decline of earlier civilizations. The key to restoring our nation to its Christian base requires a return to the fundamental principles of the gospel of Jesus Christ. Our homes are the place where this movement must begin. If our homes fall apart, the nation cannot prosper. God bless America! In God We Trust!

Application: Express gratitude to the Lord for the privilege to live in a 'promised land,' established by "wise men whom I raised up unto this very purpose" (D&C 101:80).

JULY 5

Jeffrey R. Holland: "A life without problems or limitations or challenges—life without "opposition in all things," (2 Nephi 2:11), as Lehi phrased it—would paradoxically but in very fact be less rewarding and less ennobling than one which confronts—even frequently confronts—difficulty and disappointment and sorrow" ("The Peaceable Things of the Kingdom," *Ensign*, Nov. 1996, 84).

One of the more interesting statements in scripture comes from Lehi's conclusion that there *must* be opposition in all things in order for us to appreciate the lessons of life. But, who wants or desires opposition? Who wants to confront opposites, especially when we are committed to do the right things? Yet the contrast between good and evil, health and sickness, pain versus good health —all contribute to our maturity. These are lessons that we signed up to take even before we entered this mortal university. The plan of our Father calls for us to use our agency to make choices in a day when there are many opposing options. Marriage brings together two people with opposing views, with different habits, perspectives, talents, and beliefs. Learning to deal with "problems or limitations or challenges" that arise in marriage in Christlike ways is part of the valuable lessons we learn in mortality.

Application: How do opposites contribute to our learning and maturity? How does pain and sickness, for example, cause us to appreciate good health?

JULY 6

Joseph Fielding Smith, Jr.: "The family is the most important organization in time or in eternity. Our purpose in life is to create for ourselves eternal family units. There is nothing that will ever come into your family life that is as important as the sealing blessings of the temple and then keeping the covenants made in connection with this order of celestial marriage" ("Counsel to the Saints and to the World," *Ensign*, July 1972, 27).

What an interesting world God created for His children and agency is one of its more fascinating aspects. In recent times, people are trying to change the Father's plan by deciding that they don't need to marry or have children. In some countries of the world, couples are fined or persecuted if they have more than one child. A modern trend in our country is to limit family size, the ideal, of course, is to have a boy and a girl, one of each kind! The Father's plan is being hijacked by those who have no idea that our children are His children. And this despite the invention of technologies that free up time for couples to make parenting 'easier' for them. (Imagine having to hook up the horses to a buggy to get them to school!) Sometimes health and other factors limit family size, of course, but Latter-day Saints remain 'pro-family' because family, from an eternal perspective, is what our lives are all about. The experience and growth we gain in these intimate relationships are among the few things that we take with us from this life.

Application: Imagine the difficulty your ancestors had in finding the Church and then traveling long distances to a temple. Express gratitude to Heavenly Father that you live in a day when you are able to organize an eternal family unit rather easily.

JULY 7

Spencer W. Kimball: "Supreme happiness in marriage is governed considerably by a primary factor—that of the bearing and rearing of children. Too many young people set their minds, determining they will not marry or have children until they are more secure, until the military service period is over; until the college degree is secured; until the occupation is more well-defined; until the debts are paid; or until it is more convenient. They have forgotten that the first commandment is to 'be fruitful, and multiply, and replenish the earth, and subdue it" (The *Teachings of Spencer W. Kimball*, 328-29).

Birth control pills were approved by the FDA in 1960. Preventing the conception and birth of children is rather simple. Knowing when to stop taking the 'pill' and start a family is increasingly more difficult for young couples because of the material things they think they need to acquire or pay off. A better car, a bigger TV, more electronic 'toys,' and an even a larger savings account comes before children. Family size has dropped off in recent years, even among Latter-day Saint families. Now, a family with more than 2 or 3 children is considered 'big.' The Lord reserved some of His 'most valiant' spirit children to come to earth in this day, and faithful Latter-day Saints obey the command, where health and circumstances allow, to 'multiply and replenish the earth.'

Application: Is a marriage or children mentioned in either of your patriarchal blessings? Retain a copy of your children's blessings. As they mature and move away for school, missions, and marriage, you will observe the hand of the Lord in their lives.

JULY 8

Joseph Fielding Smith, Jr.: "No nation can endure for any length of time, if the marriage covenants are abused and treated with contempt. The anger of the Almighty was kindled against ancient nations for their immorality. There is nothing that should be held in greater sacredness than this covenant by which the spirits of men are clothed with mortal tabernacles" (*Doctrines of Salvation*, 2:86-87).

A temple marriage, in most countries, conveys both civil and ecclesiastical authority to live together and enjoy the privileges of sexual intimacy. Why is this sacred union treated so casually in our culture? Why do singles think that they have any authority to participate in this intimate coupling? One of the Ten Commandments says "Thou Shalt not commit adultery" (Exodus 20:14). World-wide this commandment has been ignored or violated with impunity, and is one reason why divine judgments have come in the past, and will yet come in the future upon the earth. Outside of marriage, this relationship is simply a selfish use of another person to gratify one's sexual urges. In marriage, it represents a renewal of the covenant entered into by both spouses during the ceremony, whether civil or ecclesiastical.

Application: Fornication and adultery have always existed in spite of divine commands to the contrary. In your opinion, how do people justify sexual sins and transgressions?

JULY 9

Howard W. Hunter: "Honor your wife's unique and divinely appointed role as a mother in Israel and her special capacity to bear and nurture children. We are under divine commandment to multiply and replenish the earth and to bring up our children and grandchildren in light and truth. You share, as a loving partner, the care of the children. Help her to manage and keep up your home. Help teach, train, and discipline your children" ("Being a Righteous Husband and Father," *Ensign*, Nov. 1994, 50).

Unfortunately the cost of living has forced more and more women into the work force, leaving children off at day-care centers, pre-schools, babysitters, or to fend for themselves in front of the television set. Hopefully, wives who must work out of the home find that their husbands are more willing to pitch in by helping with housework and child care. In earlier days, men were accused of letting their wives assume the responsibilities of child care and home maintenance. Wives are happier when husbands wash dishes, assist with laundry, with child care, and with parenting.

Application: As a wife, express appreciation to your husband as a father. If both of you are 'breadwinners,' how well are you cooperating in carrying out housekeeping and parenting roles?

JULY 10

Gordon B. Hinckley: "An extravagant husband or wife can jeopardize any marriage. I think it is a good principle that each have some freedom and independence with everyday, necessary expenditures, while at the same time always discussing and consulting and agreeing on large expenditures. There would be fewer rash decisions, fewer unwise investments, fewer consequent losses, fewer bankruptcies if husbands and wives would counsel together on such matters and unitedly seek counsel from others" (Cornerstones of a Happy Home," *Satellite broadcast fireside for husbands and wives*, 29 January 1984).

What would life be like if you were married to a spendthrift, one with little control over spending habits? How destructive and upsetting would that be to a marriage? Of course, every spouse needs some money to spend on personal items, money for which they need not account to the spouse. But major expenses should require mutual agreement. Otherwise as President Hinckley indicates, "an extravagant husband or wife can jeopardize any marriage."

Application: Since marriage, have you become more conservative or more liberal in your spending habits? Do you each have funds to spend on personal items?

JULY 11

Marvin J. Ashton: "Perhaps the greatest charity comes when we are kind to each other, when we don't judge or categorize someone else, when we simply give each other the benefit of the doubt or remain quiet. Charity is accepting someone's differences, weaknesses, and shortcomings; having patience with someone who has let us down; or resisting the impulse to become offended when someone doesn't handle something the way we might have hoped. Charity is refusing to take advantage of another's weakness and being willing to forgive someone who has hurt us. Charity is expecting the best of each other" ("The Tongue Can Be A Sharp Sword," *Ensign*, May 1992, 19).

Charity is the 'mother' of all virtues. Paul and Moroni both discourse on charity. It is the motto of Relief Society: 'Charity never faileth.' This attribute amounts to an emotional interest and concern for the welfare of others and is the 'pure love of Christ.' In marriage, this attribute is especially important to a couple's happiness; in fact, exaltation is impossible to attain without it. Charity comes into play in parenting because youth lack maturity and often make unwise choices. Parents must exercise patience and charity as they assist their children to grow from infancy to adulthood.

Application: Read Moroni 7:44-48 and explore various aspects of charity as they apply to your relationship.

JULY 12

Boyd K. Packer: "A man who holds the priesthood does not have an advantage over a woman in qualifying for exaltation. The woman, by her very nature, is also co-creator with God and the primary nurturer of the children. Virtues and attributes upon which perfection and exaltation depend come naturally to a woman and are refined through marriage and motherhood" ("For Time and All Eternity," *Ensign*, November 1993, 22).

What an elevating concept of women! In this life we learn to be a spouse and a parent because that is the work of couples in eternity. Exaltation is the highest of all attainments and can only be reached by a man and a woman married by divine authority, and who acquire the divine qualities and characteristics of charity, love, and compassion. The man, in holding the priesthood, is never superior to his wife, for priesthood can only be exercised in behalf of others. There is no ordinance where a man lays his hands upon his own head and gives himself a blessing. His priesthood is always to bless others. Women, in their own natures, possess virtues and attributes that bless her husband and children in ways that are unique to her 'softer' side.

Application: As a wife, explain how marriage has helped you more fully develop your strengths as a woman. As her husband, explain what marriage to her has meant to you.

JULY 13

James E. Faust: "Spiritual peace is not to be found in race or culture or nationality but rather through our commitment to God and to the covenants and ordinances of the gospel. Each of us, regardless of our nationality, needs to reach down into the innermost recesses of our souls to find the divinity that is deep within us and to earnestly petition the Lord for an endowment of special wisdom and inspiration" ("Heirs to the Kingdom of God," *Ensign*, May 1995, 63).

As Latter-day Saints, we seek genuine spiritual peace for ourselves and for our families. That peace only comes through living the principles of the gospel of Jesus Christ. Once we obtain a testimony of God and understand our relationship to Him and to each other, we willingly commit ourselves to service in the Kingdom. We fill many different callings over the course of a lifetime: Home and visiting teachers, Sunday School teachers, priesthood quorum leaders, administrators, and officers in the auxiliaries. A 'lay church' calls for us to serve each other, and it is because of what we know about the nature of God and our relationship to each other as brothers and sisters, that we willingly serve. It is not because of race or cultural traditions. President Faust was right: Spiritual peace comes through honoring our covenants.

Application: Consider life without the Church. What would you do on Sunday? What would you do with the money you now contribute in tithing, fast offerings, etc. How valuable is your temple marriage?

JULY 14

Dallin H. Oaks: "The gospel teaches us that we are the spirit children of heavenly parents. Before our mortal birth we had 'a pre-existent spiritual personality, as the sons and daughters of the Eternal Father' (statement of the First Presidency, *Improvement Era*, Mar. 1912, p. 417; see also Jer. 1:5). We were placed here on earth to progress toward our destiny of eternal life. These truths give us a unique perspective and different values to guide our decisions from those who doubt the existence of God and believe that life is the result of random processes" ("The Great Plan of Happiness," *Ensign*, Nov. 1993, 72).

Can you imagine people believing that we came into existence as a result of natural laws; that we evolved from lower life forms? "In the gospel of Jesus Christ the family is at the pinnacle of dignity because the first man and the first woman, Adam and Eve, were the direct and first generation, literal offspring of heavenly parents both in the spirit body and in the physical body," writes Robert J. Matthews, former dean of religion at BYU Provo. "The human family is literally, in every sense, the offspring of God. This is according to divine law, for the scriptural accounts state that living things reproduce and bring forth 'after their kind' and that the 'seed could only bring forth the same in itself, after his kind' (Abr. 4:11-12, 21, 24-25) (*Selected Writings of Robert J. Matthews*, Deseret Book, 1999, 468).

The fact is that we did not descend from lower animals, but from the Highest Form of life— Heavenly Parents.

Application: What difference would it make in the way people behave if they thought they descended from animals? Re-read the first three paragraphs of "The Family: A Proclamation to the World," (*Ensign,* Nov. 1995, 102, or access at *lds.org*).

JULY 15

James E. Faust: "The family relationship of father, mother, and child is the oldest and most enduring institution in the world. It has survived vast differences of geography and culture. This is because marriage between man and woman is a natural state and is ordained of God. It is a moral imperative. Those marriages performed in our temples, meant to be eternal relationships, then, become the most sacred covenants we can make" ("Father, Come Home," *Ensign*, May 1993, 36).

Here Elder Faust reflects on the permanence of marriage as a divine institution. It has endured over the millennia, and it is only in recent times that its value has been questioned. Latter-day Saints are interested in forming an eternal alliance. Mortality is our time to learn how to function in the eternal roles of spouse and parent. Inasmuch as divorce has become a convenient and acceptable outlet to many, some couples bail out of marriage without making a real effort to keep it together. On the other hand, some people put up with marital abuse far beyond what God would expect as reasonable. These individuals remain in the relationship despite suffering physical attacks, apostasy of a spouse, emotional and spiritual abuse, and occasionally the ultimate of sins—adultery. We are not a church that believes that divorce is never justified.

Application: What is the driving force behind attacks on the family? How did we come to the point where people mock this sacred institution?

JULY 16

Wilford Woodruff: "For over half a century, the leaders of this Church have counseled with parents in the home to gather their children around them in a weekly Home Evening and there teach the truths of salvation—honesty, sobriety, integrity, and chastity. One of our leaders has promised that if parents would do this, "ninety-nine out of every hundred children…will observe them through life" (*The Discourses of Wilford Woodruff*, 267-268).

Family Home Evening is a special time for Latter-day Saint families to spend an evening each week to develop individual spirituality and to strengthen family relationships. Parents may read from scripture, from the *Ensign*, and from a variety of Church publications, or find ideas from the Church's *Family Home Evening* manual. We gather each week to sing the songs of Zion, to learn the doctrines of the Church, to calendar activities, and to relax and enjoy one another. Coordinating schedules, expressing love, and sharing insights about school instruction, friends, and while we remind ourselves of a gospel principle or two, pays later dividends.

Application: Evaluate the quality of your Family Home Evenings. Are they too long to hold your children's attention given their ages? Do you allow them to share ideas and insights as well as participate in teaching lessons?

JULY 17

James E. Faust: "In my opinion, members of the Church have the most effective cure for our decaying family life. It is for men, women, and children to honor and respect the divine roles of both fathers and mothers in the home. In so doing, mutual respect and appreciation among the members of the Church will be fostered by the righteousness found there" ("Father, Come Home," *Ensign*, May 1993, 36-37).

When a husband regularly conveys appreciation to his wife for specific things that she does, and she reciprocates by commenting on specific positive things he does, feelings of love are strengthened. All of us have a need to feel loved, appreciated, valued, and reasonably competent in the way we carry out our roles in our family. When a husband compliments his wife on a specific trait, activity, or meal, and when a wife compliments her husband on a specific accomplishment, activity, or trait, these expressions remain fixed in our minds and hearts. We can even remember the day, the time and the subject of the comment! On the other hand, rude comments, sarcastic jibes, and personal criticisms become rooted deeply within our souls—never to be forgotten. We all function more effectively when we receive positives. This same principle holds true with children.

Application: Select a recent act, behavior, or service your spouse did that made you happy.

JULY 18

Joe J. Christensen: "Keep your courtship alive. Make time to do things together—just the two of you. As important as it is to be with the children as a family, you need regular weekly time alone together. Scheduling it will let your children know that you feel that your marriage is so important that you need to nurture it. That takes commitment, planning, and scheduling" ("Marriage and the Great Plan of Happiness," *Ensign*, May 1995, 65).

The counsel to have a Friday night date has long been given. There is something about getting away together, away from children, and renewing your love for each other; it reminds you of why you decided to 'tie the knot.' Secure a good babysitter, or line up an in-law or a mature, dependable and trustworthy neighborhood girl or boy, and escape. Once in a while, splurge. Get acquainted with community theater, with athletic teams in your area, with parks, with recreation spots, and with movies. Why not take turns choosing the place to go. Dates don't have to be expensive outings, but they ought to be weekly. Put a few dollars aside each payday so that the budget always has a few funds to enjoy an outing. Wives need a break from children, husbands need a break from their schedule, and children need a break from both of you!

Application: Take turns planning Friday night dates. Be creative. Whether it is an ice cream cone, a shake, a hamburger, or a health food store—make it regular.

JULY 19

Gordon B. Hinckley: "Altogether too many men, leaving their wives at home in the morning and going to work, where they find attractively dressed and attractively made-up young women, regard themselves as young and handsome and as an irresistible catch. They complain that their wives do not look the same as they did twenty years ago when they married them. To which I say, 'Who would, after living with you for twenty years?'" ("Our Solemn Responsibilities," *Ensign*, Nov. 1991, 51).

President Hinckley usually had a twinkle in his eye and spoke with a sense of humor, but this time his talk was on a serious note. There are too many situations where couples break up homes and families, where covenants are violated, and sadly, he says, it is most often the husband who is responsible for the tragedy. Marriages are kept strong and viable by a consistent living of the gospel—scripture reading, temple attendance, couple and family prayer, family home evenings, paying tithing—activities that support the Spirit of the Lord in our personal lives. These are the things that happily married couples do. When we keep the commandments and merit the Spirit of the Lord individually and as a couple, the chances of something tragic becomes more and more remote. Husbands are under covenant to be men of character. Wives are under similar obligations to be faithful to their marital vows.

Application: Find ways at work during the day to remind yourself of your most precious possessions. Family pictures or children's artwork on a desk or wall is a good start. Give your spouse a call at lunch just to say hello and chat for a few minutes.

JULY 20

Ezra Taft Benson: "Fathers, yours is an eternal calling from which you are never released. Callings in the Church, as important as they are, by their very nature are only for a period of time, and then an appropriate release takes place. But a father's calling is eternal, and its importance transcends time. It is a calling for both time and eternity" (To the Fathers in Israel," *Ensign*, Nov. 1987, 48).

We call bishops and they serve for approximately five years; stake presidents typically serve nine or ten years. However, a father's calling never ends for he will be a father not only in this life but will continue that role in the next. Inasmuch as his calling lasts forever, the time he gives to fatherhood now will be invaluable. In our society we don't prepare boys very well for the magnificent calling of father. Being an effective father is an imitated skill rather than a trait inherent in a gene or chromosome. If no father was in the home as a young man was growing up, he must learn fathering skills by observing good fathers while serving as a missionary or in his home ward. If you were to ask family relations specialists for the best way to improve family life, be assured that their answer would be: "We need better fathers."

Application: Compute the number of hours you spent this past week as a father or mother with each individual child. Time together is wonderful, but occasionally each child needs time alone with a mom or dad.

JULY 21

Gordon B. Hinckley: "A husband who domineers his wife, who demeans and humiliates her, and who makes officious demands upon her not only injures her, but he also belittles himself. And in many cases, he plants a pattern of future similar behavior in his sons" ("Our Solemn Responsibilities," *Ensign*, Nov. 1991, 51).

Men initiate the dating process. Then they follow up with an offer of engagement and marriage. In order to convince a young woman that she should accept his offer, he exhibits a number of Christ-like characteristics to attract her. This behavior 'proves' beyond doubt that he *does* possess the ability to be a 'nice guy,' to function as an adequate husband. However, during the marriage, should he become domineering, or one who will not allow his wife room to 'flex her muscles' so to speak, or who leaves her out of financial decisions, or who doles out money in a miserly fashion, or who rejects her opinions, or who has no interest in an equal partner in his marriage, destroys her love. A husband, as the divinely appointed family 'head,' must be the epitome of charity and love if he wants his wife and children to follow his lead.

Application: Happy is the wife who has a husband who cherishes her. Ask your wife for a suggestion (only one) that would be helpful to you. Any suggestion should be given humbly and gently, and received in kindness!

JULY 22

Gordon B. Hinckley: "How beautiful is the marriage of a young man and a young woman who begin their lives together kneeling at the altar in the house of the Lord, pledging their love and loyalty one to another for time and all eternity. When children come into that home, they are nurtured and cared for, loved and blessed with the feeling that their father loves their mother. In that environment they find peace and strength and security. Watching their father, they develop respect for women. They are taught self-control and self-discipline, which bring the strength to avoid later tragedy" ("Our Solemn Responsibilities," *Ensign*, Nov. 1991, 52).

When we kneel at the altar during our marriage ceremony, we solemnly covenant with God that we are willing to accept each other's strengths and weaknesses not just for a few brief years, but way, way beyond; we pledge our love forever. We then bring to our home the children of God and our family is off and running. Next to the temple, home is the most sacred place on earth. It is there that we are kind and affectionate with each other. If not, then we destroy the spirit of our sanctuary. Children are greatly influenced by what they see and hear their parents say to each other and how they treat one another. Your example rings louder in their ears than any sermon you give in a family home evening. Don't disappoint your children by the way you treat each other, for much of their success in life depends on the model you display.

Application: Make a list from President Hinckley's suggestions on how to strengthen your marriage and family and then do your best to implement them.

JULY 23

Russell M. Nelson: "Marriage, especially temple marriage, and family ties involve covenant relationships. They cannot be regarded casually. With divorce rates escalating throughout the world today, it is apparent that many spouses are failing to endure to the end of their commitments to each other. And some temple marriages fail because a husband forgets that his highest and most important priesthood duty is to honor and sustain his wife" ("Endure and Be Lifted up," *Ensign*, May 1997, 71).

Temple covenants provide Latter-day Saints with power to live gospel principles in a fallen world environment. Solemn promises are made in the Home of our Father concerning certain behaviors and actions required of us if we expect to live among the righteous. It would be folly not to follow through on our commitments. We don't want to disappoint Heavenly Father or ourselves by being careless. We build temples to receive instruction on celestial principles and then are given the opportunity to subscribe to them. Ordinances become our signature that we will abide by the covenants we take upon ourselves. The Savior said, "I will raise up unto myself a pure people, that will serve me in righteousness" (D&C 100:16). Honoring temple covenants is a way for us to become sanctified. In return for our willingness to abide by our commitments, blessings are extended to us that include eventual eternal life and exaltation. Our task is simple then: *Keep our covenants*! We enter the path that leads to eternal life at baptism, and as we mature spiritually, we accept greater obligations in our temple worship. Covenant-keeping assures us of the promise of receiving "all that my Father hath" (D&C 84:38).

Application: Read D&C 109:4-5 for another reason why we build temples.

JULY 24

Russell M. Nelson: "Baptism is an extremely important ordinance. But it is only initiatory. The supreme benefits of membership in the Church can be realized only through the exalting ordinances of the temple. These blessings qualify us for 'thrones, kingdoms, principalities, and powers" in the celestial kingdom" (D&C 132:19). ("Endure and Be Lifted up," *Ensign*, May 1997, 72).

Baptism is called the 'covenant of salvation.' It is one of the essential ordinances in which we participate, typically at age eight; later for converts. Marriage is the 'covenant of exaltation,' for it is an essential ordinance if we are to qualify for the highest degree of glory in the Celestial Kingdom (see D&C 131:1-4). Baptism is the entrance into the Kingdom of God—the Church. Marriage is an ordinance whereby we obtain promises of exaltation and eternal lives. Once married, Church members have made every covenant and received every ordinance to enable them to qualify for exaltation. If you married in the temple, you were baptized and confirmed; the husband holds the higher priesthood, and both have experienced an initiatory ceremony, an endowment, and the crowning ordinance of a marriage sealing.

Application: Discuss your feelings the day you married in the temple. What was the counsel you received at the time you were sealed? If you were married civilly first, contrast the two ceremonies.

JULY 25

Ephesians 4:29 "Let no corrupt communication proceed out of your mouth, but that which is good."

There are three 'levels of communication:' Superficial, personal, and validating. In marriage we become more familiar with all three. A *superficial level* treats subjects that don't require much risk on our part—weather, sports, cars, etc. A *personal level* involves topics that we would be hesitant to share with strangers because of the uncertainty of their response or reaction. We usually limit this level to friends and family inasmuch as they represent our innermost thoughts and deeply held feelings, and which require more risk by us to impart. A v*alidation* level is one of affirmation of a spouse or child, including marital intimacy for the parents. A happy marriage involves all three levels, and happily married couples move easily between these levels as they learn that they can safely 'risk' at any of these levels with each other.

Application: Become aware of these three levels of communication. Share something superficial ("What a beautiful day"); something personal ("my heart aches for my mom with her cancer,"); and validating ("I love you with all my heart"). Notice how the personal and validation levels create emotions of love and charity as we convey deeply held feelings directly. The key to a great marriage is to be able to share thoughts and feelings at 'personal' and 'validating levels.'

JULY 26

Spencer W. Kimball: "In his wisdom and mercy, our Father made men and women dependent on each other for the full flowering of their potential. Because their natures are somewhat different, they can complement each other; because they are in many ways alike, they can understand each other. Let neither envy the other for their differences; let both discern what is superficial and what is beautifully basic in those differences, and act accordingly" ("Relief Society—Its Promise and Potential," *Ensign*, March 1976, 5).

Of course men and women are different! Hallelujah! How would you like to be married to a clone of you? What a disaster that would be! Many in the secular world either stress the differences that exist between men and women to explain a high divorce rate and the many unhappily married couples. Or, they ignore or suppress gender distinctions in the name of political correctness or of misguided social agendas. In the Lord's plan gender differences exist because of a variety of roles men and women must play. Each brings strengths that are unique to their gender to the marriage. In the gospel framework we do not pit men against women nor do we view males and females the same. We view them as complementary and capable of fulfilling their divine roles in marriage and family life.

Application: Discuss the differences you see in males and females. How do their different natures complement each other?

JULY 27

Neal A. Maxwell: "We men know the women of God as wives, mothers, sisters, daughters, associates, and friends. You seem to tame us and to gentle us, and yes, to teach us and to inspire us. For you, we have admiration as well as affection, because righteousness is not a matter of role, nor goodness a matter of gender. In the work of the Kingdom, men and women are not without each other, but do not envy each other....("The Woman of God," *Ensign*, May 1978, 10).

The Apostle Paul declared, "Neither is the man without the woman, neither the woman without the man, in the Lord. For as the woman is of the man, even so is the man also by the woman" (1 Cor. 11:11-12.) What a wonderful treatise. A man holds the priesthood and presides in his family. A wife has power with her husband over conception and birth. A woman's talents are magnified as she nourishes and cares for her newborns, infants, and young children. If the husband is the 'head' of the home, perhaps the wife is the 'heart.' Together they constitute a marriage partnership that is complementary in construction and function!

Application: Read this article by Elder Maxwell on *lds.org.*

JULY 28

Merrill J. Bateman: "When a man understands how glorious a woman is, he treats her differently. When a woman understands that a man has the seeds of divinity within him, she honors him not only for who he is but for what he may become. An understanding of the divine nature allows each person to have respect for the other. The eternal view engenders a desire in men and women to learn from and share with each other" ("The Eternal Family," *Brigham Young University Devotional Speeches*, 1998, 113).

The gospel of Jesus Christ places marriage at its forefront. If one believes that marriage and family is just something we do in mortality, how easy would it be to justify divorce, or immoral behavior, or to live together without marriage, or to avoid parenthood? This behavior evidences the need for the gospel being restored and explains why we have a missionary outreach to the world. To Latter-day Saints however, knowing that we continue as a male and a female in a resurrected state, what could be more natural than to want to continue the association we began here, there? If you think of marriage as a temporary arrangement, then why marry? Why would anyone go through the pain and hassle that accompanies marriage and parenthood? What would be the ultimate purpose of marriage? Perhaps it would be an ego stroke to see if you *are* capable of creating a child that resembles you? How foolish are the philosophies of men compared with the wisdom of God and the principles of the restored gospel revealed through the Prophet Joseph Smith.

Application: Explain how you would behave if your belief was that marriage and family was limited to this brief span of life.

JULY 29

Boyd K. Packer: "The plan of happiness requires the righteous union of male and female, man and woman, husband and wife....A body patterned after the image of God was created for Adam, and he was introduced into the Garden. At first, Adam was alone. He held the priesthood, but alone, he could not fulfill the purposes of his creation. No other man would do. Neither alone nor with other men could Adam progress. Nor could Eve with another woman. It was so then. It is so today. Eve, an helpmeet, was created. Marriage was instituted, for Adam was commanded to cleave unto his *wife* (not just to a *woman*) and "to none else' (D&C 42:22). ("For Time and All Eternity," Nov. 1993, 21).

In this telestial culture, the ultimate purposes of marriage and family life are unknown or confusing. The thinking of most people is that this life is our first existence ever, and is initiated at birth if not at conception. Latter-day Saints know of a premortal existence, a premortal realm where we were born to resurrected parents. We were born as their children and we lived with them in a celestial society for a very long period. Mortality was the next step in our progress because we required another body if we wanted to marry and create children of our own. We are now much closer to our ultimate destiny. We have married and are experiencing parenthood. We will now simply follow the 'instructions' that our Father has given us. Marriage is the culminating step in mortality that qualifies us for the highest level of salvation.

Application: Who is Elder Packer addressing here? How has this movement grown in your lifetime?

JULY 30

Marvin J. Ashton: "We often equate charity with visiting the sick, taking in casseroles to those in need, or sharing our excess with those who are less fortunate. But really, true charity is much, much more. Real charity is not something you give away it is something that you acquire and make a part of yourself. And when the virtue of charity becomes implanted in your heart, you are never the same again" ("The Tongue Can Be A Sharp Sword," *Ensign*, May 1992, 18-19).

Charity is a condition of the heart and Moroni explains that in giving gifts, we must do it wholehearted and not grudgingly. "For behold, if a man being evil giveth a gift, he doeth it grudgingly; wherefore it is counted unto him the same as if he had retained the gift; wherefore he is counted evil before God....Wherefore, a man being evil cannot do that which is good; neither will he give a good gift (Moroni 7:8, 10). The home is the laboratory where the initial feelings of charity develop and begin to mature. This 'heart condition' is shaped and refined as children observe their parents exercise this most important character trait.

Application: Are you more charitable with friends or colleagues than you are with those within the 'walls of your own home?' How is charity 'implanted in your heart?'

JULY 31

Margaret D. Nadauld: "You can recognize women who are grateful to be a daughter of God by their outward appearance. These women understand their stewardship over their bodies and treat them with dignity. They care for their bodies as they would a holy temple, for they understand the Lord's teaching, 'Know ye not that ye are the temple of God, and that the Spirit of God dwelleth in you?'" (1 Corinthians 3:16). ("The Joy of Womanhood," *Ensign*, November 2000, 15).

Is there anything more attractive than a righteous woman, one who understands her divine role as a daughter of God, one who magnifies her talents and skills in her responsibilities as a woman, as a wife, and as a mother? How glorious is a woman who cares for her body and whose outward appearance is comely and pleasing. She responds to her stewardships with verve and class. Lucky is that man who somewhat blindly chooses his eternal companion only to find out later how wise his choice turned out to be as he was blessed over and over again by her feminine qualities. The pair unites in marriage and then labors on behalf of their children in a home filled with love and compassion.

Application: What attributes did your wife possess before marriage that now endear you to her more than ever?

AUGUST

AUGUST 1

Gordon B Hinckley: "I hear so many complaints from men and women that they cannot communicate with one another. Perhaps I am naïve, but I do not understand this. Communication is essentially a matter of conversation. They must have communicated when they were [dating and] courting. Can they not continue to speak together after marriage? Can they not discuss with one another in an open and frank and candid and happy way their interests, their problems, their challenges, their desires?" (Cornerstones of a Happy Home," *Satellite broadcast fireside for husbands and wives*, 29 January 1984).

In secular circles, communication is thought to be the primary cause of most marital difficulties. The couple, it seems, simply has poor communication skills. Yet, communication is also thought to be the solution. The couple just needs to learn better communication skills. Prophets, however, point to a different problem and solution. They suggest that what appears to be a lack of communication skills is merely symptomatic of personal selfishness and pride. After all, when couples date, they communicate quite well. They are attentive, use appropriate language, display little if any temper, dress modestly, and are at their clever and humorous best. The point: If counselors simply work with couples to improve their communication skills without changing their 'hearts,' without them gaining an eternal perspective, counseling simply makes married couples more clever fighters!

Application: We all learn to communicate effectively during marriage. Yet, in our single state, if we were not fairly good at communicating, we would never have married. How has your post-marriage communication changed for the better?

AUGUST 2

Genesis 2:24 "Therefore shall a man leave his father and his mother, and shall cleave unto his wife: and they shall be one flesh."

Matthew 19:4-6 "Have ye not read, that he which made them at the beginning made them male and female, And said, For this cause shall a man leave father and mother, and shall cleave to his wife: and they twain shall be one flesh? Wherefore they are no more twain, but one flesh. What therefore God hath joined together, let not man put asunder."

This divine injunction is a clear command to married couples that they should live separate and apart from their parents. It is in making their own way that spines are strengthened, backbones are stiffened, and self-reliance develops into a core value. Becoming one flesh is authorization to use their masculine and feminine powers to create life in addition to strengthening their marital bonds. Being of one flesh means that couples share their very souls. They are to become one in purpose and in striving toward the goal of eternal life.

Application: What does it mean to 'leave' father and mother? What should the relationship be between you two and your parents on both sides? How successfully have you 'left' parents?

AUGUST 3

Joseph Fielding Smith, Jr.: "In this the final dispensation, the Prophet Joseph Smith was taught by revelation that the union between a man and his wife was to endure forever. Death, while it would intervene, was to be only a temporary separation, and the union of husband and wife would continue on through all eternity" (*Conference Report*, Apr. 1965, 10).

When a husband and a wife possess that love begotten by the Holy Spirit, their hearts are in agreement that death should not bring a permanent separation. It is only in the Lord's Church, restored in these latter days, that such a doctrine and an accompanying priesthood ordinance make such desires possible. Examine the alternatives: We are born as a mortal, then grow to adulthood, then marry, then bear children, and then spend the next few decades learning to improve as spouses and parents only to find that at death we are separated forever! We want to return to a spirit existence and live singly forever. How silly that would be. Perhaps that was why Jacob reasoned that without a Savior to reunite our physical and spirit bodies, we would end up similar to Lucifer rather than our Heavenly Parents. Jacob concludes that without a Savior we would become 'angels to a devil' (see 2 Nephi 9:9).

Application: Review the fate of married couples without a Savior. What would be our eventual destiny?

AUGUST 4

Gordon B. Hinckley: "Nurture and cultivate your marriage. Guard it and work to keep it solid and beautiful. Divorce is becoming so common, even rampant, that studies show in a few years half of those now married will be divorced. It is happening, I regret to say, even among some who are sealed in the house of the Lord. Marriage is a contract, it is a compact, it is a union between a man and a woman under the plan of the Almighty. It can be fragile. It requires nurture and very much effort" ("Pres. Hinckley Notes His 85th Birthday, Reminisces about Life," *Church News*, 24 June 1995, 6).

Both President Hinckley and President Thomas S. Monson expressed how disappointing it was for them, as Church Presidents, to receive requests from couples wanting to cancel their marriage sealing. To see a marriage that began so well falling from the lofty scenes of a temple sealing room to the low levels of mutual distain, is heartbreaking. Divorce is a scourge stalking the land, a destructive influence not only for individuals, but for most children. Because some of the younger generation lack confidence in their ability to do better in marriage than their parents, some opt to live together without covenants and without the spiritual safety net that a legal and lawful temple marriage provides. How sad that men and women, once so 'love struck,' are now determined to separate permanently.

Application: From your own observation and experience, what do you see as reasons those married in the temple divorce?

AUGUST 5

Boyd K. Packer: "A married couple may be tempted to introduce things into their relationship that are unworthy. Do not, as the scriptures warn, 'change the natural use into that which is against nature' (Romans 1:26). If, you do, the tempter will drive a wedge between you. If something unworthy has become part of your relationship, be wise and don't ever do it again." ("The Fountain of Life," *Things of the Soul*, 113).

Many assume that in marriage, any kind of sexual behavior is acceptable. President Packer joined President Kimball in saying to married couples that not everything in marital intimacy is spirit-sanctioned. There are sexual practices that will 'drive a wedge between you.' Sexual intimacy must be kept on the highest plane. This is in harmony with President David O. McKay's counsel: "The marriage covenant does not give the man the right to enslave her, or to abuse her, or to use her merely for the gratification of his passion. Your marriage ceremony does not give you that right" (*Conference Report*, April 1952, 86).

Application: There are sexual practices that pollute the fountain of life. What do you suppose President Packer means by his caution to not introduce any unworthy practice into your intimate relationship?

AUGUST 6

Gordon B. Hinckley: "I pity the man who at one time looked into the eyes of a beautiful young woman and held her hand across the altar in the house of the Lord as they made sacred and everlasting promises one to another, but who, lacking in self-discipline, fails to cultivate his better nature, sinks to coarseness and evil, and destroys the relationship which the Lord has provided for him" ("Walking in the Light of the Lord," *Ensign*, November 1998, 99).

Pornography exacts a heavy toll on marriage. Follow the logic of President Hinckley: A young woman accepts a young man's invitation of engagement and marriage. She assumes that he is living the gospel because of his mission and now insistence on a temple marriage. They make covenants with Heavenly Father to be true to each other, to be loyal, and to honor their commitments. However, the husband turns or re-turns to pornography with all of its denials, its lies, its secretiveness, its defensiveness, its justification, and its resultant loss of the Spirit of the Lord. In time, without severe repentance, he will lose his priesthood, his wife, and his children because of his spiritual death from this modern plague. What a sad ending to what might have been!

Application: Discuss the dangers of pornography to a marriage. As a wife, help your husband understand why this form of media is so repulsive to women.

AUGUST 7

Gordon B. Hinckley: "There may be now and again a legitimate cause for divorce. I am not one to say that it is never justified. But I say without hesitation that this plague among us, which seems to be growing everywhere, is not of God, but rather is the work of the adversary of righteousness and peace and truth" ("What God Hath Joined Together," *Ensign*, May 1991, 73-74).

President Hinckley is in harmony with statements of earlier prophets in acknowledging that there *are* justifiable reasons to leave a marriage. We marry intending to create a partnership of best friends. However, situations arise where a husband or wife is justified in separating. There *are* reasons to obtain a divorce, but they are never *good* reasons! Adultery, pornography, and addictions overwhelm individual judgment. Some situations make marriage a 'living hell.' "If I am not happy in my marriage, life is too short to stay married," is a common refrain. Satan must laugh when couples divorce, for it returns them to a state of singleness similar to his own. On the other hand, Satan's temptations can never overwhelm couples honoring covenants and remaining completely loyal.

Application: In what situations do you think God would agree that a divorce justifiable?

AUGUST 8

Spencer W. Kimball: "The Lord organized the whole program in the beginning with a father who procreates, provides, and loves and directs, and a mother who conceives and bears and nurtures and feeds and trains. The Lord could have organized it otherwise but

176

chose to have a unit with responsibility and purposeful associations where children train and discipline each other and come to love, honor, and appreciate each other. The family is the great plan of life as conceived and organized by our Father in Heaven" ("The Family Influence," *Ensign*, July 1973, 15).

Why did God organize the family as He did? Because it is how His family is organized. As mortals we are simply imitating the heavenly pattern. Our Heavenly Father is not only a father, but He is a husband. What kind of husband would you expect Him to be? He is also a father! How shocking would that information be to the Christian community? To the world, God is 'unknowable,' a 'mystery,' and He is 'incomprehensible.' Yet, Latter-day Saints understand that we are simply apprenticing in marriage and family life now to prepare for an opportunity following our resurrection. This *is* the Father's plan, a plan not unlike that of mortal parents who send their children 'out of the house' at an appropriate time in hopes that they will learn for themselves the laws and principles that govern relationships as well as govern the universe.

Application: What kind of husband would you assume Heavenly Father to be? What kind of parent would you expect Him to be?

AUGUST 9

Gordon B. Hinckley: "To men within the sound of my voice…if you are guilty of demeaning behavior toward your wife, if you are prone to dictate and exercise authority over her, if you are selfish and brutal in your actions in the home, then stop it! Repent! Repent now while you have the opportunity to do so. To you wives who are constantly complaining and see only the dark side of life, and feel that you are unloved and unwanted, look into your own hearts and minds. If there is something wrong, turn about. Put a smile on your faces. Make yourselves attractive. Brighten your outlook. You deny yourselves happiness and court misery if you constantly complain and do nothing to rectify your own faults. Rise above the shrill clamor over rights and prerogatives, and walk in the quiet dignity of a daughter of God" (Cornerstones of a Happy Home," *Satellite broadcast fireside for husbands and wives*, 29 January 1984).

Perhaps nothing was more frustrating to the Savior than to see the hypocrisy that existed among the Pharisees and Sadducees of His day. Here a prophet is not mincing words concerning the behavior of some men in the Church in our day, men who presumably hold priesthood authority and may even be good administrators in the Kingdom. But they have lost the Spirit of the Lord in marriage and are in need of serious repentance!

Application: Is either one of you guilty of demeaning the other? Does either one of you have a tendency to "see only the dark side of life?"

AUGUST 10

David B. Haight: "Divorce rarely occurs without immense emotional, social, and financial upheaval. Most people underestimate the alienation, bitterness, disruption, and frustration between a divorcing couple, and among their children, friends, and relatives. Some never adjust to the resulting emotional consequences. Perhaps most tragic of all is that more than 60 percent of all divorces involve children under eighteen years of age" ("Marriage and Divorce," *Ensign*, May 1984, 12-13).

Divorce wreaks havoc on homes and society. Have you ever witnessed a 'happy' divorce? Some couples try to save money by hiring the same attorney. At first, the spirit of fairness spears to be working, but when it comes down to issues of dividing up property, determining child custody, selling the family residence, and distributing resources, cooperation goes out the window. Divorce creates bitterness and acrimony on both sides. Each is convinced that the fault lies with the other. The results are often devastating to innocent children whose lives are usually seriously impacted in negative ways.

Application: Discuss the impact of divorce on individuals you have known and how it affected their children.

AUGUST 11

Gordon B. Hinckley: "It seems to me that communication is essentially a matter of talking with one another. Let that talk be quiet for quiet talk is the language of love. It is the language of peace. It is the language of God. It is when we raise our voices that tiny hills of difference become mountains of conflict" (Cornerstones of a Happy Home," *Satellite broadcast fireside for husbands and wives*, 29 January 1984).

President Hinckley points out that communication between spouses should take place with quiet, unemotional voices. Can you imagine a couple that marred in the temple now yelling and screaming at each other? Do loud exchanges ever change anyone's attitude or behavior for the better? We are able to communicate softly with colleagues and with friends. We don't use loud, boisterous language with them. Quiet talk is kind, soft, and gentle, the way married couples who love each other should talk. Living with one who is loud and temperamental is not a pleasant experience and an emotional state prevents any resolution of problems.

Application: Have you had any major contention in your marriage? If so, what topic or practice initiated it? How was it resolved? If little or no contention exists, what is it about your natures that contention is never an issue?

AUGUST 12

David B. Haight: "Middle-age divorce is particularly distressing, as it indicates that mature people, who are the backbone of our

179

society, are not working carefully enough to preserve their marriages. Divorces granted to people over forty-five have increased at an alarming rate. When middle-aged people even consider breaking up their marriage—a couple who may have reared their children, who possibly have grandchildren—and now decide to go their separate ways, they need to realize that every divorce is the result of selfishness on the part of one or both" (Marriage and Divorce," *Ensign*, May 1984, 13).

It seems reasonable to assume that after a couple has been married for twenty or more years, that any issue serious enough to threaten divorce would have been resolved years earlier. By the time a couple has logged more than twenty years, they should be well adjusted to each other's idiosyncrasies. Their love for each other should have deepened, their intimacy should be an enriching factor in their relationship, and their children should be beyond the stages of childhood where they demand great care and attention. At that point in life, each should be a leader in the community, in their employment, and in their church. What a tragedy that takes place when couples married for that length of time decide to break apart their families.

Application: How would you describe your parent's marriage? How about their friends? They have all been married more than twenty years. Have there been divorces among them; if so, for what reasons?

AUGUST 13

Gordon B. Hinckley: "The time has come for all of us to put the past behind us in a spirit of repentance and live the gospel with new dedication. The time is now for husbands and wives who may have offended one another to ask forgiveness and resolve to cultivate respect and affection one for another, standing before the Creator as sons and daughters worthy of his smile upon us" (Cornerstones of a

Happy Home," *Satellite broadcast fireside for husbands and wives*, 29 January 1984).

In every marriage there are disagreements and differences of opinion that coexist along with the wonderful vistas. Every marriage has its ups and downs. Some people handle differences well; others do not. Some individuals have grown up in homes where criticism, sarcasm, and even yelling were common practices. Others come from homes where no one in the family ever raised their voice. Marriage is a mutual commitment that we are willing to learn from each other and make whatever changes are needed to please the other. Humility is a requirement for either person to make lasting changes.

Application: List one thing your spouse brought into marriage that was totally unexpected by you. Discuss how you made adjustments.

AUGUST 14

Howard W. Hunter: "A man who holds the priesthood accepts his wife as a partner in the leadership of the home and family with full knowledge of and full participation in all decisions relating thereto. ...The Lord intended that the wife be a helpmeet for man (*meet* means equal)—that is, a companion equal and necessary in full partnership" ("Being a Righteous Husband and Father," *Ensign*, November 1994, 50-51).

President Hunter was emphatic that a man and wife should be equal partners. Of course we are never 'equal' in the sense that we possess different skills, different talents, and different temperaments. But we can be equal in the way we value each other's input, with neither one dominating the relationship. Both companions should have an equal say in decision making, in rearing children, and in keeping to a budget. Realistically there are times when a wife's wisdom prevails and times when a husband may have greater insight on an issue, and times when both come to the same conclusion. In respecting each other's opinions and feelings, it is easier to function as 'equal partners.'

Application: Would you say that you function as 'equal partners?' In what ways are you equal? In what ways are you unequal? Are there areas in your marriage where you could improve?

AUGUST 15

Gordon B. Hinckley: "I see my own companion of fifty-two years. Is her contribution less acceptable before the Lord than is mine? I am satisfied it is not. She has walked quietly at my side, sustained me in my responsibilities, reared and blessed our children, served in many capacities in the Church, and spread an unmitigated measure of cheer and goodness where she has gone. The older I grow the more I appreciate—yes, the more I love—this little woman with whom I knelt at the altar in the house of the Lord more than half a century ago" ("Rise to the Stature of the Divine within You," *Ensign*, Nov. 1989, 97).

In paying tribute to his wife, President Hinckley's love and devotion to Marjorie is touching. After more than five decades of marriage, it is clear that these two were more deeply in love than ever. The years had bonded their souls together in such a way that they worked jointly to meet the various challenges and trials they faced. A husband learns to appreciate his wife even more when she becomes a mother and a grandmother. He is impressed with her talents in homemaking, mothering, and spirituality. Her devotion to him as her husband strengthens his love for her. As a wife watches her husband preside, teach, and bless their children, her gratitude for him is magnified. What greater blessing could come to either of them than a companionship of many years that allowed them to rejoice in happy times, and gain solace from each other in times of weeping?

Application: How do you think you will feel about each other after fifty-two years of marriage? Imagine being married more than one-hundred years. Five hundred. A thousand. A million!

Boyd K. Packer: "In the home it is a partnership with husband and wife equally yoked together, sharing in decisions, always working together. While the husband, the father, has responsibility to provide worthy and inspired leadership, his wife is neither behind him nor ahead of him but at his side ("The Relief Society," *Ensign*, May 1998, 73). On another occasion, Elder Packer said: "Your wife is your partner in the leadership of the family and should have full knowledge of and full participation in all decisions relating to your home" ("The Father and the Family," *Ensign*, May 1994, 21).

One of the primary causes of marital disharmony is the dominance of one spouse over the other. No one likes to be smothered or feel that their decisions are never good enough to be taken seriously or ever implemented. Self-worth is enhanced when we work together as a full partnership. When efforts go unnoticed, are ignored or even ridiculed, feelings can be deeply wounded. Negative feelings then ripple through the entire marriage. No one likes a partner who abdicates responsibility. It is wise for husbands and wives to counsel together with some regularity to insure compatibility and a 'full participation in all decisions relating to your home.'

Application: Is there an area of marriage such as finances, where you are uninformed? Investments? Insurance coverages? 401k plans? Roth IRAs? Bring each other up-to-date on checkbooks, insurance coverages, etc.

AUGUST 17

Bruce R. McConkie: "The Lord never sends apostles and prophets and righteous men to minister to his people without placing women of like spiritual stature at their sides.…The exaltation of the one is dependent upon that of the other" (*Doctrinal New Testament Commentary*, 3:302).

When you consider the contributions of Adam, Enoch, Noah, Abraham, Issac, Jacob, Joseph Smith, and others, you are impressed with the Eves, the Sarahs, the Rebeckahs, the Emmas, and other great women who served alongside their husbands. Where would any of those men be without a righteous woman at their side? As we listen to the leaders of the Church in our day, they are quick to compliment their wives. Elder James E. Faust, in his inaugural call to the Quorum of the Twelve Apostles said: "I acknowledge the soothing and sustaining love of my beloved Ruth, who is as much a part of me as my heart and soul" ("Response to the Call," *Ensign*, Nov 1978, 20). Perhaps some men are called to important positions because of their wives! Effective Church leaders honor their sweethearts in part because the Spirit of the Lord demands it.

Application: Do your patriarchal blessings comment about a future wife or husband? Re-read your blessings together.

AUGUST 18

Spencer W. Kimball: "To be a righteous woman during the winding up scenes on this earth, before the second coming of our Savior, is an especially noble calling.…Other institutions in society may falter, and even fail, but the righteous woman can help to save the home, which may be the last and only sanctuary some mortals know in the midst of storm and strife" ("Privileges and Responsibilities of Sisters," *Ensign*, Nov. 1978, 103).

Who can count the value of righteous women who serve so admirably in the home, in the ward or stake, and in the community? Women have great responsibilities in building the Kingdom of God in these last days. Fortunate is that man who found a woman who will join him in the great tasks of this life. That man will marvel over and over at her wisdom, her influence on him and on their children. President Kimball continued: "There is a constant need to develop and to maintain tenderness. The world's ways harden us. The tenderness of our women is directly linked to the tenderness of our children. The women of the Church do so much to teach our sons and daughters and to prepare the rising generation" (*ibid.* 104).

Application: Name three great women that have influenced you in your life. Specifically, how did they impact your life?

AUGUST 19

Dallin H. Oaks: "We live in a day when there are many political, legal, and social pressures for changes that confuse gender and homogenize the differences between men and women. Our eternal perspective sets us against changes that alter those separate duties and privileges of men and women that are essential to accomplish the great plan of happiness. We do not oppose all changes in the treatment of men and women, since some changes in laws or customs simply correct old wrongs that were never grounded in eternal principles ("The Great Plan of Happiness," *Ensign*, Nov. 1993, 73-74).

In the past twenty years, same gender attraction and same gender marriage advocates have become more loud and blaring in the public square. The position of the Church has and always will be that exaltation can only take place with a married man and woman. The Church has been clear in pleading with members not to mistreat those who advocate this position. Every person deserves the love and respect due him or her as a child of God. But it is clear that the gates of the Celestial Kingdom's highest degree of glory are not open to such arrangements. It has been a constant theme of Church leaders over the years that any such behavior, acted out, is cause for church discipline. Some of these individuals may be articulate, may be talented, and may be kind and passive. It is not a question of personal worth. The issue is that this lifestyle is contrary to scriptural injunctions, the plan of our Heavenly Father, and the counsel of his prophets.

Application: Find time to read and discuss Elder Oak's article: "Same-Gender Attraction," *Ensign*, Oct. 1995, 7-14; access at *lds.org*.

AUGUST 20

Spencer W. Kimball: "The more clearly we see eternity, the more obvious it becomes that the Lord's work in which we are engaged is one vast and grand work with striking similarities on each side of the veil....If we live in such a way that the considerations of eternity press upon us, we will make better decisions" (*Teachings of Spencer W. Kimball*, 25).

This idea of 'seeing eternity' is a major theme of this 'tune-up kit,' as you have gleaned by now, for marriage partners treat each other better when they know their relationship can be eternal. Without this perspective, 'anything goes' in the behavior of people and we are surrounded by that philosophy in our culture. If death ended marriage, if death ended our relationship with our children, Latter-day Saints, of all people, would be most miserable. With an eternal perspective, however, mortality is seen as a school which we attend and from which we must graduate with 'highest honors.' It is a place much like a simulator where we practice living the principles that will go with us into eternity. Just as mortal children grow to adulthood and become friends with their parents, the same is true of us and our Heavenly Parents. As the prophet explained, an eternal view, especially with regard to marriage and family relations, helps couples make better decisions in all areas of their lives.

Application: Discuss how an eternal perspective makes a difference in your own lives as to the way you treat each other.

AUGUST 21

Quentin L. Cook: "Much of what we accomplish in the Church is due to the selfless service of women. Whether in the Church or in the home, it is a beautiful thing to see the priesthood and the Relief Society work in perfect harmony. Such a relationship is like a well-tuned orchestra, and the resulting symphony inspires all of us" ("LDS Women Are Incredible!" *Ensign*, May 2011, 18).

This address is a reminder of the incredible nature of women who have played a major role in the progress of the Church from its inception. A righteous woman, admirably filling the roles of wife and mother, is one of God's finest creations. A woman must pass through the 'valley of the shadow of death' to become a mother. In doing so, she presents her husband with the greatest of all her many gifts to him—fatherhood. A mother understands more fully the mission of the Savior as she experiences severe pain, and sheds her own blood in bringing forth mortal life. She sees the parallel of what she experiences with the Savior's need to pass through intense pain and the shedding of His own blood to bring forth eternal life.

Application: As a husband, were you present when your wife gave birth? What were your feelings as you witnessed the sacrifice of your wife and the wondrous miracle of birth?

AUGUST 22

Ezra Taft Benson: "One apparent impact of the women's movement has been the feelings of discontent it has created among young women who have chosen the role of wife and mother. They are often made to feel that there are more exciting and self-fulfilling roles for women than housework, diaper changing, and children calling for mother. This view loses sight of the eternal perspective that God elected women to the noble role of mother and that exaltation is eternal fatherhood and eternal motherhood" (To The Elect Women of the Kingdom of God,' Nauvoo Illinois Relief Society Dedication, 30 June 1978, in *Teachings of Ezra Taft Benson*, 548).

When did the noble vocations of wife and mother come under criticism? Who would dare look down on the valuable contribution made by women in their homes? When did a woman working out of the home supersede the home work of mothers? What could be more ennobling in the eternal scheme of things than to have a mother to influence her sons and daughters to grow up into responsible adults? Part-time mothers and single mothers have difficulty fulfilling the role of mother because of the heavy burdens they bear in having to work *and* manage a home. In the Lord's plan, the most cherished callings of women are those of wife and mother. To those in our culture who denigrate motherhood in favor of the workplace, who think that punching a time clock to earn a few more shekels at the factory is of more value than a conscientious mother rearing her children, is stunning. No wonder forty percent of children born in our land are born to unwed mothers!

Application: Husbands, is it your goal to allow your wife to be a mother? What do you see as the impact on children when children come home to an empty house?

AUGUST 23

Bruce R. McConkie: "Marriage and the family unit are the central part of the plan of progression and exaltation. All things center in and around the family unit in the eternal perspective. Exaltation consists in the continuation of the family unit in eternity" (*Doctrinal New Testament Commentary*, 1:546).

Elder McConkie confirms the point that marriage and family life are the central part of the Father's plan for His children. The lack of belief in eternal marriage among Christians stems from a misunderstanding of a conversation between the Savior and the Sadducees. The Sadducees did not believe in angels, in an individual spirit, in a Messiah, or, most seriously, in a resurrection. With a limited understanding of true theology, no wonder Jesus' statement to them was: "Ye do err, not knowing the scriptures, nor the power of God. For in the resurrection they (Sadducees and those with limited doctrinal understanding), neither marry, nor are given in marriage, but are as the angels of God in heaven" (Matt. 22:29-30). Without a belief in a resurrection and with other false doctrines, Sadducees could never qualify for the highest degree of glory. Therefore there could be no marriage for them after death and that is what the Savior said to them. Christians have falsely concluded from this passage that there will be no marriage in eternity, or heaven. It is one of the great theological stumbling blocks of the Christian community. No other non-Christian religions believe in an eternal marriage either.

Application: Read the account of the Savior's response to the Sadducees in Matthew 22. Then re-read D&C 131:1-4 in contrast.

AUGUST 24

James E. Faust: "I wonder if it is possible for one marriage partner to jettison the other and become completely whole. Either partner who diminishes the divine role of the other in the presence of the children demeans the budding femininity within the daughters and the emerging manhood of the sons. I suppose there are always some honest differences between husband and wife, but let them be settled in private" ("Father, Come Home, *Ensign*, May 1993, 36).

Here is an important comment on marriage and its nemesis, divorce. Elder Faust continued: "In recent times, society has been plagued with a cancer from which few families have escaped. I speak of the disintegration of our homes. Immediate corrective treatment is urgent.... I also believe that there is no greater good in all the world than motherhood" (*Ibid.* 35). How disappointing it is that in our society couples divorce and leave children without the very ones who brought them into the world. As Latter-day Saints we must do all that we can to avoid this tragedy that is so common in our culture when a happy marriage is within the reach of all.

Application: Read the entire talk. See *lds.org*, "Father, Come Home," Ensign, May 1993, 35-37.

AUGUST 25

Merrill J. Bateman: "One can assume that the longer the view a woman and man have regarding the marital relationship, the greater the probability of success. The divorce rate for temple marriages is well below that of civil marriages, and civil divorce rates are exceeded by separation rates for open marriages....A view of marriage and the family based on eternal principles increases the probability of success. When one takes the long view, one tries harder to be patient, long-suffering, kind, gentle, and meek. These characteristics, in turn, strengthen the marriage" ("The Eternal Family," Brigham Young University, *Devotional Speeches of the Year, 1998*, 115).

In the United States, there are more people living in an unmarried relationship than there are Latter-day Saints living in the entire world! How did this arrangement gain traction? Perhaps the increase in divorces over the years has had some effect. Individuals worry about their ability to function as marriage partners and parents. They began to use as an excuse the argument that the best way to prepare for marriage was to live together first! "I'm not going to marry someone if we are not sexually compatible!" This non-marriage arrangement was thought to allow them to explore areas such as finances, sexual responses, personalities and other issues they thought important—before they made any serious commitments. When it came time to marry, goes the argument, there would be no surprises and marriage would be much 'easier' because of fewer adjustments. They could 'practice' marriage. In actuality, few of these couples ever marry and many do not remain together very long unless there is an economic benefit such as sharing rent and utilities.

Application: Why has traditional marriage lost its glamour to the extent that many would resort to this arrangement? What is its appeal? Why is it contrary to LDS theology?

AUGUST 26

Spencer W. Kimball: "The love of which the Lord speaks is not only physical attraction, but also faith, confidence, understanding, and partnership. It is devotion and companionship, parenthood, common ideals and standards. It is cleanliness of life and sacrifice and unselfishness" (*Teachings of Spencer W. Kimball,* 248).

President Kimball, in his ministry, gave a number of classic talks on marriage. Here he defines important elements of love, the type that should exist in a marriage. "Your love, like a flower, must be nourished," he said. "There will come a great love and interdependence between you, for your love is a divine one. It is deep, all-inclusive, most comprehensive. It is not like that association of the world which is misnamed love, but which is mostly physical attraction. When marriage is based on this only, the parties soon tire of each other" (*ibid*). The love that should exist between two sweethearts who have eternity as their goal is a sweet love, a mature love which has grown from a mutual attraction, to a flowering shrub, into a magnificent companionship.

Application: What is the difference between love and infatuation? Do you see different 'levels' of love in marriages? In your mind, what constitutes the ideals of marital love?

AUGUST 27

Gordon B. Hinckley: "I know of no other practice that will have so salutary an effect upon your lives as will the practice of kneeling together in prayer. The very words, Our Father in Heaven, have a tremendous effect. You cannot speak them with sincerity and with recognition without having some feeling of accountability to God. The little storms that seem to afflict every marriage become of small consequence while kneeling before the Lord and addressing him as a suppliant son and daughter" (*Cornerstones of a Happy Home*, 216).

Oh that every couple would begin and end the day together on their knees in supplication *and* appreciation to the God in heaven. He is interested in their progress. He is interested in their counseling with Him for there is not a marital problem that He could not solve. Most couple prayers are expressions of gratitude for the privilege of marriage in a stunning age of enlightenment when we enjoy a fulness of the gospel and we have priesthood authority with its sacred and saving ordinances. Couple prayer is a 'window into the soul' of your spouse. As you listen to the righteous pleadings of your spouse, you fall more deeply in love with each other. Love is enriched and strengthened when you kneel together and plead for divine help. Do not neglect this simple practice that will enrich your lives beyond measure.

Application: Share your feelings about how daily prayer together has blessed your marriage. How is prayer a 'window into the soul' of your spouse?

AUGUST 28

Lorenzo Snow: "We are the offspring of God, begotten by Him in the spirit world, where we partook of His nature as children here partake of the likeness of their parents. Our trials and suffering give us experience, and establish within us principles of godliness" (*Journal of Discourses*, 26:368).

The 'Proclamation on the Family' states that "Each is a beloved spirit son or daughter of heavenly parents, and, as such, each has a divine nature and destiny. Gender is an essential characteristic of individual premortal, mortal, and eternal identity and purpose" (*Ensign*, Nov. 1995, 105). How exciting to understand this doctrine! We did not descend from animals, but from a *divine* species. We are made in the image of our Heavenly Parents who are resurrected and perfect Companions and Parents. This understanding of true doctrine, as President Packer has stated a number of times to the saints, has the power to change behavior more effectively than will the secular doctrines and teachings that emanate from worldly philosophies.

Application: Were our spirit bodies born in an actual 'spirit world,' or were we born as spirit children to Heavenly Parents in a celestial kingdom? What is meant by a premortal 'spirit world?'

AUGUST 29

Gordon B. Hinckley: "There is a remedy for all of this [marital problems]. It is not found in divorce. It is found in the gospel of the Son of God. He it was who said, 'What therefore God hath joined together, let no man put asunder' (Matt. 19:6). The remedy for most marriage stress is not in divorce. It is in repentance. It is not in separation" ("What God Hath Joined Together," *Ensign*, May 1991, 73-74).

Why is divorce so prevalent in today's culture? What happens to couples who pledge their love to each other, even in sacred

193

precincts, yet before long they are anxious to renounce their pledges? Do we not disappoint God the Father, our Savior, and the Holy Ghost by this decision? Remember that marriage is performed in the name of all three members of the Godhead. You do not want to embarrass any of them by your behavior! How embarrassing to parents who gave of their substance to inaugurate the launching of the newlyweds. Divorce is difficult on children too who sometimes feel like they are responsible for the divorce of their parents. The best solution to marital problems is to seek forgiveness when we err, and completely forgive. Surely you have learned that divorce never ends! Even in a re-marriage, children from the previous marriage still need braces and are shifted back and forth between angry parents. Surely repentance and forgiveness and getting back to the 'business' of being an active Latter-day Saint is a much shorter route.

Application: Why would divorce disappoint Heavenly Father? Why would it be embarrassing to family members? In what way is it an embarrassment to the reputation of the Church?

AUGUST 30

Boyd K. Packer: "The single purpose of Lucifer is to oppose the great plan of happiness, to corrupt the purest, most beautiful and appealing experiences of life: romance, love, marriage, and parenthood. The specters of heartbreak and guilt [see Alma 39:5; Moroni 9:9] follow him about. Only repentance can heal what he hurts" ("For Time and All Eternity," *Ensign*, Nov. 1993, 21).

We must ever remember that there is one character and his followers who are determined to prevent you from receiving the full blessings that were conferred upon you in your temple sealing. Satan is damned in his inability to ever marry or exercise procreative power. We, on the other hand, can generate life during most of our lives. Without this mortal body that we inherited from our first parents, Adam and Eve, family life would not be possible. There is nothing that pleases Satan more than to see couples fight and quarrel and misuse and abuse the heavenly gift of procreation. He especially is pleased when a temple marriage ends in separation. Here Elder Packer lists areas where Satan centers his attention on destroying you. Surely among the important events of life in which you are engaged are 'romance, love, marriage, and parenthood.'

Application: How does Satan gain power over mortals who possess bodies? What are you doing to prevent his intrusion into your lives?

AUGUST 31

Gordon B. Hinckley: "Why all of these broken homes? What happens to marriages that begin with sincere love and a desire to be loyal and faithful and true one to another? There is no simple answer. I acknowledge that. But it appears to me that there are some obvious reasons that account for a very high percentage of these problems. I say this out of experience in dealing with such tragedies. I find selfishness to be the root cause of most of it" ("What God Hath Joined Together," *Ensign*, May 1991, 73).

Every couple, regardless of how much they regard each other at the time they marry, will be challenged in their stability and quality of their marriage. That is a given. The issue is not if there will be differences between the two, but how they handle those differences. Will they handle them as true Christians or will they more closely imitate the Adversary? Satan has a temper himself (see Moses 1:19), and it is his desire to see us angry and contentious. Selfishness and pride prevent us from repairing any damage we do by repentance, so we blame each other for our difficulties. Interestingly, many who divorce later confess that they 'could have made it if they had both tried harder.' Being single again after being married is not as easy as it is touted to be prior to a divorce. A sincere apology can go a long way towards healing troubled relationships.

Application: Some people say they can 'forgive' but not 'forget.' Is it possible to do both? What is the relationship between the two —forgiving and forgetting?

SEPTEMBER

SEPTEMBER 1

Spencer W. Kimball: "If we will sue for peace, taking the initiative in settling differences—if we can forgive and forget with all our hearts—if we can cleanse our own souls of sin, accusations, bitterness, and guilt before we cast a stone at others—if we forgive all real or fancied offenses before we ask forgiveness for our own sins—if we pay our own debts, large or small, before we press our debtors—if we manage to clear our own eyes of the blinding beams before we magnify the motes in the eyes of others—what a glorious world this would be. Divorce would be reduced to a minimum, courts would be freed from disgusting routines, family life would be heavenly" (Conference Report, Oct. 1949, 133).

Why is it so hard to apologize, to initiate peace, to forgive and forget? As mortals we know that we are not perfect. We make frequent mistakes and misjudgments, so why do we find acknowledging them so difficult? The Savior mentioned motes and beams, accusing us of being anxious to extract a splinter from the eye of a neighbor while a two-by-four is poking out of our own! In a healthy marriage, sincere apologies and forgiving hearts are mandatory. Sometimes we treat each other as if our spouse planned the offense in advance. Elder Kimball was right. The key to a great marriage is the ability of both spouses to overlook trivial offenses, and even better, to refuse to take offense in the first place. Don't we all say and do things at times that do not reflect what is in our hearts?

Application: How easy is it for you to initiate peace? To apologize? To forgive? To forget?

SEPTEMBER 2

Dallin H. Oaks: "When married couples postpone childbearing until after they have satisfied their material goals, the mere passage of time assures that they seriously reduce their potential to participate in furthering our Heavenly Father's plan for all of his spirit children. Faithful Latter-day Saints cannot afford to look upon children as an interference with what the world calls "self-fulfillment." Our covenants with God and the ultimate purpose of life are tied up in those little ones who reach for our time, our love, and our sacrifices" ("The Great Plan of Happiness," *Ensign*, Nov. 1993, 75).

When couples marry and begin the new adventure of sexual relations, of course the possibility of conception and pregnancy arises and the question of family size is an obvious subject. The cultural media blares out the message that one or two children are sufficient for any couple; three is max. We already have an 'overcrowding' condition on the planet and our 'carbon footprint' is excessive! What better way for Satan to prevent more of the Father's family from coming to mortality than to convince mankind that the earth cannot sustain any more people. Latter-day Saints take a different point of view. D&C 104:17 explains that "the earth is full, and there is enough and to spare; yea I prepared all things...." In this final dispensation, Latter-day Saints have multiple tasks: (1) Take the gospel to the world; (2) Establish a Zion people; and (3) Research and identify progenitors and perform their temple ordinances. To achieve these important goals, we bring to earth the valiant spirits of the Father. Given these divine purposes, Latter-day Saints are pro-children.

Application: Share your thoughts about family size? What has been the typical family size in your respective families?

SEPTEMBER 3

D&C 64:8-10 "My disciples, in days of old, sought occasion against one another and forgave not one another in their hearts; and for this evil they were afflicted and sorely chastened. Wherefore, I say unto you, that ye ought to forgive one another; for he that forgiveth not his brother his trespasses standeth condemned before the Lord; for there remaineth in him the greater sin. I, the Lord, will forgive whom I will forgive, but of you it is required to forgive all men."

Our Father, like any mortal parent, must cringe to see His children fight amongst themselves. In Moses 7:33, we feel His groaning: "And unto thy brethren have I said, and also given commandment, that they should love one another, and that they should choose me, their Father; but behold, they are without affection, and they hate their own blood." Earthly parents know that their children lack maturity, and selfishness is prominent in the early stages of their development. As adults, eliminating temper and anger are signs of maturity, after having witnessed for themselves their destructive power over the years. Can you imagine the inhabitants of the Celestial Kingdom ever fighting or quarrelling? Why would they? After death, our new perspective of 'eternity' will no doubt significantly affect our behavior.

Application: Read D&C 64:8-10 again. What disciples was Jesus referring to? Do you ever see contention among Church members? Why do you suppose mortals become agitated over things that really have little long-term importance?

SEPTEMBER 4

Spencer W. Kimball: "It is not enough to refrain from adultery. We need to make the marriage relationship sacred, to sacrifice and work to maintain the warmth and respect which we enjoyed during courtship. God intended marriage to be eternal, sealed by the power of the priesthood, to last beyond the grave. Daily acts of courtesy and kindness, conscientiously and lovingly carried out, are part of what the Lord expects" ("Hold Fast to the Iron Rod," *Ensign*, November 1978, 6).

The Ten Commandments are powerful, yet terrestrial at best. They are couched in 'thou shalt not's' rather than positive commands. President Kimball points out that just refraining from adultery is insufficient. One who truly loves his spouse would not harm that spouse through immoral acts; not because they are incapable, but because it is contrary to the basis of happiness as well as common sense. Sexual sins destroy bonds of trust that are only developed through complete loyalty. Not killing someone is a good start, but it falls short of "love thy neighbor as thyself." The law of chastity protects singles and married couples from the severe damage that results from its violation.

Application: In today's multi-media, the law of chastity is mocked or ignored. What safeguards do you have in place to avoid violating this law?

SEPTEMBER 5

Howard W. Hunter: "Any man who abuses or demeans his wife physically or spiritually is guilty of grievous sin and in need of sincere and serious repentance. Differences should be worked out in love and kindness and with a spirit of mutual reconciliation. A man should always speak to his wife lovingly and kindly, treating her with the utmost respect. Marriage is like a tender flower, brethren, and must be nourished constantly with expressions of love and affection" ("Being a Righteous Husband and Father," *Ensign*, November 1994, 50-51).

In this classic address, President Hunter reminds a husband of his responsibility to treat his sweetheart, the one he invited to join him in marriage, in loving and thoughtful ways. It would be the height of foolishness for a man to abuse or demean his eternal companion. President Hunter calls abuse a 'grievous sin,' meaning that such treatment requires sincere repentance on the part of the offender. His comparing marriage to a 'tender flower' gives meaningful perspective to the significance of marriage as a relationship that requires gentleness, softness, tenderness, and respect as we regard each other's feelings.

Application: What did President Hunter mean by "differences should be worked out in love and kindness and with a spirit of mutual reconciliation?"

SEPTEMBER 6

Gordon B. Hinckley: "Selfishness so often is the basis of money problems, which are a very serious and real factor affecting the stability of family life. Selfishness is at the root of adultery, the breaking of solemn and sacred covenants to satisfy selfish lust. Selfishness is the antithesis of love. It is a cankering expression of greed. It destroys self-discipline. It obliterates loyalty. It tears up sacred covenants. It afflicts both men and women" ("What God Hath Joined Together," *Ensign*, May 1991, 73).

No wonder Presidents Kimball and Hinckley were in agreement that selfishness is responsible for the majority of problems in marriages. We live in a day when there are so many ways to be selfish. We have a plethora of goods and services to attract our resources, and the technology of the day requires that we update electronic gadgets when the new model comes out. There are pressures on couples and families to have the latest in cars, appliances, clothing, and other items that demand our attention. President Hinckley condemns selfishness in its most serious forms from money issues to the most serious one of all—adultery.

Application: Make a brief list of the serious consequences that selfishness distorts.

SEPTEMBER 7

Ephesians 4:31-32 "Let all bitterness, and wrath, and anger, and clamor, and evil speaking, be put away from you, with all malice: And be ye kind one to another, tenderhearted, forgiving one another, even as God for Christ's sake hath forgiven you."

Of all the places you spend time, energy, and effort, home must be the center of your lives. It is the place where you teach, pray, love, express appreciation, compliment, touch, hug, and relate daily with the most important people in your life. Anger and temper destroy family relations regardless of nation or clime. No child should grow up in a home where either parent is angry, temperamental, or critical. Homes are to be sanctuaries in the crazy world in which we live; each member finding solace in family associations. Home should be a place where parents and children rejoice together, where spiritual and emotional batteries are charged before the next day requires another separation of its members.

Application: Evaluate the emotional climate in your home. Ask your children: "Do you think your mom and I love each other?" "How do you know that we do?" "Are you comfortable bringing friends home?" "What could we do to improve things around here?"

SEPTEMBER 8

L. Tom Perry: "Teaching children the joy of honest labor is one of the greatest of all gifts you can bestow upon them. I am convinced that one of the reasons for the breakup of so many couples today is the failure of parents to teach and train sons in their responsibility to provide and care for their families and to enjoy the challenge this responsibility brings. Many of us also have fallen short in instilling within our daughters the desire of bringing beauty and order into their homes through homemaking" ("The Joy of Honest Labor," *Ensign*, Nov. 1986, 62).

From time to time our nation finds itself fluctuating in employment numbers. On those occasions when unemployment is high, securing a decent paying job may be difficult. It may require great creativity to find ways to support a family. When parents train their children to work and complete tasks efficiently, they are better prepared to deal with the ups and downs of the economy. Teaching children the value of work is one of the more important principles parents pass on to their children. Boys learn to work in preparation for supporting a family, while girls develop a work ethic to earn their own income and become capable organizers and managers of a home.

Application: What chores do your children have? How much time do they spend on the computer, phone, or electronic gadgets? If no children, think back to what kinds of jobs you were given at home? What is the value of a strong work ethic?

SEPTEMBER 9

L. Tom Perry: "Marriage is a divine institution, ordained of God. Achieving success in the home is a supernal challenge—no other success can compensate for it. Unless, however, a husband and wife learn to work together as one, marriage can also be an infernal ordeal. There are too many unhappy marriages in the world today. There are too many marriages that do not stay the course, ending prematurely in divorce" ("An Elect Lady," *Ensign*, May 1995, 72).

In this article Elder Perry pays tribute to the wife of President Gordon B. Hinckley. Elder Perry quoted the prophet's comment about his wife: "She is a woman of great faith. She is a wonderful mother. How I love her" (*ibid*, 74). Oh that every husband felt that way about his wife. There are so many marriages that struggle simply to find happiness and to regard each other with appropriate love and respect. Far too many relationships wither and die prematurely. What a terrible scourge has been unleashed upon mankind, the separation of a man and woman who at one time thought so much of each other that they hated to be separated even for brief periods. Divorce is a spiritual tragedy, and its frequency is too high even among active Church couples. Of course situations arise that justify divorce, but it is not the plan of our Father in Heaven that His children, after being sealed together by His authority, should break that union, especially for reasons that are unjustifiable.

Application: Has your marriage ever been in jeopardy? Perhaps every couple thinks about divorce, maybe after the first major argument! But most couples have enough good sense to ignore the idea and clear up any animosities.

SEPTEMBER 10

Joseph B. Wirthlin: "Husbands, be patient with your wives; and wives, be patient with your husbands. Don't expect perfection. Find agreeable ways to work out the differences that arise" ("Patience, A Key to Happiness," *Ensign*, May 1987, 32).

Elder Wirthlin quoted a suggestion which President David O. McKay was fond of repeating: "Keep your eyes wide open before marriage and half closed afterward" (Conference Report, April 1956, 9). Then Elder Wirthlin humorously recommended: "Perhaps, on occasion, our wives could get into the car and honk the horn while we, as husbands, get the children ready" (*ibid.*) Patience is of utmost relevance in marriage on the part of both spouses. We live in such a fast-paced world with access to electronic information at the push of a key on a keyboard or on a mobile phone. We become impatient with traffic lights, other drivers, machinery, automobiles, and even others of our own species. Patience is a celestial attribute and one in which most of us could improve dramatically. However, recall how patient we were with each other while dating—proof that we can be patient when we want to be.

Application: Where do you fit on the patience scale—from 1-10? Which one of you is the more patient? Why is patience an important attribute for parents?

SEPTEMBER 11

Dean L. Larsen: "Marriage is not an easy venture. It is largely a one-time-through, do-it yourself project for the husband and wife. I repeatedly encounter the illusion today, especially among younger people, that perfect marriages happen simply if the right two people come together. This is untrue. Marriages don't succeed automatically. Those who build happy, secure, successful marriages pay the price to do so. They work at it constantly" ("Enriching Marriage," *Ensign*, March 1985, 20).

Marriage is a new adventure that involves major adjustments that we couldn't anticipate when we are dating, when we are so much 'in love.' We have never been married before to this particular spouse! We behaved well enough dating each other to convince the other that we were worthy of taking a chance. After settling into marriage, daily living together requires us to 'pay the price' if we want to build a 'happy, secure, and successful marriage.' Actually, neither one of us came from the 'true family,' the family where everything was done perfectly. So we will have to learn from each other. Sometimes individuals think that if a serious difference develops in their marriage, they must have married the 'wrong person.'

Application: In what ways has marriage required you to 'work at it constantly?' What concerns did you have about each other before marriage that turned out to be unimportant or became marital strengths?

SEPTEMBER 12

Spencer W. Kimball: "Too much leisure for children leaves them in a state of boredom, and it is natural for them to want more and more of the expensive things for their recreation. We must bring dignity to labor in sharing the responsibilities of the home and the yard" ("The Stone Cut Without Hands," *Ensign*, May 1976, 5).

In a society as advanced technologically as the one in which we live, parents must be ever vigilant that their children are involved in useful, productive activities—music, athletics, helping others—instead of just staring at their smartphone or texting away their time. There is a concern that today's children may be losing social skills because of the time they spend on video games and electronic gadgets. Idle time benefits no one. Chores teach responsibility, accountability, and help children develop a work ethic. Parents who fail to require their young children to work will end up with regret when those same children depart home and have difficulty out in the 'real world.' Too many children grow up thinking the world owes them a living, and when they do find employment, to put in a full day of work is difficult for them. In some homes, parents discourage their children from working in the summers. "You have 'Especially for Youth,' Scout Camp or Girls Camp, and Youth Conference, so you really can't get a job."

Application: Review your 'job/chore' chart. Discuss your philosophy of work with your children. Is your work ethic being passed on to them? If there are no children yet, share your ideas about what you expect work-wise of your children.

SEPTEMBER 13

Ezra Taft Benson: "The earth was cursed for Adam's sake. Work is our blessing, not our doom....Wholesome recreation is part of our religion and a change of pace is necessary, and even its anticipation can lift the spirit" ("Do Not Despair," *Ensign*, Nov. 1974, 66).

One of nine suggestions in 'The Family: A Proclamation to the World' is that of "work." Another is "wholesome recreational activities." Family home evening is a great time to review work schedules. But 'all work and no play' can create hostility in children. Families need time to re-create together. Working together presents parents with an excellent opportunity to teach, to listen, and to insure that a job is done well. The satisfaction that comes from completing a task is invaluable. As a parent you learn that sometimes relationships are strengthened more at play than at work. Children function best with incentives—not bribes. (A bribe is where money is paid to do something illegal!) There ought to be something good happen at the end of the job. Playing together at the park or athletic field, eating out at a restaurant, or even a backyard barbeque or picnic can create lasting memories.

Application: When are your clean up, fix up, repair or paint times? Involve children in keeping a tidy home inside and out. As children mature, give them more responsibilities.

SEPTEMBER 14

3 Nephi 11:29-30 "I say unto you, he that hath the spirit of contention is not of me, but is of the devil, who is the father of contention, and he stirreth up the hearts of men (and women) to contend with anger, one with another....This is my doctrine that such things should be done away."

Consider how foolish it would be for resurrected companions to fight and argue. Can you imagine any of our recent prophets fighting with their spouse? If a person believes that every couple ought to 'get it off their chest' occasionally just to 'clear the air,' it indicates a lack of understanding of the gospel and the requirements for retaining the Spirit of the Lord in marriage. Couples that marry in the temple and yet consistently argue have lost sight of their marriage covenants. They forgot how they felt about each other at one time. This statement of the Savior puts fighting and contention in marriage out of bounds. It is not something Celestial people do! If we expect to live among those who are exalted, we must learn to avoid contention.

Application: Discuss a past disagreement. Did you handle it as two people who understand the gospel and the importance of marriage? Do you find that as your love and respect grows for each other there is less frustration, anger, and temper issues?

SEPTEMBER 15

Thomas S. Monson: "Our house is to be a house of order. 'To *every thing* there is a season, and a time to every purpose under the heaven' (Ecclesiastes 3:1), advised Ecclesiastes, the Preacher. Such is true in our lives. Let us provide time for family, time for work, time for study, time for service, time for recreation, time for self—but above all, time for Christ" ("Building Your Eternal Home," *Ensign*, May 1984, 18).

Have you ever been in a home (maybe you came from one) that frankly, was a mess both inside and out. Here President Monson reminds us of the importance of establishing a house of order, an organized residence that is attractive and is a blessing to the entire family. All members of the family have a responsibility to keep the home orderly. There are times when you work, when you play, when you study, and times when you serve others. But home ought to be tidy. Even small children can help with house work: Washing dishes, setting tables, taking out trash, putting away dishes, vacuuming floors, picking up toys, and making beds. Don't think that children must wait until they reach a certain age before they contribute to orderliness.

Application: How does your home rate as to 'orderliness?' Who does the laundry? The vacuuming? The dishes? Don't let the burden for these tasks fall solely on the mother.

SEPTEMBER 16

James E. Faust: *"Develop family traditions.* Some of the great strengths of families can be found in their own traditions, which may consist of many things: making special occasions of the blessing of children, baptisms, ordinations to the priesthood, birthdays, fishing trips, skits on Christmas Eve, family home evening, and so forth. The traditions of each family are unique and are provided in large measure by the mother's imprint" ("Enriching Family Life," *Ensign,* May 1983, 41).

One of the more memorable things parents do for their children is to establish family traditions. Elder Faust lists several. Prayer may not be thought of as a tradition, but it is, in fact, one of the most important of all. Family vacations are important as is saving money to attend a theme park. Children, in looking back at their home life, recall leisure and vacation times as being most memorable. Visiting cousins, traveling cross-country together, trips to visit historical places, and enjoying theme parks tend to be events children never forget. One hint to dad: Exercise great patience and kindness. Children get rambunctious cooped up in a car or SUV, but games ("how many miles to the top of the next hill," counting cars, playing the alphabet game—looking for letters on billboards), help pass the time for wiggly children. Remember that the destination is not the most important part of the activity. It is to enjoy being together on a trip! Take a few breaks, stop at interesting points along the way, and don't become overly focused on logistics.

Application: What do you recall as the most 'fun times' growing up? What family traditions do you recall? What tradition(s) are you working to establish?

SEPTEMBER 17

Carlos E. Asay: "A few years ago…Elder James E. Faust, then of the Quorum of the Twelve Apostles, told about his being called to serve as a General Authority. He was asked only one question by President Harold B. Lee: "Do you wear the garments properly?" to which he answered in the affirmative. He then asked if President Lee wasn't going to ask him about his worthiness. President Lee replied that he didn't need to, for he had learned from experience that how one wears the garment is the expression of how the individual feels about the Church and everything that relates to it. It is a measure of one's worthiness and devotion to the gospel" ("The Temple Garment, An Outward Expression of an Inward Commitment," *Ensign*, August 1997, 19).

The proper wearing of temple clothing signifies to God that we are serious about honoring our covenants. We want to be the recipients of the blessings promised us in our marriage ceremony. We want to return back to our Father together as a couple. In the close proximity of home life, our children see how reverently or casually we treat the garment. The principle stressed by Church leaders is to look for ways to wear it rather than ways to avoid wearing it. There are appropriate activities in which the garment should not be worn such as swimming or certain sporting activities.

Application: How well prepared were you for temple worship? Did any interesting things take place on the way to the temple, at the reception, or during the honeymoon?

SEPTEMBER 18

D&C 132:19 "And again, verily I say unto you, if a man marry a wife by my word, which is my law, and by the new and everlasting covenant, and it is sealed unto them by the Holy Spirit of promise, by him who is anointed, unto whom I have appointed this power and the keys of this priesthood; and it shall be said unto them—Ye shall come forth in the first resurrection;...and shall inherit thrones, kingdoms, principalities, and powers, dominions, all heights and depths—then shall it be written in the Lamb's Book of Life...and shall be of full force when they are out of the world, and they shall pass by the angels, and the gods, which are set there, to their exaltation and glory in all things, as hath been sealed upon their heads, which glory shall be a fulness and a continuation of the seeds forever and ever."

Here the Lord outlines the blessings that are associated with a temple marriage. In verses 15-18, the Lord specifies the outcome of a secular marriage which is only temporary. In verse 19, however, the Lord outlines what conditions must be met for a marriage to be valid forever: The ordinance must be His law, it must be performed by one holding proper authority, and it must take place in His house. Our Father is a God of order, and when we marry, we receive blessings that pertain to eternity.

Application: Read D&C 132:18-25. Notice in verse 25 the penalty that comes to those who do not attain exaltation. What do you suppose the phrase 'the deaths' refers to?

SEPTEMBER 19

Dallin H. Oaks: "The ultimate act of destruction is to take a life. That is why abortion is such a serious sin. Our attitude toward abortion is not based on revealed knowledge of when mortal life begins for legal purposes. It is fixed by our knowledge that according to an eternal plan all of the spirit children of God must come to this earth for a glorious purpose, and that individual identity began long before conception and will continue for all the eternities to come" ("The Great Plan of Happiness," *Ensign*, Nov. 1993, 74).

Imagine a society where a woman is given a legal right to destroy the life that is growing within her body. You might expect such a thing in a primitive society, but not in a modern, industrialized nation like ours. However, since the Supreme Court Decision of Roe vs. Wade in 1973 gave a woman a legal right to abort a pregnancy, millions of abortions have occurred in just our land alone. And to think that it is legal! The scripture against abortion is found in D&C 59:6: "Thou shalt not...kill, nor do anything like unto it." Abortion is similar to killing in that if the fetus were allowed to grow, it would receive a spirit at an appropriate time and be given birth. With this doctrinal understanding, we need not get caught up in the fine distinctions of fetal development upon which legislation and public opinion try to create justification for this atrocious act.

Application: The penalty for an abortion by an active member of the Church, either to obtain an abortion or to perform an abortion, is severe discipline. Is abortion forgivable? What constitutes a 'late-term' abortion?

SEPTEMBER 20

Henry B. Eyring: "Eternal life means to become like the Father and to live in families in happiness and joy forever, so of course what he wants for us will require help beyond our powers. That feeling of our inadequacy can make it easier to repent and to be ready to rely on the Lord's help" ("The Family," CES fireside for college-age young adults, 5 November 1995).

Eternal life and exaltation are synonymous. Through the resurrection of Jesus Christ, all mankind will be resurrected in which, of course, we retain our gender. Since at that point death is no longer possible, it only makes sense that there be a way provided for husbands and wives who love each other to continue as a married couple into the eternities. What a blessing it is to live in a day when this ordinance is available. Temple marriage places us on the path to eternal life, and this covenant should affect the way we date and choose a spouse, and it should impact the way we treat each other as husband and wife.

Application: Review the marriage covenant. What do you pledge on your part and what does God expect of you as married partners? What are the ultimate blessings of a temple marriage?

SEPTEMBER 21

David B. Haight: "A few years ago I sat in the Los Angeles Temple in a little sealing room with my wife, Ruby. We had our sons there with their wives....And as I looked around the room I then realized that this was the great moment of my life, because I had in that room everything that was precious to me—everything. My wife was there, my eternal sweetheart and companion. Our three children were there with their eternal companions. And I thought, David, in your youth you had things all wrong. You thought some worldly event of some kind might be the great event of your life. But now, I was witnessing that great event. I was there, I was feeling it, I felt a part of it, and I knew in that little white sealing room—clean, sweet, pure, in that room—with all of my family there that this was the great moment of my life" ("Hymn of the Obedient: 'All is Well,'" *Ensign*, Nov. 1997, 71).

What a wonderful reflection by Elder Haight. Surely, for a righteous Latter-day Saint, that event would be the greatest.

Application: What can you do to insure that your entire family will be worthy to gather in the temple? Would you consider an event like Elder Haight's the greatest in your lives?

<h2 style="text-align:center">SEPTEMBER 22</h2>

Spencer W. Kimball: "Husband and wife…are authorized, in fact they are commanded, to have proper sex when they are properly married for time and eternity. That does not mean that we need to go to great extremes. That does not mean that a woman is the servant of her husband. It does not mean that any man has a right to demand sex anytime that he might want it. He should be reasonable and understanding and it should be a general program between the two, so they understand and everybody is happy about it.…(*The Teachings of Spencer W. Kimball*, 312).

In many of today's cultures, women are treated like chattel, as if they were a man's property. How different is the gospel's perspective on women who are to be equal partners with their husbands. It is true that women are still not treated as equal to men in wages and employment mobility, but in America, women continue to make progress in these areas. President Kimball's counsel that no "man has a right to *demand sex* anytime that he might want it" is in response to the way some women are treated by their husbands in their own homes. President Gordon B. Hinckley said something similar: "A husband who domineers his wife, who demeans and humiliates her, and who makes officious demands upon her not only injures her, but he also belittles himself." ("Our Solemn Responsibilities," *Ensign,* Nov. 1991, 51).

Application: Look up the definition of 'officious.' Do either of you feel any spirit of domination from the other? Are you ever guilty of demeaning the other? Are you both happy with the frequency and quality of your intimacy?

SEPTEMBER 23

Gordon B. Hinckley: "Selfishness so often is the basis of money problems, which are a very serious and real factor affecting the stability of family life. Selfishness is at the root of adultery, the breaking of solemn and sacred covenants to satisfy selfish lust. Selfishness is the antithesis of love. It is a cankering expression of greed. It destroys self-discipline. It obliterates loyalty. It tears up sacred covenants. It afflicts both men and women" ("What God Hath Joined Together," *Ensign*, May 1991, 74).

Though many in the world consider money, sex, in-laws, ineffective communication, or other elements to be at the heart of marital problems, President Hinckley lays the blame at the feet of selfishness. Like President Kimball before him, he declared that selfishness is the cause of many marital issues—serious issues. He outlines the consequences of selfishness. You might expect selfishness to rear its ugly head in a society like ours which is filled with commercialism and advertisements that remind you that you 'deserve' their products. Selfishness and pride brought down entire Book of Mormon civilizations. Question: How can Latter-day Saints be a humble people when they enjoy unprecedented economic, technological, and educational blessings that surpass anything had by Book of Mormon civilizations?

Application: In what ways does selfishness destroy marriages? How do you fight against selfishness when you are surrounded by so many material options?

SEPTEMBER 24

Thomas S. Monson: "Because sexual intimacy is so sacred, the Lord requires self-control and purity before marriage, as well as full fidelity after marriage.…Tears inevitably follow transgression.

215

Men, take care not to make women weep, for God counts their tears" ("That We May Touch Heaven," *Ensign*, Nov. 1990, 47).

The Lord accused the Nephites of gross treatment of their women: "For they shall not lead away captive the daughters of my people because of their tenderness, save I shall visit them with a sore curse, even unto destruction; for they shall not commit whoredoms" (Jacob 2:33). Could there be any more repulsive behavior than for a member of the Lord's Church to commit adultery or participate in sexual sins that befoul and besmirch marriage? Alma indicates that sexual sins are "most abominable above all sins save it be the shedding of innocent blood or denying the Holy Ghost" (Alma 39:5). It is incumbent on the 'saints' to live the law of chastity to avoid the heartbreak and misery that attends its violation.

Application: Read Alma 39:5. What the three most serious sins that a Latter-day Saint could commit?

SEPTEMBER 25

Richard G. Scott: "Adultery, fornication, committing homosexual acts, and other deviations approaching these in gravity are not acceptable alternate lifestyles. They are serious sins. Committing physical and sexual abuse are major sins. Such grave sins require deep repentance to be forgiven" ("Finding Forgiveness," *Ensign*, May 1995, 77).

The argument is often made by those advocating for more liberal sexual standards, (think same sex attraction) that 'they are not bothering you." Or, "I thought Christians were supposed to be tolerant of other people,' as if Christians should tolerate the most abhorrent kinds of sexual behavior. Immorality, in its many forms, violates the commands of God. Elder Scott labels sexual behavior outside of marriage as deviant and 'not acceptable' as an alternate lifestyle. It was the sin of homosexuality among the inhabitants of Sodom and Gomorrah that led to their destruction. And who destroyed it? The Lord. Despite the Church coming under attack for its moral stand, its leaders speak in behalf of Deity and cannot do otherwise than to speak out against behavior offensive to God and decent men and women.

Application: Elder Scott called immoral sexual acts 'serious sins.' Why? What is 'serious' about them and why are they offensive to God when people only claim to 'love' each other?

SEPTEMBER 26

Ezra Taft Benson: "If you are married, avoid flirtations of any kind. ...If you are married, avoid being alone with members of the opposite sex whenever possible. Many of the tragedies of immorality begin when a man and woman are alone in the office or at church or driving in a car. At first there may be no intent or even thought of sin. But the circumstances provide a fertile seedbed for temptation....It is so much easier to avoid such circumstances from the start so that temptation gets no chance for nourishment" ("The Law of Chastity," *BYU 1987-88 Devotional and Fireside Speeches*, 52).

Of all the serious sins that mankind can commit in mortality, sexual sins are among the most abhorrent. A healthy and vibrant marital relationship is the best deterrent to the commission of adultery. No spouse begins the day intending to commit adultery. But this serious sin is usually the culmination of a series of events over time. Oftentimes, feelings of dissatisfaction are generated over marital difficulties and Satan is ever ready to plant ideas into the heads of those who stray from their covenants. Avoid the very appearance of evil and remember that honoring covenants is a sure guide in sustaining fidelity. Don't let marital disagreements fester or go unresolved. It is okay to be friendly with others at work, at

Church, and elsewhere, but don't let friendliness become, or be misunderstood, as flirtatious.

Application: President Benson counseled the saints to avoid being alone with members of the opposite sex where possible. Do you two have any rules about being alone with someone of the opposite sex? (Riding in cars, taking someone to the store or home from work, to Church?)

SEPTEMBER 27

Richard G. Scott: "Brethren, do you lead out in family activities such as scripture study, family prayer, and family home evening, or does your wife fill in the gap your lack of attention leaves in the home? Do you tell your wife often how very much you love her? It will bring her great happiness. I've heard men tell me when I say that, "Oh, she knows." You need to tell her. A woman grows and is greatly blessed by that reassurance. Express gratitude for what your spouse does for you. Express that love and gratitude often. That will make life far richer and more pleasant and purposeful. Don't withhold those natural expressions of love. And it works a lot better if you are holding her close while you tell her" ("The Eternal Blessings of Marriage," *Ensign*, May 2011, 95-96).

Men are generally thought of as being less expressive of love and affection in marriage—except perhaps in initiating sexual contact. Here Elder Scott lists a number of ways in which a husband can retain the 'spark' in his marriage through his sensitivity to his wife's needs. However, it is not just women who need to hear and feel expressions of devotion. Men also need to know they are loved and appreciated. When both partners find that compliments flow easily back and forth between them, such marriages thrive. Love sends its roots deep into such fertile soil.

Application: 'Holding her close while you tell her,' express your love for her and let it be reciprocated.

SEPTEMBER 28

Spencer W. Kimball: "We have come to realize that the mere performance of a ceremony does not bring happiness and a successful marriage. Happiness does not come by pressing a button, as does the electric light; happiness is a state of mind and comes from within. It must be earned. It cannot be purchased with money; it cannot be taken for nothing. . . true marriage is based on a happiness...which comes from giving, serving, sharing, sacrificing, and selflessness" ("Oneness in Marriage," *Ensign*, March 1977, 3).

It has often been observed that brides-to-be spend much of their time picking out wedding colors, the cake, various decorations, and a dress and then refine reception details as if those were the most important elements of marriage. President Kimball suggests a higher principle. It is not 'the mere performance of a ceremony' that brings happiness to a married couple, but the spiritual preparation that comes from "giving, serving, sharing, sacrificing, and selflessness.' The doctrines and ordinances of the gospel, especially temple instruction and ordinances—initiatory, endowment, and sealing, help keep priorities right. It is interesting how the distractions of commercialism appear at the very outset of this important ordinance. Entire industries have sprung up around the simple symbolism embodied in an engagement ring. The 'trappings' of marriage are important because they provide an appropriate event for friends and family to celebrate with you (they do bring nice presents), but after the reception, on your own, spirituality now becomes your most valuable trait.

Application: Think back to your reception. How important were colors? The cake? The cost of the reception center? If you had to do it over again, what changes would you make?

SEPTEMBER 29

Joe J. Christensen: "The more our hearts and minds are turned to assisting others less fortunate than we, the more we will avoid the spiritually cankering effects that result from greed, selfishness, and overindulgence. Our resources are a stewardship, not our possessions. I am confident that we will literally be called upon to make an accounting before God concerning how we have used them to bless lives and build the kingdom" ("Greed, Selfishness, and Overindulgence," *Ensign*, May 1999, 11).

In our day many families struggle to make ends meet. As parents we want to rear children who are sensitive to the needs of others. Help children to learn the value of reaching out to those in need by volunteering their services—mowing lawns, baking bread, visiting the sick, babysitting for single moms—to those who are less fortunate. Charitable acts bless the giver as well as the receiver. Teach children to serve in and out of the home and thereby avoid the plague of selfishness that is so destructive of marriage.

Application: How do you teach children to give of themselves when they tend to focus on their own wants?

SEPTEMBER 30

Richard G. Scott: "The most important principle I can share: Anchor your life in Jesus Christ, your Redeemer. Make your Eternal Father and His Beloved Son the most important priority in your life —more important than life itself, more important than a beloved companion or children or anyone on earth. Make their will your central desire. Then all that you need for happiness will come to you" ("The Power of Correct Principles," *Ensign*, May 1993, 34).

Keeping priorities in perspective is an important part of marriage. There are so many distractions, and among the alternatives, some are good and honorable. Elder Scott explains that the Father and the

Savior ought to be the highest of priorities in our lives, and if a couple succeeds in doing so, other issues are more easily resolved. Does it seem counterintuitive to you to put something higher than the love of your partner or children? The point is that when we anchor our lives firmly in the Father and His Son, we know that we can trust them because of their love for us. In loving them, we do not take away from our love of friends and family. Practically speaking, what husband would not like to 'catch' his wife kneeling in solitary prayer; or a wife 'catch' her husband on bended knee? The promise of Elder Scott is that everything associated with true happiness is based on this fundamental priority of placing the Godhead at the forefront of our lives.

Application: Practically speaking, how do you make the Father and the Son important priorities? Read Mosiah 7:33 and apply it to marriage.

OCTOBER

OCTOBER 1

Gordon B. Hinckley: "It is difficult for me to understand the tragic accounts of troubled marriages that come to me. They speak of abuse. They speak of dictatorial attitudes and of some husbands who are bullies in their own homes. They speak of violations of trust and of broken covenants. They speak of divorce and tears and heartache" (Cornerstones of a Happy Home," *Satellite broadcast fireside for husbands and wives*, 29 January 1984).

Recent data indicate that "nearly half of first marriages break up within 20 years" ("Move-in before marriage no longer predicts divorce," *Deseret News*, Wed. March 21, 2012.) President Hinckley speaks here of Church members who are guilty of serious marital offenses. What circumstances could change so much over the years of marriage that individuals once so 'in love,' could turn on each other and treat each other so poorly? The answer is that they have lost the Spirit of the Lord, first of all, and they have stopped doing what happily married couples do. The solution is to repent and get the Spirit of the Lord back in their lives. The fruits of the Spirit are kindness, peace, and charity. Husbands seem to attract most of the blame from prophets. However, women are not completely blameless. It is not always the man who is at fault.

Application: Of divorced couples that you know, to which person would you ascribe primary blame?

OCTOBER 2

David B. Haight: "It would seem that a major underlying cause of divorce is in not understanding that marriage and families are God-given and God-ordained. If we understood the full meaning we would have less divorce and its attendant unhappiness. Couples would plan for a happy marriage relationship based on divine instruction. If couples understood from the beginning of their romance that their marriage relationship could be blessed with promises and conditions extending into the eternities, divorce would not even be a considered alternative when difficulties arise. The current philosophy—get a divorce if it doesn't work out—handicaps a marriage from the beginning" ("Marriage and Divorce," *Ensign*, May 1984, 12).

How true! If you believe that marriage and family life is limited to this brief span of mortality, could you not justify almost any kind of behavior? For example, one could argue: 'Why bother to marry if it is only a temporary arrangement anyway? Why can't I just live with someone and enjoy a sexual relationship without the responsibility of children? Children are a drain on financial resources anyway and they make rude teenagers! Why complicate life? Birth control is the key to a less stressful life.' With such a short-term perspective, it is easier to justify sterilization, or abortion, or to leave a spouse for a 'better one' if that is what you decide. Too many men, women, and children in today's culture live shattered lives spawned by selfishness.

Application: Discuss Elder Haight's statement that divorce results from a lack of knowing that "their marriage relationship could be blessed with promises and conditions extending into the eternities?"

OCTOBER 3

Boyd K. Packer: "Fathers and mothers, next time you cradle a newborn child in your arms, you can have an inner vision of the mysteries and purposes of life. You will better understand why the Church is as it is and why the family is the basic organization in time and in eternity. I bear witness that the gospel of Jesus Christ is true, that the plan of redemption, which has been called the plan of happiness, is a plan for families" ("And a Little Child Shall Lead Them," *Ensign*, May, 2012, 9).

What is more thrilling than to hold a newborn as you contemplate the miracle of birth? Such an experience brings a confirmation to one's spirit that we are God's children, that we are created in His image, that we must have had a prior existence, and that we have the responsibility to care for this child who is really one of Heavenly Father's spirit children. A profound appreciation of the power of procreation settles in on you as you realize that in your intimate expressions of love for each other, you created this new little body. A miracle of this magnitude is overwhelming. The power to generate life and rear these infants to adulthood is a profound source of joy.

Application: What were your impressions as you looked into the eyes of your first newborn?

OCTOBER 4

Margaret D. Nadauld: "Women of God can never be like women of the world. The world has enough women who are tough; we need women who are tender. There are enough women who are coarse; we need women who are kind. There are enough women who are rude; we need women who are refined. We have enough women of fame and fortune; we need more women of faith. We have enough greed; we need more goodness. We have enough vanity; we need more virtue. We have enough popularity; we need more purity" ("The Joy of Womanhood," *Ensign*, Nov. 2000, 15).

How clearly Sister Nadauld contrasts the impact that the gospel has on women with those unacquainted with their potential as the daughters of God. Unfortunately, the 'natural woman,' one who knows nothing of the workings of the Lord, is lacking in vision as to her marvelous potential. Is it possible that working outside of the home toughens women as they are forced to compete with men for employment, for equal wages, and for advancement? Perhaps the spirit of competition causes them to develop a coarseness, a spirit of greed, a spirit of toughness that is unbecoming. The God-given inclination of women as wives and mothers is to be kind, gentle, and soft hearted. The Lord loves His daughters and values their contribution to the lives of His children.

Application: Discuss ways in which the 'world' can have a negative effect on women. In what ways has the role of women changed in your lifetime? What can women do to retain the Christlike traits of humility, softness, tenderness, and kindness?

OCTOBER 5

David B. Haight: "Considering the enormous importance of marriage, it is rather astonishing that we don't make better preparation for success. Usually, young couples date for a few months or for a year or two, enjoying romance and getting acquainted, and then get married. Once married, they soon learn that romance must blend with spiritual beliefs, in-law relationships, money issues, and serious discussions involving ethics, children, and the running of a home" ("Marriage and Divorce," *Ensign*, May 1984, 13).

Preparation for marriage begins in the home, and parents are the most obvious example their children see. When parents love each other and their mutual adoration is infectious, their children are more apt to look forward to their own future marriage. As children mature and must face life on their own, they harken back to the model they saw in their home. Their feelings about marriage are positive and they look forward to parenthood themselves. On the other hand, when parents fight and argue, such contention destroys the confidence of their children to succeed. How parents treat each other is a powerful model for children. What greater gift could parents give their children than to demonstrate a healthy relationship of a husband and a wife who love and cherish one another?

Application: Discuss your parent's marriage and how it impacted you—for better or worse. What can be done to better prepare our youth for the inevitable adjustments in marriage?

OCTOBER 6

Homer Ellsworth: ". . . I have always found it helpful to use a basic measuring stick: *Is it selfish?* I have concluded that most of our sins are really sins of selfishness. If you don't pay your tithing, selfishness is at the heart of it. If you commit adultery, selfishness is at the heart of it. If you are dishonest, selfishness is at the heart of it. I have noted that many times in the scriptures we observe the Lord chastising people because of their selfishness. Thus, on the family questions, if we limit our families because we are self-centered or materialistic, we will surely develop a character based on selfishness" ("I Have a Question," *Ensign*, August 1979, 23-24).

Many of today's couples use birth control to limit family size. Of course the number of children is a personal decision that couples make as they counsel with each other and the Lord. There are a variety of artificial barriers to prevent conception. The health of the mother should be the paramount decision (including mental, physical, and emotional health). Over the years prophets have counseled couples to move ahead with their families even before graduation or acquiring a home. 'Replace fear with faith,' has been the general admonition. The command to 'multiply and replenish' the earth has not been rescinded. You don't have to do it all by yourselves, of course, but what a wonderful privilege it is to become parents. Dr. Ellsworth's counsel is to beware of 'selfishness' when it comes to 'family planning.'

Application: Are you two in agreement as to family size? What do you consider to be important factors in making this decision?

OCTOBER 7

Spencer W. Kimball: "Honorable, happy, and successful marriage is surely the principal goal of every normal person. Marriage is perhaps the most vital of all the decisions and has the most far-reaching effects, for it has to do not only with immediate happiness, but also with eternal joys. It affects not only the two people involved, but also their families and particularly their children and their children's children down through the many generations" ("Oneness in Marriage," *Ensign*, March 1977, 3).

Sometimes religious people are thought to have 'boring marriages' because of their conservative lifestyle. A couple that avoids social drinking, that never skips church, who never swears and never attends R-rated movies, must be missing out on the 'good things' of life! But Latter-day Saints have happy marriages because of what it means to be sealed together as sweethearts, to rear children together, and to live as God has directed. Actually, marriage is the most 'fun' thing active members of the Church do. They simply have a different outlook, a different standard and perspective, and the wholesome things they enjoy doing together, and the feelings of love that they share, make life anything but boring.

Application: President Kimball said that marriage is 'the most vital of all the decisions' we make in this life. Why is that a true statement?

OCTOBER 8

Boyd K. Packer: "I believe in marriage. I believe it to be the ideal pattern for human living. I know it to be ordained of God. The restraints relating to it were designed to protect our happiness. I do not know of any better time in all of the history of the world for a young couple who are of age and prepared and who are in love to think of marriage. There is no better time because it is *your* time" ("Marriage," *Ensign*, 1981, 15).

Currently, sixty percent of Americans live together with someone before they actually marry! How different that is from the standards of Latter-day Saints! Ironically, these individuals don't usually marry the person with whom they live for a period of time anyway! Do you think the percentages are likely to drop in the coming years? How disappointing it must be for Heavenly Father to watch His children mismanage their mortal probation. No wonder we send out missionaries to the world. We must inform them of a better way, of a better lifestyle. Every married couple in the Church has the responsibility to reach out to others and share the gospel which is a gospel of happy marriages and happy children and the way to achieve this happiness.

Application: What do your neighbors and non-member friends think about you as a Mormon couple? Do they know that you are members of the Lord's Church? What is the best way for you two to share the correct view of marriage with others?

OCTOBER 9

James E. Faust: "Happiness in marriage and parenthood can exceed a thousand times any other happiness....Parenthood should bring the greatest of all happiness. Men grow because as fathers they must take care of their families. Women blossom because as mothers they must forget themselves. We understand best the full meaning of love when we become parents" ("The Enriching of Marriage," *Ensign*, Nov. 1977, 11).

Marriage is what Latter-day Saints do if they can find a compatible partner. Parenthood is what Latter-day Saints do if they are physically able. Some couples find that they are unable to conceive a child of their own, and it is a great disappointment to them. For those who can marry and become parents, their responsibility is to be the kind of marriage partners whose love for each other is obvious to all who know them. Imagine how the gospel would spread if people could say: "I've never met a Mormon who was divorced. There must be a number of them who are because it is so common these days, but I have never met one!" Or, if they could say, "I don't know how those Mormons have so many kids. But those kids are terrific. If you hire one, you know you'll get the job done right. They are great neighbors."

Application: What would happen to the growth of the Church if all Church couples had strong, stable marriages? What if our children developed a great work ethic and were happy to serve their neighbors?

OCTOBER 10

Gordon B. Hinckley: "Perhaps our greatest concern is with families. The family is falling apart all over the world. The old ties that bound together father and mother and children are breaking everywhere. We must face this is our own midst. There are too many broken homes among our own. The love that led to marriage somehow evaporates, and hatred fills its place. Hearts are broken; children weep. Can we not do better? Of course we can. It is selfishness that brings about most of these tragedies. If there is forbearance, if there is forgiveness, if there is an anxious looking after the happiness of one's companion, then love will flourish and blossom" ("What God Hath Joined Together," *Ensign*, May 1991, 74).

In 1995, the First Presidency and Council of Twelve Apostles issued a proclamation entitled: "The Family: A Proclamation to the World." In this inspired document, apostles and prophets recorded the basic principles on which marriage and family life are to be established among men and women. This treatise was necessary because the family *is still* falling apart all over the world. The Church of Jesus Christ of Latter-day Saints is now a world-wide religion, and as we send missionaries to all points of the compass, the purposes of marriage and family life, as God designed them, are among our primary messages.

Application: How tragic it is when Latter-day Saints struggle in their marriages when they are supposed to be the example for the world to follow. Read the last three paragraphs of the Proclamation.

OCTOBER 11

Spencer W. Kimball: "The union of the sexes, husband and wife (and *only* husband and wife), was for the principal purpose of bringing children into the world. Sexual experiences were never intended by the Lord to be a mere plaything or merely to satisfy passions and lusts. We know of no directive from the Lord that proper sexual experience between husbands and wives need be limited totally to the procreation of children, but we find much evidence from Adam until now that no provision was ever made by the Lord for indiscriminate sex" ("The Lord's Plan for Men and Women," *Ensign*, Oct 1975, 2).

This statement is a prophet's response to events in our culture. President Kimball reviewed the basic principles of the gospel because there are too many marital arrangements and practices that are foreign to God's plan for His children. For Latter-day Saints, it is difficult to believe that people actually live together in some kind of 'trial marriage,' outside the divine pattern given by the Lord to Adam and Eve. We were created male and female to marry and create a family patterned after that of our Heavenly Parents. President Kimball clarifies the point that sexual relations in marriage is not limited to procreation, but it is an ennobling principle that enlarges the souls of a husband and his wife.

Application: How do you explain the attraction of two people of the same gender? Many of these couples are now able to adopt children. Are you in agreement with that policy?

OCTOBER 12

Parley P. Pratt: ". . . our natural affections are planted in us by the Spirit of God, for a wise purpose; and they are the very main-springs of life and happiness—they are the cement of all virtuous and heavenly society—they are the essence of charity, or love; and therefore never fail, but endure forever. There is not a more pure and holy principle in existence than the affection which glows in the bosom of a virtuous man for his companion;....The fact is, God made man, male and female; he planted in their bosoms those affections which are calculated to promote their happiness and union" (*Writings of Parley Parker Pratt*, Parker Pratt Robison, ed. and publisher, 1952, 52-53).

Often in the Church, perhaps most frequently in 'Standard Night' talks, speakers treat sex as if it were something terrible. Well, it is for those who are single and not under the covenant of marriage. But sexual relations in marriage are an integral part of marriage and are 'commanded' of the couple at the time they marry. The greatest joy, the deepest satisfaction, and the most poignant impressions of the soul come to a man and a woman in a covenant marriage as they share emotional and physical intimacy. Therefore, Latter-day

Saints should have the most positive attitudes about marital intimacy, for this union allows a couple to share feelings of love and devotion for one another and to reaffirm their commitment to be trustworthy, faithful, and loyal.

Application: What is your recollection growing up in the Church of instruction on morality? How well did your parents prepare you for the adventure of marital intimacy?

OCTOBER 13

Lorenzo Snow: "Think of the promises that are made to you in the beautiful and glorious ceremony that is used in the marriage covenant in the temple. When two Latter-day Saints are united together in marriage, promises are made to them concerning their offspring, that reach from eternity to eternity. They are promised that they shall have the power and the right to govern and control and administer salvation and exaltation and glory to their offspring worlds without end" (*Teachings of Lorenzo Snow*, 138).

The Restoration of the gospel and priesthood came through angels that appeared to the Prophet Joseph Smith. They brought back to the earth important truths and ordinances lost over the previous millennia. To think that the family we create in mortality can be ours forever, is the most important truth to Latter-day Saints, and is a reason for our missionary outreach. No matter where we end up after the final judgment, our earthly father will always be known to us as our earthly father. The mother of our earthly body will always be known as the mother of our mortal body. That is one reason why we want to be sealed together as a family and then live so that we all inherit the same degree of glory. Ordinances in mortality have eternal implications, and to our mortal parents we owe our love and allegiance.

Application: Your children are eternal beings. Their spirit can never die; it cannot be annihilated. You were privileged to be their earthly parents. Discuss the significance of being a parent to an eternal being!

OCTOBER 14

David O. McKay: "Let us instruct young people who come to us, first, young men throughout the Church, to know that a woman should be queen of her own body. The marriage covenant does not give the man the right to enslave her, or to abuse her, or to use her merely for the gratification of his passion. Your marriage ceremony does not give you that right" (*Conference Report*, April 1952, 86).

President McKay was a powerful exponent of the sanctity of womanhood. His emphasis here is that a woman is not to be subject to her husband's sexual fantasies; she is not his possession. She is the queen of her own body, and even in marriage there can be sexual conduct that is repulsive to her. Every wife has a right to enjoy her sexuality with her husband, and he is to respect her feelings and preferences. Unfortunately, pornography portrays sexual behavior that belittles women and treats them as objects of sexual desire rather than as a warm, loving, sweetheart with divine sensitivity. Where young men were exposed to the erotic sleaze of pornographic images, first they must repent to be worthy of marriage to her; then they must not bring such fantasies to the marital bed.

Application: Are you both comfortable with the sexual arousal techniques of each other? Is either one of you trying to persuade the other to perform sex acts that are offensive to the other?

OCTOBER 15

Henry B. Eyring. "There is an old formula which goes something like this: Income five dollars and expenses six dollars: misery.

Income four dollars and expenses three dollars: happiness." ("The Family," *Ensign*, Feb. 1998, 16).

In a day of relative abundance, there is a tendency to think that we need things when in fact we can do quite well without them. When we fail to differentiate between needs and wants, we find ourselves in debt—easily owing more than we take in. A classic warning was given by President Gordon B. Hinckley in 1998: ". . . I am suggesting that the time has come to get our houses in order....So many of our people are living on the very edge of their incomes. In fact, some are living on borrowings....There is a portent of stormy weather ahead to which we had better give heed....I urge you, brethren, to look to the condition of your finances. I urge you to be modest in your expenditures; discipline yourselves in your purchases to avoid debt to the extent possible. Pay off debt as quickly as you can, and free yourselves from bondage" ("To the Boys and to the Men," *Ensign*, Nov. 1998, 51).

Such counsel is always relevant in marriage. We live in a debt-ridden society where it is easy to slide into debt situations from which it is not easy to extricate ourselves.

Application: Discuss the financial practices of your parents. Were they good money managers? Are your attitudes and practices about spending and saving similar to theirs?

OCTOBER 16

Boyd K. Packer: "There are covenants we can make if we are willing, and bounds we can seal if we are worthy, that will keep marriage safe and intact beyond the veil of death....Eternal love, eternal marriage, eternal increase! This ideal, which is new to many, when thoughtfully considered, can keep a marriage strong and safe. No relationship has more potential to exalt a man and a woman than the marriage covenant. No obligation in society or in the Church supersedes it in importance" ("Marriage," *Ensign*, May 1981, 15).

What a glorious concept—eternal marriage! It required a new dispensation to restore this doctrine. The work of the Father and the efforts of Jesus Christ through His Atonement and resurrection provide a way for a husband and wife to escape the sting of death that would place their bodies in the grave forever. Because of Him, they will rise together in the resurrection in a state of never-ending companionship. Their great hope is that all of their children will follow them. We thank our Father in Heaven daily for our temple marriage and the privilege to be sweethearts now and evermore.

Application: Where did your 'sealer' receive the authority to unite you as a couple together forever? When you next attend a sealing, ask the sealer when, where, and from whom he received his authority.

OCTOBER 17

Boyd K. Packer: "And if you suppose that the full-blown rapture of young romantic love is the sum of the possibilities which spring from the fountain of life, you have not yet lived to see the devotion and the comfort of longtime married love. Married couples are tried by temptation, misunderstandings, separation, financial problems, family crises, illness; and all the while love grows stronger, the mature love enjoys a bliss not even imagined by newlyweds" ("The Fountain of Life," *Things of the Soul*, 106-07).

Ideally we marry at an appropriate age, in our twenties. That is the period of time that nature gives us our best physical attributes, when bodies are lithe and energetic, when the physical attraction between genders peaks. Couples that weather the storms of life together feel their love ripen into a full-blown, mature companionship. President Kimball said: "The love of which the

Lord speaks is not only physical attraction, but also faith, confidence, understanding, and partnership. It is devotion and companionship, parenthood, common ideals and standards. It is cleanliness of life and sacrifice and unselfishness. This kind of love never tires nor wanes. It lives on through sickness and sorrow, through prosperity and privation, through accomplishment and disappointment, through time and eternity" (*The Teachings of Spencer W. Kimball*, 248).

Application: If one of you were severely injured or disfigured and your beauty scarred, would it affect your feelings of love for one another?

OCTOBER 18

Boyd K. Packer: "Temptations are ever present in mortal life. The adversary is jealous toward all who have power to beget life. He cannot beget life; he is *impotent*. He and those who followed him were cast out of heaven and forfeited the right to a mortal body....He knows the supernal value of our power of procreation and jealously desires to rule those who have it....He will tempt you, if he can, to degrade, to corrupt, if possible to destroy this gift by which we may, if we are worthy, have eternal increase" ("The Fountain of Life," *Things of the Soul*, 110).

In this classic address, President Packer outlines the major limitation of Lucifer—impotence, the inability to procreate. He is denied this privilege which mortals may take for granted. Married couples express their love for each other in wholesome ways, something denied the arch-tempter. He is denied this power because of his rejection of the Father's plan and the consequence of his choice is that he will never obtain a physical body of element. Two bodies, one of spirit and one of element, are required to generate life. Spirits, by themselves are impotent. Not only Lucifer, but all those in the premortal life who chose to follow him, suffer the same outcome. No wonder these evil spirits do all that they can to ruin marriages and to destroy family life.

Application: If there were no resurrection we would revert to a spirit existence. Re-read the above statement by President Packer and discuss the consequences of Satan's rebellion.

OCTOBER 19

Spencer W. Kimball: "Soul mates" are fiction and an illusion; and while every young man and young woman will seek with all diligence and prayerfulness to find a mate with whom life can be most compatible and beautiful, yet it is certain that *almost* any good man and any good woman can have happiness and a successful marriage if both are willing to pay the price" ("Oneness in Marriage," *Ensign*, Mar. 1977, 4; italics added).

It is not uncommon for many Latter-day Saints to believe that there is a 'one and only' for every person. In this quote, however, the Lord's prophet clearly states that there are a number of people with whom we could 'fall in love.' After all, love is a product of sharing and risking feelings and personal thoughts with each other in an environment devoid of criticism or ridicule. It is the product of life's experiences that draw a couple closer to each other as they become dependent on one another. However, the fact that some lose their companions to sickness or accident and yet find another compatible and loving companion, confirms the truth of President Kimball's point. However, it would be wise for you to treat each other as real soul mates!

Application: Before marriage, did you believe there was only one other person on the planet meant for you? How does this statement by President Kimball influence your thinking?

OCTOBER 20

Boyd K. Packer: "Reverently now I use the word *temple*. As I do, there comes to mind the words: 'Put off thy shoes from off thy feet, for the place whereon thou standest is holy ground' (Ex. 3:5). I envision a sealing room and an altar, with a young couple kneeling there, or perhaps a more mature couple who joined the Church a year ago. This sacred temple ordinance is more, much more, than a wedding, for this marriage is sealed by the Holy Spirit of Promise, and the scriptures promise that the participants, if they remain worthy, 'shall inherit thrones, kingdoms, principalities, and powers, dominions' (D&C 132:19). I think of the words of the sealing ordinance, which cannot be written here. I understand, in a small measure at least, the sacred nature of the fountain of life which is in us. And I see the joy that awaits those who accept this supernal gift and use it worthily" ("The Fountain of Life," *Things of the Soul*, 117).

Why would anyone who understands the gospel settle for less than a temple marriage? The words of the marriage ordinance are not written or published for us to review, but it is our privilege to return again and again to the temple, and in performing ordinances for our ancestors, we can listen again to the blessings we received when we were sealed.

Application: Plan a temple visit with the intent of listening carefully to the blessings conferred in the initiatory, endowment, or sealing ordinances.

OCTOBER 21

Gordon B. Hinckley: "It takes effort. It takes self-control. It takes unselfishness. It requires the true essence of love, which is an anxious concern for the well-being and happiness of one's companion. I could wish nothing better for all of you than this, and

I pray that this may be your individual blessing" ("Our Solemn responsibilities," *Ensign*, Nov. 1991, 52).

There is nothing that brings more happiness to the God of Heaven and His prophets then when two saints unite in marriage in one of God's temples. That is the way of the Lord. The living prophet holds every priesthood key necessary to unite a couple together for 'time and all eternity.' The prophet is also the only person on the earth who can cancel the original temple sealing. This allows divorced individuals to be able to marry again. Of course, we want to avoid divorce, we want to make our marriage an eternal companionship by the way we treat each other and honor our covenants. But there is a way for individuals who need to leave a marriage to recover from a difficult situation, to divorce and yet be able to marry again in the House of the Lord.

Application: How do you manifest 'an anxious concern for the well-being and happiness' of each other? What do you do that shows you have an 'anxious concern?'

OCTOBER 22

Dean L. Larsen. "Discover things you enjoy doing together, and then do them regularly. Appreciate one another's talents, and encourage and foster them. A wise bishop told me recently that every Friday night is date night for him and his wife. The older children in the family know that they have a babysitting assignment every Friday evening. It is a tradition that they enjoy with their parents" ("Enriching Marriage," *Ensign,* March 1985, 23.)

The leaders of the Church encourage couples to renew their marriages by dating at least weekly. Every couple needs a break from their normal schedules and routines. There is value in getting away from children and work as a couple or with friends. Such 'wholesome recreational activities' may involve a movie, a dinner, a walk in the park, a joint hobby, a temple session, or visiting a nearby historical place of interest. The point is to get away together where you can renew romantic feelings, revive your dreams, and enjoy your companionship.

Application: Read this article by Elder Larsen at *lds.org* or the *Ensign,* March, 1985, 20-23.

OCTOBER 23

Joe J. Christensen: "Pray for the success of your marriage. Elder Kimball shared this wise counsel [with returned missionaries]: 'Well don't just pray to marry the one you love. Instead pray to love the one you marry'" ("Marriage and the Great Plan of Happiness," *Ensign*, May, 1995, 64).

In addition to couple prayer, individuals should have their own individual conversation with their Father in Heaven. It is axiomatic that you can't 'get mad' at someone for whom you pray. When we pray to "love the one [we] marry," we are more apt to keep our hearts and minds completely pure and chaste. Love is a fruit of the Spirit of the Lord, and when we pray in behalf of each other, we not only do we have our thoughts centered in our companion, but the Lord can extend His blessings and protection to our sweetheart as they go about their daily fare. There are influences inside the home (media) and outside the home (colleagues) that can test our commitments, but praying individually and as a companionship, we are more likely to receive divine warnings and protection.

Application: Do you pray daily for each other? What specifically do you ask of the Lord for your companion?

OCTOBER 24

David O. McKay: "'Well,' you may ask, 'how may I know when I am in love?'. . . if you meet a girl in whose presence you feel a desire to achieve, who inspires you to do your best, and to make the most of yourself, such a young woman is worthy of your love and is awakening love in your heart'…In the presence of the girl you truly love you do not feel to grovel; in her presence you not attempt to take advantage of her; in her presence you feel that you would be everything that a [righteous man] should become, for she will inspire you to that ideal" (*Improvement Era*, March 1938, 139; *Eternal Marriage, Student Manual* Religion 234 and 235, 154).

This is important counsel for single individuals but has application to marriage as well. Are you still meeting the standard laid out by this prophet? Do you still find that in each other's presence you want to be the very best person you can be? Do you continue to uplift each other? Is one of you trying to take advantage of the other in some way? In each other's presence do you feel a desire to only bless one another? When one of you has a difficult day, is the other one sympathetic? Do you inspire each other to rise to your tallest spiritual stature? After these years together, have you two turned out to be a good match?

Application: What 'proof' can you point to that you two are still in love?

OCTOBER 25

John A. Widtsoe: "Marriage that lasts only during earth life is a sad one, for the love established between man and woman, as they live together and rear their family, should not die, but live and grow richer with the eternal years. True love hopes and prays for an endless continuation of association with the loved one. To those who are sealed to each other for all existence, love is ever warm, more hopeful, believing, courageous, and fearless. Such people live the richer, more joyful life. To them happiness and the making of it have no end" (*Evidences and Reconciliations*, 299).

Even though Elder Widtsoe wrote these comments many years ago, this counsel is even more valuable in a day when the benefits of marriage are being questioned and when the divorce rate is embarrassingly high. How silly to spend our adult years in marriage and family relations with all that it entails, only to say 'goodbye' to each other at the time of death. If that were the case, we would ask ourselves at some point: "Was that it? That is what I spent my time doing? For what purpose? What a terrible plan! I would not sustain a God who designed such a shortsighted plan?" Latter-day Saints rejoice in the knowledge that marriage is forever!

Application: Remind each other of the length of time you committed to be companions! This life is your time to perfect your partnership and to acquire parenting skills that will carry over into eternity.

OCTOBER 26

Spencer W. Kimball: "What is love? Many people think of it as mere physical attraction and they casually speak of 'falling in love' and 'love at first sight.' This may be Hollywood's version and the interpretation of those who write love songs and love fiction. True love is not wrapped in such flimsy material. One might become immediately attracted to another individual, but love is far more than physical attraction. It is deep, inclusive and comprehensive. Physical attraction is only one of the many elements, but there must be faith and confidence and understanding and partnership...." (*Love versus Lust*, 18).

President Kimball focuses on the meaning of love which he clearly states is more than simple 'physical attraction.' After couples live together through the vicissitudes of life—marriage and children, limited finances, physical challenges, and a multitude of sacrifice in behalf of each other and the couple's children, love comes to permeate the heart and soul of each companion. Love is best expressed in the form of verbal and non-verbal appreciation for the contributions each one makes to the marital partnership.

Application: Discuss your feelings of love for each other. Are they 'deep, inclusive, and comprehensive?' Are you setting a good example for your children/grandchildren?

OCTOBER 27

John Taylor: "Do you have prayers in your family? And when you do, do you go through the operation like the grinding of a piece of machinery, or do you bow in meekness and with a sincere desire to seek the blessing of God upon you and your household? This is the way that we ought to do, and cultivate a spirit of devotion and trust in God, dedicating ourselves to him, and seeking his blessings" (*Journal of Discourses*, 2:118-119).

We repeat ourselves about prayer often because we believe that the single most important activity that will insure happiness as a married couple is to kneel in prayer both in the mornings and at night. We are convinced that pride prevents this practice for who could deny its value? It is best at your bedside, morning and evening, kneeling together, hand in hand. Family prayer is important for children to learn to pray, but couple prayer is where you pour out your heart and soul to your Father in behalf of the members of your little kingdom. You plead together for His help. You are rearing His children too, you know. The success of marriage depends to such a great extent on retaining the Spirit of the Lord in a relationship, and praying as a couple is the best 'guarantee' to retain that Spirit. It is almost impossible for negatives to infiltrate and destroy your marriage when you jointly call upon the powers of heaven in your behalf.

Application: Kneel in prayer morning and night to supplicate God's blessings for you and your family. Share with each other the value of this practice if it has been on-going.

OCTOBER 28

Boyd K. Packer: "The greatest deception foisted upon the human race in our day is that overemphasis of physical gratification as it is related to romantic love. It is merely a repetition of the same delusion that has been impressed on every generation in ages past. When we learn that physical gratification is only incident to, and not the compelling force of love itself, we have made a supreme discovery. If only physical gratification should interest you, you need not be selective at all. This power is possessed by almost everyone. Alone, without attendant love, this relationship becomes nothing—indeed, less and worse than nothing" (*Eternal Love*, 15).

Any male or female of any race can successfully mate. For the sons and daughters of God, however, the procreative act has a higher meaning and purpose beyond mere pleasure or propagation. For that reason, God places safeguards and sanctions against the improper use of this marvelous power. Sadly, we live in a world were sexual relations are no longer limited to marriage. The 'sexual revolution' in recent decades prostitutes the sacred union of a man and a wife to the point where few movies or media presentations portray 'married love.' The portrayal of sex in these productions is almost always between singles who have little interest in marriage and parenthood.

Application: List shows or movies you have seen where there was little regard for moral behavior. Would you predict that future movies will return to more conservative themes?

OCTOBER 29

Gordon B. Hinckley: "The complaint of a husband, after eighteen years of marriage and five children, that he no longer loves his wife is, in my judgment, a feeble excuse for the violation of covenants made before God and also the evasion of the responsibilities that are the very strength of the society of which we are a part. The finding of fault with consequent divorce is usually preceded by a long period in which little mistakes are spoken of in harsh and angry language, where tiny molehills of difference grow into great mountains of conflict" ("Our Solemn Responsibilities," *Ensign*, Nov. 1991, 51).

Divorce is the worst of scourges, often more serious than that caused by bacteria and viruses. Statistics reflect the sad fact that nearly half of the marriages in our land will end prematurely. President Hinckley continued: "I am satisfied that the more unkindly a wife is treated, the less attractive she becomes. She loses pride in herself. She develops a feeling of worthlessness. Of course it shows" (*ibid.*) The human pain that is caused by divorce takes a serious toll on the human family. Husbands and wives disappoint not only themselves in breaking apart their marriage, but the children typically suffer emotional damage as well. Some individuals come from families where fault-finding was honed to a fine edge. Let such behavior stop with you two.

Application: Were sarcasm and criticism main staples in your family? How do you stop negative behavior from passing to the next generation?

OCTOBER 30

Spencer W. Kimball: "If two people love the Lord more than their own lives and then love each other more than their own lives, working together in total harmony with the gospel program as their basic structure, they are sure to have this great happiness. When a husband and wife go together frequently to the holy temple, kneel in prayer together in their home with their family, go hand in hand to their religious meetings, keep their lies wholly chaste—mentally and physically—so that their whole thoughts and desires and loves are all centered in the one being, their companion, and both work together for the upbuilding of the kingdom of God, then happiness is at its pinnacle" ("Oneness in Marriage," *Ensign*, March 1977, 5).

President Kimball presents a simple formula to avoid divorce. Attending the temple, kneeling in prayer together as a couple and as a family, putting the Lord first in priorities, understanding the place of marriage and family in the eternal plan, attending religious services, avoiding immoral themes, and keeping our minds and hearts centered in each other's happiness and welfare, allow us to fulfill our destiny as loving companions.

Application: Sketch out a rough pie chart of your time together. Okay, sleep wins, so stick to your waking hours. How much time do you actually spend together in the course of a day?

OCTOBER 31

Jeffrey R. Holland: "I have heard President Hinckley teach publicly and privately what I suppose all leaders have said—that most problems in love and marriage ultimately start with selfishness....True love blooms when we care more about another person than we care about ourselves....Love is a fragile thing, and some elements in life can try to break it. Much damage can be done if we are not in tender hands, caring hands. To give ourselves totally to another person, as we do in marriage, is the most trusting step we take in any human relationship. It is a real act of faith— faith all of us must be willing to exercise. If we do it right, we end up sharing everything—all our hopes, all our fears, all our dreams, all our weaknesses, and all our joys—with another person" ("How Do I Love Thee?" BYU 1999-2000 Speeches, 158-62)

Strengthening marriages involves a willingness to risk our innermost thoughts and feelings with each other. The open and honest communication required for a healthy marital companionship leaves us vulnerable to hurtful, sarcastic and critical responses if a companion chooses to violate the trust of a spouse. Violating trust constitutes a major obstacle to developing a deeper companionship. Be wise and careful with the information shared with you by a spouse who felt safe at the time in revealing the very thoughts and feelings of his or her heart when such risking was meant for your eyes and ears only.

Application: Are you two able to easily share your deepest thoughts and feelings with each other without receiving a negative or critical response? Are you able to share your "hopes and fears and dreams" as well as any weaknesses?

NOVEMBER

NOVEMBER 1

Jeffrey R. Holland: "Temper tantrums are not cute even in children; they are despicable in adults, especially adults who are supposed to love each other. We are too easily provoked; we are too inclined to think that our partner meant to hurt us—meant to do us evil, so to speak; and in defensive or jealous response we too often rejoice when we see them make a mistake and find them in a fault….At least one difference between a tolerable marriage and a great one may be that willingness in the latter to allow some things to pass without comment, without response" ("How Do I Love Thee?" *BYU 1999-2000 Speeches, 158-62*).

Does speaking in angry tones ever help resolve issues in a relationship? Of course, it is important that a balance exist between being candid versus holding things inside that later fester and surface in emotional outbursts. Some people won't discuss subjects openly and allow resentment to grow until they withdraw emotionally. Others say anything on their mind regardless of any hurt or damage to feelings they may cause. Elder Holland contrasts an 'average' marriage with a 'great one.' The difference, he says, is when one spouse allows minor irritants to pass without comment.

Application: In what way should we allow 'some things to pass without comment?' For example, you come home and find the lawn sprinklers still on, or a garage light has been on the entire day. What is the best way to handle these situations?

NOVEMBER 2

Melvin J. Ballard: "What do we mean by endless or eternal increase? We mean that through the righteousness and faithfulness of men and women who keep the commandments of God they will come forth with celestial bodies, fitted and prepared to enter into their great, high and eternal glory in the celestial kingdom of God; and unto them through their preparation, there will come spirit children. I don't think that is very difficult to comprehend. The nature of the offspring is determined by the nature of the substance that flows in the veins of the being. When blood flows in the veins of the being the offspring will be what blood produces, which is tangible flesh and bone; but when that which flows in the veins is spirit matter, a substance which is more refined and pure and glorious than blood, the offspring of such beings will be spirit children" (*Melvin J. Ballard—Crusader for Righteousness*, 211).

The spirits we bring into our homes are the offspring of Heavenly Parents. The origin of a spirit body is best explained in this explanation by Elder Ballard. Mortal parents create 'blood children.' Resurrected parents create 'spirit children.' Apparently, it is the substance that flows in the veins of the parents that makes a major difference—mortal blood versus spirit element. Both bodies, one of spirit and one of element, constitute our soul and joined together allow us to become parents.

Application: Re-read the above statement by Elder Ballard. Then read D&C 131:7-8 and draw your own conclusions.

NOVEMBER 3

Marlin K. Jensen: "We were living in Salt Lake City, where I was attending law school and Kathy was teaching first grade. Under the stress of being new to the city, our respective schools, and each other, our relationship became a bit testy. One night at about dinnertime, we had a quarrel that convinced me that I need not hope for nourishment at home. So I left our modest apartment and walked to the nearest fast-food restaurant, a block away. As I entered the north door of the establishment, I looked to my right— and much to my surprise, I saw Kathy entering through the south door! We exchanged angry glances and advanced to opposing cash registers to place our orders. We continued to ignore each other as we sat alone on opposite ends of the restaurant, sullenly eating our evening meals. We then left as we had entered and took our separate routes home. It wasn't until later that we reconciled and laughed together about how infantile we had been" ("A Union of Love and Understanding," *Ensign*, Oct. 1994, 47).

What drives individuals to allow the truly insignificant to flare into arguments and disputes? Is it anger, frustration, ego, pride, competitiveness, or selfishness? We each must examine our temperament to discover what drives both anger and happiness.

Application: What was the cause of your last disagreement? Chances are it wasn't something monumental but rather a small, silly, ego driven reaction to a routine event. Right?

NOVEMBER 4

Gordon B. Hinckley: "Eve was given as a helpmeet to Adam. The facts are that they stood side by side in the garden. They were expelled from the garden together, and they worked together, side by side, in gaining their bread by the sweat of their brows" ("Our Solemn Responsibilities," *Ensign,* Nov. 1991: 51).

Adam and Eve, by their Fall, provided us with the opportunity to come to earth to experience a different kind of life than that which we experienced in the premortal realm. How grateful Latter-day Saints are to these first parents who made a momentous decision. Had we remained in the spirit world, we never would have the opportunity to marry and become parents. In LDS theology, Adam and Eve are heroes, whereas other faiths think that this couple betrayed God's trust; they disappointed God after all He had done for them. Besides working side by side, they suffered the murder of a righteous son by an older brother—the first murder on the planet. This tragedy undoubtedly broke their hearts. Adam and Eve will be forever revered by Latter-day Saints for their courage and bravery in initiating the Father's plan for the rest of us.

Application: To read of the majesty of Adam, see D&C 107:53-56. No doubt Eve was Adam's equal.

NOVEMBER 5

Howard W. Hunter: "Together with your wife, you determine the spiritual climate of your home. Our first obligation is to get our own spiritual life in order through regular scriptural study and daily prayer. Secure and honor your priesthood and temple covenants; encourage your family to do the same" ("Being a Righteous Husband and Father," *Ensign*, Nov. 1994, 51).

What is readily observable in LDS couples experiencing marital difficulties is that they have stopped doing what happily married couples do on a regular basis. Instead, they are doing what miserable people do and then wonder why they are miserable! President Hunter lists a number of suggestions that strengthens marriages: Daily prayer, temple worship, reading and studying gospel literature, paying an honest tithe and fast offering, holding family home evenings and maintaining a regular schedule of intimate contact. These simple suggestions bless every couple and they will find the Spirit of the Lord more evident in their lives.

Application: Look at the above list of activities and determine which ones you could add to what you are already doing. Add to the list items important to you.

NOVEMBER 6

Boyd K. Packer: "True doctrine, understood, will change behavior quicker than will the study of behavior change behavior." ("Do Not Fear," *Ensign*, May 2004, 73).

Doctrines of the Restored Church are basic concepts that comprise the plan of salvation. Doctrine explains our origins, the purposes of mortality, and outlines our ultimate potential. With an understanding of doctrine we are motivated to match our behavior with the doctrine. Once it is clear to us that life is eternal, that mortality is our time to apprentice in marriage and family relations, we are better prepared to handle life's challenges. The Father said to Jehovah, "Behold, the man is become as one of us to know good and evil" (Moses 4:28). Doctrines keep us on course while we are learning the differences between good and evil. With this knowledge, we can now be trusted to use our agency wisely in making those decisions that lead us to our ultimate destiny— exaltation.

Application: Read through the list of doctrines in Appendix A which outlines the elements of the plan of salvation. How do these doctrines provide you with a greater perspective on spouse and parent roles?

NOVEMBER 7

Thomas S. Monson: "We live in troubled times. I assure you that our Heavenly Father is mindful of the challenges we face. He loves each of us and desires to bless us and to help us. May we call upon Him in prayer, as He admonished [quotes D&C 19:38)....My dear brothers and sisters, may your homes be filled with love and courtesy and with the Spirit of the Lord. Love your families. If there are disagreements or contentions among you, I urge you to settle them now" ("As We Close This Conference," *Ensign*, May 2012, 115-116).

We do live in troubled times. This is the last dispensation of the gospel and priesthood to the earth prior to the Lord coming again to usher in the Millennium. President Monson assures us that our Heavenly Father loves us and is interested and involved in our lives. We have a perfect Father. The prophet stresses the need for prayer in our homes and pleads with us to live in love and harmony as couples and as families. There is too much contention, bitterness, anger, and wounded hearts in our homes, which is antithetical to what we espouse.

Application: Read D&C 19:38 and 3 Nephi 11:28-30. President Monson quoted these two scriptures in his closing remarks. We cannot be much of an example of being 'saints' if we fight and contend.

NOVEMBER 8

Jeffrey R. Holland: "One of the great purposes of true love is to help each other in these times. No one ought to have to face such trials alone. We can endure almost anything if we have someone at our side who truly loves us, who is easing the burden and lightening the load....Together we need to monitor the load levels and be helpful in shedding or at least readjusting some cargo if we see our sweetheart is sinking. Friends, sweethearts, and spouses need to be able to monitor each other's stress" ("How Do I Love Thee?" *BYU 1999-2000 Speeches*, 158-62).

The grand sweeping romances of the silver screen are enjoyable as escape entertainment. Sometimes they are even inspiring. However, true love is manifested in the small, every day, sometimes monotonous interactions we have with each other. Constancy, loyalty, and attentiveness are the mortar of a solid relationship. Life throws us enough trials and stress without creating our own. One of our chief desires we should all have is to lessen the burdens of our spouse.

Application: Think about what stress your companion is under. What can you do to help alleviate the stress that he or she feels?

NOVEMBER 9

Boyd K. Packer: "It takes the steady strength of a father to hammer out the metal of it and the tender hands of a mother to polish and fit it on. Sometimes one parent is left to do it alone. It is difficult, but it can be done. In the Church we can teach about the materials from which a shield of faith is made: reverence, courage, chastity, repentance, forgiveness, compassion. In church we can learn how to assemble and fit them together. But the actual making of and fitting on of the shield of faith belongs in the family circle. Otherwise it may loosen and come off in a crisis" ("The Shield of Faith," *Ensign*, May 1995, 8).

Next to the temple, home is the most sacred of earthly places. It is from these crucibles that individuals emerge and enter the social order. Schools help train, Sunday School and Youth leaders may instruct, church programs and summer camps may inspire, and weekly meetings may lift. But it is in the home, overseen by a loving father and mother, where the soldiers of God are reared and prepared for the battles of life. This labor requires a righteous mother and father to rear their sons and daughters to be socially, mentally, spiritually, and physically prepared to enter the field of battle. If we fail in our homes, society is in jeopardy.

Application: Practically speaking, what would represent the 'shield of faith?' What are the 'materials' from which parents fashion the shield?

NOVEMBER 10

Marlin K. Jensen: "Consider the power of the idea that of all people on earth, we Latter-day Saints know the most about genuine romantic love and have the greatest opportunity to achieve truly happy and enduring marriages. Will it not be a memorable day when as a people we are best known not just for our large families but for our truly exceptional marriages?" ("A Union of Love and Understanding," *Ensign*, Oct. 1994, 48).

What are Latter-day Saints known for in the larger society? Our Word of Wisdom? Polygamy? Genealogy? What we would like them to know about us is our doctrine on marriage and families. We are unique among religious organizations in asserting that marriage and families are to be forever. That knowledge, alone, should strengthen the saints so that divorce would be practically unknown among those who marry in the temple. Perhaps in the past, we were known for having more children than those not of our faith. But imagine the impact we would have on the citizens of the world if divorce were unknown among our people; if families portrayed the finest examples of work ethics, of charity, of kindness, and of serviceability. That is our larger task as a people. It is an important way in which we can influence the world for good. Our example must exceed our preaching.

Application: What do you suppose our influence would be on the 'world' if among Latter-day Saints divorce was extremely rare?

NOVEMBER 11

Spencer W. Kimball: "These things worry us considerably because there are too many divorces and they are increasing. It has come to be a common thing to talk about divorce. The minute there is a little crisis or a little argument in the family, we talk about divorce, and we rush and see an attorney. This is not the way of the Lord. We should go back and adjust our problems and make our marriage compatible and sweet and blessed" ("Marriage and Divorce," *1976 Devotional Speeches of the Year*, 155; or see, *CES Eternal Marriage Student Manual*, 174).

It seems that every day we read of a Hollywood couple filing for divorce, often after only a few months of marriage, or of a break-up after simply living together. This phenomenon, like so many things in our modern society, epitomizes the pop culture view of marriage as an arrangement of convenience to be discarded when the convenience ends. How different is the way of the Lord, where everything He does is designed to last forever. Marriage is the most important of the Lord's work, for in that relationship we most approximate the heavenly pattern.

Application: Why do you suppose so many people in our culture want to avoid the responsibilities of marriage?

NOVEMBER 12

Boyd K. Packer: "Some years ago an associate of mine lost his beloved wife. She died after a lingering illness....One day near the end she told him that when she was gone she wanted him to marry again and he was not to wait too long a time. He protested! The children were nearly grown and he would go the rest of the way alone. She turned away and wept and said, 'Have I been such a failure that after all our years together you would rather go unmarried? Have I been such a failure?' In due time there came another....I have the feeling that his first beloved wife is deeply grateful to the second one, who filled the place that she could not keep" ("Marriage," *Ensign*, May 1981, 15).

We are subject to the vagaries of mortality. Death takes away many in their youth, their middle-age, and in their later years. It is especially tragic when a young spouse or parent is lost. In this story the wife was insistent that her husband not 'go the rest of the way alone.' We learn from scripture that "It is not good for man to be alone." That premise is true even after a lifetime of loving compatibility. It applies also to a wife whose husband dies first. There is much labor that can be done by older couples. Though they marry for 'time only,' they may serve as missionaries, as temple workers, and as ward and stake officers.

Application: If either one of you died, would you feel comfortable if the other re-married? Would you give your spouse the same counsel as did this wife?

NOVEMBER 13

Brigham Young: "Those who attain to the blessing of the first or celestial resurrection will be pure and holy, and perfect in body. Every man and woman that reaches to this unspeakable attainment will be as beautiful as the angels that surround the throne of God. If you can by faithfulness in this life, obtain the right to come up in the morning of the resurrection, you need entertain no fears that the wife will be dissatisfied with her husband, or the husband with the wife; for those of the first resurrection will be free from sin and from the consequences and power of sin" ("Future State of Existence," *Contributor*, May 1890, 241).

When we die and return to our spirit existence after death in the 'spirit world' of this earth, it will be clear to us that the plan of salvation we were taught in mortality was *really true*. Though losing our earthly body in death, we are still alive as spirit entities. This existence will simply confirm what we already knew. Yes, we will miss our earthly bodies (see D&C 45:17 and D&C 138:50). But a clearer perspective of eternity will motivate us to learn more and conform to every commandment and principle of the gospel. Our spouse will not be 'dissatisfied' with us, nor we with him or her, for we will see things in a new light. Our Christlike behavior will also make us more lovable! Interestingly enough the near obsession of our society with physical appearance will, ironically, will be granted freely to all when they obtain their resurrected bodies.

Application: Spirit bodies are perfect in form and shape. Imagine what your spirit body really looks like compared to your mortal tabernacle. Read the two scriptures above.

November 14

James E. Faust: "Some years ago, I was consulted by a woman who desired a divorce from her husband on grounds which, in my opinion, were justified. After the divorce was concluded, I did not see her again for many years. A chance meeting with her on the street was very surprising. The years of loneliness and discouragement were evident in her once beautiful face. After passing a few pleasantries, she was quick to say that life had not been rich and rewarding for her and that she was tired of facing the struggle alone. Then came a most startling disclosure, which, with her permission, I share. She said, "Bad as it was, if I had to do it over again, knowing what I do now, I would not have sought the divorce. This is worse" ("The Enriching of Marriage," *Ensign*, Nov. 1977, 9).

A majority of the seemingly intractable problems in marriage are artificial, meaning that they exist because we allow them to exist, or in some cases, we create and even foster them. Being annoyed at something your partner does is a state of mind. It's annoying because you choose to be annoyed. This is also true of anger. It's also true of things that delight or humor us. Being single again after a divorce affects us in ways not envisioned when we thought it necessary to exit the marriage. Pride and selfishness are the primary culprits that cause marital dissatisfaction and prevent repentance and apologies from taking place that could repair damaged relationships. Divorce brings, often too late, a clearer vision of our own failings.

Application: What would life be like to be divorced? Can you imagine the pain and anguish that come with trying to divide property and determine custody of the children?

NOVEMBER 15

Spencer W. Kimball. "Marriage is perhaps the most vital of all the decisions [we make] and has the most far-reaching effects, for it has to do not only with immediate happiness, but also with eternal joys." ("Marriage & Divorce," *1976 Devotional Speeches of the Year*, Brigham Young University Press, 143).

What decision could be more significant for mortals than the decision of whom we marry? Though there is no one and only, there is 'only one.' Sometimes singles are so concerned about marrying the right person, as if *they* were *already* the right person. Each of us has many things to improve before marriage but especially after. Healthy marriages require mature adults. Even though we do our best to screen each other before we marry, happiness is a result of how we treat one another *after marriage*. Anyone can be pleasant dating. But too often we see couples treat each other differently after marriage than before. In marriage we do our best to please each other and thereby maximize happiness.

Application: What trait most evident in dating continues to be your spouse's strength in marriage?

NOVEMBER 16

Gordon B. Hinckley: "Marriage is not all romance. Marriage is work. Marriage is effort. You have to accommodate one another.

You have to look after one another. Another thing is to do everything you can to develop the talents, the resources, the opportunities of your companion" (Hinckleys to Note 60th Anniversary," *Church News*, 19 April, 1997, 3).

Libraries are filled with self-help books. Some argue that we do not train people well for marriage, that we provide more training to obtain a driver's license than we do to marry! What training *is* available to individuals to prepare them for marriage? If marriage is work, if marriage requires effort, if marriage requires looking after someone else, then we need help before we enter this relationship. Being a husband or wife, a father or mother, is to a large extent an imitated skill that we learn from our parents. Marriage requires a humility to learn how to improve in our marriage and parenting roles. Marriage is a commitment that we make with each other that we will assist each other to learn to live more perfectly.

Application: Examine the possibility of starting a new hobby together: Family history, tennis, walking, running, preparing for a marathon, gardening, or something of interest to both. Pry a little cash loose from your wallet for tuition or an activity fee.

NOVEMBER 17

James E. Faust: "I learned in serving almost twenty years as bishop and stake president that an excellent insurance against divorce is the payment of tithing. Payment of tithing seems to facilitate keeping the spiritual battery charged in order to make it through the times when the spiritual generator has been idle or not working" ("The Enriching of Marriage," *Ensign*, Nov. 1977, 11).

Paying a full tithing requires personal discipline. Tithing seems to be easier as we age because of the Lord's blessings to us in the past. You do not want to go ahead in life without His blessings. But in the beginning of a marriage, when funds are scarce, there may be the temptation to resist paying tithing. Accept it on faith if you must, but always pay tithing, for you are in need of the Lord's blessings. Should you run out of food, contact the bishop who will assist you with food from the Church storehouse.

Application: Did you both come from homes where tithing was paid? Do your recall your first tithing settlement?

NOVEMBER 18

Boyd K. Packer: "The creation of life is a great responsibility for a married couple. It is the challenge of mortality to be a worthy and responsible parent. Neither man nor woman can bear children alone. It was meant that children have two parents—both a father and a mother. No other pattern or process can replace this one" ("And a Little Child Shall Lead Them," *Ensign*, May, 2012, 8).

Is there anything more difficult than rearing children from infancy to adulthood? Never mind the costs involved, children bring their own set of challenges at every stage of life. Little ones require constant care, toddlers are dangerous home wreckers and get into jams because they do toddle, young adults search for acne cures while teenagers wreck the family car! Fathers help boys learn to be boys while mothers instill in their daughters the finer points of being feminine. Together, couples are deeply involved in the development and maturity of children who, surprisingly, turn out to be fairly normal!

Application: What would you say is one of the more important lessons you have learned from your children?

NOVEMBER 19

David B. Haight: "Latter-day Saints need not divorce—there are solutions to marriage problems. If, as husband and wife, you are having serious misunderstandings or if you feel some strain or tension building up in your marriage, you should humbly get on your knees together and ask God our Father, with a sincere heart and real intent, to lift the darkness that is over your relationship, that you may receive the needed light, see your errors, repent of your wrongs, forgive each other, and receive each unto yourselves as you did in the beginning. I solemnly assure you that God lives and will answer your humble pleas, for he has said, 'Ye shall ask whatsoever you will in the name of Jesus and it shall be done' (D&C 50:29), (Marriage and Divorce," *Ensign*, May 1984, 14).

Nephi said to his father that he would "go and do the things which the Lord hath commanded, for I know that the Lord giveth no commandments unto the children of men, save he shall prepare a way for them that they may accomplish the thing which he commandeth them (1 Nephi 3:7). The most important 'commandment' you two are now living is that of marriage. When two people marry, the command given them is to be one. That means that they stay together through 'thick and thin.' They married in the Lord's House and are under covenant to make their marriage 'sure' by the way they live and treat each other. Living the gospel softens hearts. It causes love to bloom and relationships to prosper. Elder Haight counsels couples who may be contemplating divorce to "humbly get on your knees together and ask God our Father" for assistance. As Nephi knew, no one cares more about your success in life than the One to whom we pray.

Application: Make it a practice to not leave home in the mornings or go to bed at night without making contact with heaven.

NOVEMBER 20

Dallin H. Oaks: "I pray that we will not let the challenges and temporary diversions of mortality cause us to forget our covenants and lose sight of our eternity destiny. We who know God's plan for his children, we who have covenanted to participate, have a clear responsibility. We must desire to do what is right, and we must do all that we can in our own circumstances in mortality" ("The Great Plan of Happiness," *Ensign*, Nov. 1993, 75).

The gospel teaches a simple message: Honor your covenants and you will be safe. Violate your covenants and you have no promises. There are 'Latter-day Saints' who fail to appreciate their membership in the Church. They may have been faithful as youth, they may have even served missions and married in the temple, but for some reason they are no longer honoring their covenants. This lifestyle exposes them to the wiles of Satan. Furthermore, they are kidding themselves about exaltation. One of the main differences between those who attain to the Celestial Kingdom and those that receive the Terrestrial glory, is one of being valiant 'in the testimony of Jesus' (see D&C 76:79). There are diversions that throw people off the path leading to eternal life. If our lives are centered in the Savior and His teachings, the Father's plan will bring us home.

Application: Read D&C 89:4. This scripture reminds us there are "evils and designs which do and will exist in the hearts of conspiring men in the last days." What evils and designs do you see leading married couples from the gospel path?

NOVEMBER 21

Spencer W. Kimball: "Two years make a tremendous difference in the life of a young man. He goes out a boy and comes back a man. He goes out immature, he comes back mature and strong, gracious, and a worker and willing to serve. He goes back to college in most cases and there he will make higher grades than he ever made before, because he has purpose in his life" (*Teachings of Spencer W. Kimball*, 590-91).

Serving a mission is the best training for marriage the Lord has devised. Where else (college dorm life has some similairites) does a person learn to live 24/7 with an individual from a different family and background? He or she is 'forced' to make compromises and adjustments not unlike those of marriage—sharing time and space, learning and teaching gospel principles, serving, praying and fasting for others, sharing household tasks, developing leadership skills, cleaning apartments, managing finances, and a host of other marriage-helpful lessons.

Application: From your own experience, list a few additional blessings of missions that relate to marriage.

NOVEMBER 22

Father, Consider Your Ways: "Marriage, as ordained of God, is the lawful union and man and wife, not only for this earth life, but for all eternity. A paramount purpose of marriage is to clothe spirit children of our Father in heaven with earthly bodies. When your first child is born, you become a father [and mother]. The title father is sacred and eternal. It is significant that of all the titles of respect and honor and admiration that are given to Deity, he has asked us to address him as Father" ("A Message from The Church of Jesus Christ of Latter-day Saints," by the Quorum of the Twelve Apostles, pamphlet, 1973).

Where does the role of father fit in the many titles you carry such as manager, coach, friend, husband, breadwinner, quorum leader, and so forth? Does the role of father take high priority in your life or would it finish a distant third behind sports, TV, the gym, or other selections? Sometimes it's easy to be home together, but not really be there or home *together*. Take the opportunity to spend meaningful time with your children and grandchildren. Nothing else you give to them will come anywhere near the value of your time and attention.

Application: Being a father is no easy task in today's world. An old research study indicated that fathers spend less than 10 minutes per week with *an individual child*. Do better than that. Keep track this week with your children and exceed that mark.

NOVEMBER 23

Carlos E. Asay: "This garment, worn day and night, serves three important purposes: it is a reminder of the sacred covenants made with the Lord in His holy house, a protective covering for the body, and a symbol of the modesty of dress and living that should characterize the lives of all the humble followers of Christ" ("The Temple Garment: An Outward Expression of an Inward Commitment," *Ensign*, Aug. 1997, 20.)

We live in a day of extreme fashion styles that show little regard for modesty and the sanctity of our bodies. Such fashions can be a temptation for the opposite sex and, sadly, people sometimes yield to temptation with the consequence that adultery and other sexual sins ruin their marriages and families. Latter-day Saints have a divine protection when they properly wear the garment, a reminder of our covenants. Though there are times when it is appropriate to remove the garment—bathing, sports, sexual relations—Elder Asay counseled: "The fundamental principle ought to be to wear the garment and not to find occasions to remove it" (*ibid.* 22).

Application: Help each other be modest in dress and appearance. Low cut dresses, blouses, and tight clothing are unwise.

NOVEMBER 24

Gordon B. Hinckley: "The tragedy is that some men are ensnared by their own foolishness and their own weakness. They throw to the wind the most sacred and solemn of covenants, entered into in the house of the Lord and sealed under the authority of the holy priesthood. They set aside their wives who have been faithful, who have loved and cared for them, who have struggled with them in times of poverty only to be discarded in times of affluence. They have left their children fatherless. They have avoided with every kind of artifice the payment of court-mandated alimony and child support" ("Our Solemn Responsibilities," *Ensign*, Nov. 1991, 51).

Occasionally we are stunned to learn that someone we thought we knew quite well has divorced. It shocks us, and we wonder what events or decisions could have brought about this ending. Who knew that they were having problems? What went wrong is usually related to how well they were living the gospel. Couples stop praying together, temple attendance becomes less frequent or ceases, there is carelessness around members of the opposite sex, or individuals have their faith shaken by reading anti-Mormon material. Satan is always on the prowl looking for individuals who are 'bored' with life, with the Church, and with their same old routine.

Application: Have you been shocked by close family members or personal friends who separated? Are you aware of the primary reason for their separation?

NOVEMBER 25

Ezra Taft Benson: "Fathers, another vital aspect of providing for the material needs of your family is the provision you should be making for your family in case of an emergency. Family preparedness has been a long-established welfare principle. It is even more urgent today. I ask you earnestly, have you provided for your family a year's supply of food, clothing, and where possible, fuel? The revelation to produce and store food may be as essential to our temporal welfare today as boarding the ark was to the people in the days of . Noah" ("To the Fathers in Israel," *Ensign*, Nov. 1987, 49).

These provisions for families aren't as immediately gratifying as electronic toys, sporting events trips, or vacations. But for the price of an average family holiday, we can give our families what might be a lifesaving bequest in times of emergency. Have we not seen in recent years the devastation that accompanies hurricanes, earthquakes, tsunamis, volcanoes, drought, and tainted food? Commercial enterprises now produce food storage items that are affordable and can be preserved for years. When you purchase groceries, buy a few extra items for storage. Be sure to rotate the food you store by using it on a regular basis.

Application: In a family council, discuss what items need to be replenished in your food storage program. Involve your children in this list of items.

NOVEMBER 26

Gordon B. Hinckley: "No man who abuses his wife or children is worthy to hold the priesthood of God. No man who abuses his wife or children is worthy to be a member in good standing in this Church. The abuse of one's spouse and children is a most serious offense before God, and any who indulge in it may expect to be disciplined by the Church" ("What Are People Asking About us?" *Ensign*, Nov. 1998, 72).

In a rebuke of men who fail to honor their wives' goodness, President Hinckley often referred to letters written by women complaining of their husband's treatment. After reading his condemnation of such men, it is incumbent on each husband to search his own soul as to how he treats his wife. It was the husband that 'made the offer' of marriage. Probably the quickest way to keep a man from reaching the highest degree of glory is for him to mistreat a daughter of God, especially the one who became his wife and the mother of his children. On the other hand, when a husband loves his wife and she feels his genuine love and appreciation for her, she more cheerfully fills her roles as a wife and a mother.

Application: How serious is abuse in marriage? What would be some examples of how a man might abuse his wife? In what ways could a wife be abusive to her husband?

NOVEMBER 27

Howard W. Hunter: "The priesthood cannot work out its destiny, nor can God's purposes be fulfilled, without our helpmates. Mothers perform a labor the priesthood cannot do. For this gift of life, the priesthood should have love unbounded for the mothers of their children....You should express regularly to your wife and children your reverence and respect for her. Indeed, one of the greatest things a father can do for his children is to love their mother" ("Being a Righteous Husband and Father," *Ensign*, Nov. 1994, 50).

Feelings emerge from expressions of love and appreciation. Many individuals are starved for affection and attention. Do not assume that your partner knows how you feel about him or her, or that your children already know the extent of your love for them. As a wife, appreciate the work of your husband to fight daily traffic and deal with individuals who may not appreciate his efforts. Husbands, are you cognizant of the efforts your wife makes, especially those who pull double duty in working away from home as well as being a homemaker? The easiest 'work' we do ought to be simple and frequent expressions of appreciation.

Application: What labors do mothers perform that men can't? As a wife, do you hear your husband expressing, on a regular basis, his love and respect for you? How are you at reciprocating?

NOVEMBER 28

Gordon B. Hinckley: "[Your wife] will be yours and yours alone, regardless of the circumstances of your lives. You will be hers and hers alone. There can be eyes for none other. There must be absolute loyalty, undeviating loyalty one to another....Through all the days of your lives you must be as true one to another as the polar star" ("Living Worthy of the Girl You Will Someday Marry," *Ensign*, May 1998, 49).

You just enjoyed the Thanksgiving season, a special time to verbally express gratitude and appreciation to the Lord and to your companion for the blessings that have come your way. Each of you is among your greatest treasures and your temple sealing protects you against the unknowns of mortality. Of all the meaningful blessings you share, the association you have with each other on a daily basis is among the greatest. We all function much better with compliments, with genuine words of appreciation whether as adults or children. Don't limit your expressions of love to this season.

Application: Keep a picture of your sweetheart at your desk, your cubicle, your counter, or your wallet or purse. Set a phone/ computer reminder to phone and express your love to your sweetheart.

NOVEMBER 29

D&C 131:1-4 "In the celestial glory there are three heavens or degrees; And in order to obtain the highest, a man must enter into this order of the priesthood [meaning the new and everlasting covenant of marriage]; And if he does not, he cannot obtain it. He may enter into the other, but that is the end of his kingdom; he cannot have an increase."

The privileges that go with exaltation—marriage and family life— are open only to those who reach or qualify for the highest degree of glory in the highest degree of glory! To attain that level requires a lifetime of serving each other and honoring marriage covenants. However, at the time we marry, we know little about each other. As

270

we mature and gain experience in living the principles of the Restoration, we come to see that marriage is the crowning ordinance of the entire gospel plan. There is no doubt that many will look back on their time as mortal marriage partners with disappointment, knowing they failed to live by the principles that could have qualified them to live together forever.

Application: Read D&C 131:1-4. What kind of marriage must a couple have to qualify for the highest degree? Now is your time to acquire the necessary attributes you will need to live there.

NOVEMBER 30

Gordon B. Hinckley: "I constantly deal with those cases of members of the Church who have been married in the temple and who later divorce and then apply for a cancellation of their temple sealing. When first married, they are full of great expectations, with a wonderful spirit of happiness. But the flower of love fades in an atmosphere of criticism and carping, of mean words and uncontrolled anger. Love flies out the window as contention enters. I repeat, my brethren, if any of you...men have trouble controlling your temper, I plead with you to begin the work of making that correction now. Otherwise you will bring only tears and sorrow into [your] homes" ("Living Worthy of the Girl You Will Someday Marry," *Ensign*, May 1998, 50).

It is inevitable that the novelty and freshness of marriage will wear off to some extent over time. Perhaps you have experienced a little of it already. However, consider what has changed. If you do, you will conclude that it is *you* that has changed. Your sweetheart's physical and mental features are unlikely to have undergone dramatic alteration. It is your perception of each other that has changed from earlier times in your relationship. The good news is that this is an area under your control, something you can actually improve through a change in behavior. It is true that most problems are not solely the fault of one spouse, but the most effective way to begin resolving them is to make the changes that *you* need to make—now.

Application: Recall the feelings you had during those early days of marriage. Briefly talk about those feelings. Reflect on why we treated each other so well then. Has the attraction that drew you together waned or grown stronger?

DECEMBER

DECEMBER 1

Gordon B. Hinckley: "Be modest in your wants. You do not need a big home with a big mortgage as you begin your lives together. You can and should avoid overwhelming debt. There is nothing that will cause greater tensions in marriage than grinding debt, which will make of you a slave to your creditors. You may have to borrow money to begin ownership of a home. But do not let it be so costly that it will preoccupy your thoughts day and night" ("Living Worthy of the Girl You Will Someday Marry," *Ensign*, May 1998, 50).

As the Christmas season approaches, be aware that this is a difficult time for some families. It is a time for children to learn the differences between needs and wants. Plan now to limit your spending this Christmas and bless your children in ways other than with a deluge of presents. Debt places great stress on marriages, and Christmas is no time to add to that burden. Perhaps more importantly, piles of commercial goods are a distraction from the real significance of this holiday.

Application: Avoid a toy overload this Christmas! Plan now. Perhaps you could pick out a family in the ward or neighborhood that needs your help or attention.

DECEMBER 2

Ezra Taft Benson. "Thou shalt 'love thy wife with all thy heart, and shalt cleave unto her and none else' (D&C 42:22)…What does it mean to love someone with all our hearts? It means with all our emotional feelings and our devotion. Surely when you love your wife with all your heart, you cannot demean her, criticize her, find fault with her, nor abuse her by words, sullen behavior, or actions" ("What Manner of Men Ought We to Be?" *Ensign*, Nov. 1983, 43).

How sad to hear a husband or a wife criticize a spouse. Marriage is designed to bring out the best in us as did dating. We learn from each other how to be a spouse (we never played this role before now) and to be critical and negative with each other is foolishness. We ought to be enthusiastic students and kind teachers as we learn from each other how to function as marriage partners. To be critical of a companion when he or she is doing his or her best during this 'spouse school' of mortality is unbecoming of a Latter-day Saint. We learn more quickly from positive comments than negative ones. We know that we have weaknesses and to have a spouse continually harp on our inadequacies is unproductive and contrary to the spirit of marriage, charity, and the Golden Rule.

Application: Can you both say that you love each other with heart and soul, and that you are cleaving? (This is a different use of the word 'cleave.' Look it up if necessary).

DECEMBER 3

Gordon B. Hinckley: "The girl you marry will be yours forever. You will love her and she will love you through thick and thin, through sunshine and storm. She will become the mother of your children. What greater thing in all this world can there be than to become the father of a precious child, a son or daughter of God, our Father in Heaven, for whom we are given the rights and responsibilities of mortal stewardship" ("Living Worthy of the Girl You Will Someday Marry," *Ensign*, May 1998, 51).

The old saw, "familiarity breeds contempt," contains the essence of a problem many of us experience in marriage. After the novelty and excitement of marriage has worn off to some extent, we may lessen our expressions of appreciation, and even our intimate lives can become perfunctory. Don't let your marriage grow tiresome, dull, or boring. If one or both of you work away from home, you already spend most of your waking hours in different locations and environments. Staying in contact daily is one of the purposes of this 'tune-up kit.' Find a competent babysitter and at least once a week get out together. A babysitter is always cheaper than a divorce! Don't stop your expressions of appreciation even for the 'small stuff.' Human beings never tire of genuine compliments.

Application: Re-create, or recall, as best you can, one of your early dates. Recall what you did, where you went, and how you felt about each other at that point in time.

DECEMBER 4

Russell M. Nelson: "....I warn against pornography. It is degrading of women. It is evil. It is infectious, destructive, and addictive. The body has means by which it can cleanse itself from harmful effects of contaminated food or drink. But it cannot vomit back the poison of pornography. Once recorded, it always remains subject to recall, flashing its perverted images across your mind, with power to draw you away from the wholesome things in life. Avoid it like the plague!" ("Our Sacred Duty to Honor Women," *Ensign*, May 1999, 39).

Avoiding pornography is a frequent theme of the Brethren in conference addresses because of its prevalence and ease of access in our culture and its destructive power on marriages. The

275

seriousness of this media form has reached epidemic proportions. Pornography is spiritually deadening. This plague is a major deterrent to exaltation. Its addictive impact is such that some researchers consider it to be more powerful in its grip than some of the 'hard drugs' such as cocaine or heroin! The latest research also indicates that pornography alters normal brain functions!

Application: How prevalent is pornography in your environment? What defenses do you have in place to prevent anyone accessing pornographic sites in your home?

DECEMBER 5

Spencer W. Kimball: "Immorality does not begin in adultery or perversion. It begins with little indiscretions like sex thoughts, sex discussions, passionate kissing, petting and such, growing with every exercise. The small indiscretion seems powerless compared to the sturdy body, the strong mind, the sweet spirit of youth who give way to the first temptation. But soon the strong has become weak, the master the slave, spiritual growth curtailed. But if the first unrighteous act is never given root, the tree will grow to beautiful maturity and the youthful life will grow toward God, our Father" ("President Kimball Speaks Out on Morality," *Ensign*, Nov. 1980, 95).

Harmless flirting at the office, working late hours alone with an individual of the opposite sex, or suggestive jokes on a 'Facebook' posting, may seem far distant from anything truly dangerous. But as President Kimball noted, sexual attraction that leads to immorality does not happen all at once. Satan knows that he is unlikely to tempt us directly into an inappropriate relationship. He is a patient, long-term planner whose goal is designed to lead us "carefully down to hell" (2 Nephi 28:21).

Application: Evaluate your work and social environments. Consider situations where you are in close and regular contact with colleagues. Are all your relationships appropriate?

DECEMBER 6

Bible Dictionary: "Charity. The highest, noblest, strongest kind of love, not merely affection; the pure love of Christ" (632).

Moroni reminds us that "charity suffereth long, and is kind, and envieth not, and is not puffed up, seeketh not her own, is not easily provoked, thinketh no evil, and rejoiceth not in iniquity but rejoiceth in the truth, beareth all things, believeth all things, hopeth all things, endureth all things. Wherefore…if ye have not charity, ye are nothing, for charity never faileth…. Charity is the pure love of Christ, and it endureth forever; and whoso is found possessed of it at the last day, it shall be well with him" (Moroni 7:45-47.) Could a divorce take place if both husband and wife possess this trait? Charity is an essential key in a happy and lasting marriage. Were we not charitable when we dated? Had we not been, it is doubtful we would have married. The challenge now is to continue charitable behavior in spite of our familiarity.

Application: Read the topic of *charity* in the Bible Dictionary. Which of the charitable attributes listed are most important to you in your marriage? Which is your spouse's best 'charity trait?'

DECEMBER 7

N. Eldon Tanner: "Modesty in dress is a quality of mind and heart, born of respect for oneself, one's fellowmen, and the Creator of us all. Modesty reflects an attitude of humility, decency, and propriety. Consistent with these principles and guided by the Holy Spirit, let parents, teachers, and youth discuss the particulars of dress, grooming, and personal appearance, and with free agency accept responsibility and choose the right" ("Friend to Friend," *Friend*, June 1971, 2).

We seem to live in a 'clothing obsessed' world. Multi-billion dollar industries pedal products that fill entire malls and warehouses. Somehow we are made to believe that our self-worth revolves around the clothing we wear. Fashions seem to change with each Spring and Fall season in Milan or London. For the most part, designers could care less about modesty in their styling. In fact, much that passes for modern fashion is designed to shock or titillate. Clothing has become an expensive budget item. Clothing purchases ought to be made while keeping in mind comfort, utility, and modesty.

Application: What does a new pair of designer jeans cost? Shoes? How important are clothes to your self-esteem? Do you view clothes differently now compared to when you were single?

DECEMBER 8

Mosiah 4:29-30 "I cannot tell you all the things whereby ye may commit sin; for there are diverse ways and means, even so many that I cannot number them. But this much I can tell you, that if ye do not watch yourselves, and your thoughts, and your words, and your deeds, and observe the commandments of God, and continue in the faith of what ye have heard concerning the coming of our Lord, even unto the end of your lives, ye must perish. And now, O man, remember, and perish not."

Even with the safeguards that come from personal and family prayer, scripture reading, church attendance and family time, most of us work out of the home or maintain electronic connection with the outside world via television, the Internet, a smartphone, via social media. With all of these amazing gadgets, it is difficult to avoid provocative material. Sadly, in only a few unguarded moments in the world of technological accessibility, a few clicks of a mouse, or sliding a screen across a phone or tablet can lead to untold damage.

Application: King Benjamin, rather than listing ways that mankind can sin, simply concludes his sermon with the counsel to 'watch yourselves.' What might be a practical way to do this?

DECEMBER 9

James E. Faust: "Upon returning from living in South America I was struck by the lack of self-esteem revealed in the manner by which so many people now clothe themselves in public. To attract attention or in the name of comfort and informality, many have sunk not only to immodesty but to slovenliness. Against their own self-interest, they present themselves to others in the worst possible way" ("The Dignity of Self," *Ensign*, May 1981, 9).

Sometimes our worst dress is reserved for times with spouse and family because our level of familiarity is such that we are not concerned with impressing them. While the Book of Mormon is filled with references to pride and vanity associated with costly apparel, we ought to dress in a neat and comely fashion at home and around our children. We ought to clothe ourselves modestly, yet comfortably. Being well-groomed, even in casual situations, allows us to present our best self to others.

Application: What outfit do you like best on your wife? Which suit do you think makes your husband look his best? Would your spouse choose different clothes for you than you do?

DECEMBER 10

Ezra Taft Benson: *"If you are married, avoid flirtations of any kind.* Sometimes we hear of a married man going to lunch with his secretary or other women in the office. Men and women who are married sometimes flirt with and tease members of the opposite sex. So-called harmless meetings are arranged or inordinate amounts of time are spent together. In all of these cases, people rationalize by saying that these are natural expressions of friendship. But what may appear to be harmless teasing or simply having a little fun with someone of the opposite sex can easily lead to more serious involvement and eventual infidelity. A good question to ask ourselves is this: Would my spouse be pleased if he or she knew I was doing this? Would a wife be pleased to know that her husband lunches alone with his secretary? Would a husband be pleased if he saw his wife flirting and being coy with another man? My beloved brothers and sisters, this is what Paul meant when he said: "Abstain from all appearance of evil" (1 Thessalonians 5:22). ("The Law of Chastity," *Devotional and Fireside Speeches of the Year, 1987-88*, 53).

How would a Church president know of these types of situations? Records of court proceedings in which members are disciplined, are sent to the First Presidency.

Application: Read President Benson's quote again and commit each other to its safe principles.

DECEMBER 11

Thomas S. Monson: "As we go about living from day to day, it is almost inevitable that our faith will be challenged....Increasingly, some celebrities and others who—for one reason or another—are in the public eye have a tendency to ridicule religion in general and, at times, the Church in particular. If our testimonies are not firmly enough rooted, such criticisms can cause us to doubt our own beliefs or to waver in our resolves" ("Dare To Stand Alone," *Ensign*, Nov. 2011, 60.)

Have you heard or seen 'celebrities' who live and behave far differently than the standards the Lord has set for members of His Church? Why do actors and talented athletes have any influence anyway? What do they know about eternal marriage? Are they defending marriage and morality? In fact, many of them bear children out of wedlock with little regard for legalizing the relationship. Some seem to change partners on a regular basis and proudly enter into relationships of temporary convenience. With little regard for the Ten Commandments and other Biblical standards, perhaps that is their motivation to ridicule religion and its adherents.

Application: Have you had a favorite actor only to learn that he or she was living with someone outside of marriage with perhaps a child or two out of wedlock, or who was atheistic and an outright foe of religion?

DECEMBER 12

First Presidency: "The Lord's law of moral conduct is abstinence outside of lawful marriage and fidelity within marriage. Sexual relations are proper only between husband and wife appropriately expressed within the bonds of marriage" ("To All Members of the Church of Jesus Christ of Latter-day Saints." Letter read in Sacrament meetings, Nov. 14, 1991).

When contrasted to modern legislative and other governmental attempts to combat what are effectively moral issues, the Lord's laws are simple and clear. Abstinence is unambiguous. It is not like tennis where a skillful hit on or near the boundary line is viewed as advantageous. There are no advantages in marriage where behavior places us anywhere near the simple boundaries the Lord set. Fidelity in marriage encompasses loyalty to spouse, to self, and to God.

Application: What are the three most serious sins that could be committed by a member of the Church? Read Alma 39:5 if you need a review.

DECEMBER 13

Dallin H. Oaks: "Our understanding of life begins with a council in heaven. There the spirit children of God were taught his eternal plan for their destiny. We had progressed as far as we could without a physical body and an experience in mortality. To realize a fulness of joy, we had to prove our willingness to keep the commandments of God in a circumstance where we had no memory of what preceded our mortal birth....Maleness and femaleness, marriage, and the bearing and nurturing of children are all essential to the great plan of happiness" ("The Great Plan of Happiness," *Ensign*, Nov. 1993, 72).

The de-evolution of marriage and family relationships promoted by those who know nothing of the true purposes of marriage and family relations, is one of the sad social trends of our day. Nevertheless, attacks against marriage and traditional families do not alter the pattern outlined by God. The nuclear family was established by the Father in the beginning with Adam and Eve and is not to be changed or modified by the whims of man.

Application: What have you noticed are the primary strengths of males? Of females? How do their separate traits and attributes combine to make the ideal marriage?'

DECEMBER 14

Russell M. Nelson: "The highest ordinances in the house of the Lord are received by husband and wife together and equally—or not at all!....An ideal marriage is a true partnership between two imperfect people, each striving to complement the other, to keep the commandments, and to do the will of the Lord" ("Our Sacred Duty to Honor Women," *Ensign*, May 1999, 39.)

The Apostle Paul instructed men: "Husbands, love your wives, even as Christ also loved the church, and gave himself for it" (Ephesians 5:25). While extending love to one another, we learn that we are, in fact, 'imperfect' people; we don't always perform at our best. Yet because of our love for each other and our desire to be faithful members of the Church, we consider obedience to God's laws as paramount. Our potential for exaltation inspires us to work as a couple to build a 'forever marriage.'

Application: In what ways do you sometimes feel 'imperfect,' or inadequate? Yet, even with our mortal weaknesses, we can build a true partnership.

DECEMBER 15

Gordon B. Hinckley: "Keep yourself worthy through all the days of your life. Be good and true and kind one to another. There is so much of bitterness in the world. There is so much of pain and sorrow that come of angry words. There is so much of tears that follow disloyalty. But there can be so much of happiness if there is an effort to please and an overwhelming desire to make comfortable and happy one's companion" ("Living Worthy of the Girl You Will Someday Marry," *Ensign*, May 1998, 51.)

We often measure our worthiness by the questions associated with a temple recommend. However, recommends are now valid for a period longer than a year. In effect, we must evaluate our worthiness frequently, and certainly each time we attend the temple. Worthiness is a state of mind as well as a reflection of behavior. Personal worthiness is an essential element of personal happiness. As Alma taught his son Corianton: "Behold, I say unto you, wickedness never was happiness" (Alma 41:10). And, it never will be.

Application: Happiness is surely your goal as a couple. At this point in your lives, what brings you happiness on a daily basis?

DECEMBER 16

Thomas S. Monson: "....I believe the saddest and most discouraging responsibility I have each week is the handling of cancellations of sealings. Each one was preceded by a joyous marriage in the house of the Lord, where a loving couple was beginning a new life together and looking forward to spending the rest of eternity with each other. And then months and years go by, and for one reason or another, love dies. It may be the result of financial problems, lack of communication, uncontrolled tempers, interference from in-laws, entanglement in sin" ("Priesthood Power," *Ensign*, May 2011, 68).

Imagine the prophet reading letters of unhappy couples seeking a cancellation of their temple sealing. He is 'forced' to read about the situations that lead them to want to end their relationship. No wonder these letters tug at his heartstrings. No one who divorced usually has positive things to say of their former spouse. Their hearts are usually filled with anger and bitterness. For that reason, a cancellation of sealing usually requires sufficient time for both individuals to eliminate any bitterness or acrimony. Surely the two who seek a permanent separation, at one time had a quiet, touching ceremony in a temple setting followed by a reception where close friends and family members gathered to celebrate with them. What a tragic ending to what was an impressive beginning.

Application: Count your blessings that you are still in love with each other and that you treasure sacred as well as mundane moments together.

DECEMBER 17

Thomas S. Monson: "If any of you are having difficulty in your marriage, I urge you to do all that you can to make whatever repairs are necessary, that you might be as happy as you were when your marriage started out. We who are married in the house of the Lord do so for time and for all eternity, and then we must put forth the necessary effort to make it so....Do not let your marriage get to the point where it is in jeopardy" ("Priesthood Power", *Ensign*, May 2011, 69).

Is there a married couple without differences of opinion? Though we could not see it the days before we joined hands and hearts and made solemn covenants in the temple, we did agree to accept each other as we are. Before marriage we were blind to so many things. But now they are in plain sight. They are no longer hidden. Though we can easily spot them in a spouse, it may be that our weaknesses are the most glaring—recall the story of motes and beams. We must not let our weaknesses throw us off course just because we are now more familiar with each other. We realize that our love for each other stems from the unique inner strengths each of us have developed over the years together, and the good news is that we are more in love than ever before!

Application: No one wants to be reminded of physical signs of aging. Be wise and refrain from making comments; they contribute few positives to the relationship!

DECEMBER 18

Spencer W. Kimball: "If we looked at mortality as the whole of existence, then pain, sorrow, failure, and short life would be calamity. But if we look upon life as an eternal thing stretching far into the premortal past and on into the eternal post-death future, then all happenings may be put in proper perspective" (*Faith Precedes the Miracle*, 97).

The Prophet Joseph Smith literally brought heaven down to earth. No longer are men and women bound by a this-life-only perspective. He restored the vision of an eternal family. Unfortunately, the world is unaware of this doctrine which, by itself, would be sufficient reason for us to be a missionary church. Though in other faiths there is talk of a resurrection, it is not thought to be one of physical matter, but of a spirit substance. What a bitter ending that would be to an otherwise wonderful existence? Would it not be a monumental waste of time and effort if, after decades of marriage, all that you created and cherished vanished in death? Who could respect a God who developed such a shallow plan? If our God is Endless, why would He put together a plan that is only temporary? If Joseph Smith had restored no other doctrine than that of eternal marriage, how greatly we would honor him.

Application: What would be your feelings if there were no concept of an eternal relationship for you two? Why do you think that only Latter-day Saints teach this doctrine of eternal marriage and family when other faiths believe in a resurrection?

DECEMBER 19

Joe J. Christensen: "In our day many children grow up with distorted values because we as parents overindulge them. Whether you are well-to-do or, like most of us, of more modest means, we as parents often attempt to provide children with almost everything they want, thus taking away from them the blessing of anticipating, of longing for something they do not have. One of the most important things we can teach our children is to deny themselves. Instant gratification generally makes for weak people. How many truly great individuals do you know who never had to struggle? ("Greed, Selfishness, and Overindulgence," *Ensign*, May 1999 9).

Elder Christensen pleads with parents to not overindulge their children. There are so many 'toys' and 'gadgets' that appeal to children, and parents must be wise in not catering to their every whim. In an effort to prevent children from sacrificing or 'going without' (perhaps as they did growing up), parents may distort the relationship between effort and reward by removing the thrill of anticipation or the need to save first for things of value. For example, we live in a day when the cost of athletic shoes easily exceeds $100. Wise parents let children earn their own money if their efforts to dissuade them go unheeded. Learning to sacrifice is an important lesson that youth must learn for they will yet be called upon to serve missions, marry, and become parents themselves. Children must learn the differences between needs and wants early in life; otherwise, life itself will teach them difficult lessons later on.

Application: Recall the past Christmas. How many presents did your children receive? Probably way too many? Plan now to change that this Christmas. Define overindulgence. If childless, share your philosophy about gift-giving.

DECEMBER 20

Richard G. Scott: "Pure love is an incomparable, potent power for good. Righteous love is the foundation of a successful marriage. It is the primary cause of contented, well-developed children. Who can justly measure the righteous influence of a mother's love?" ("The Eternal Blessings of Marriage," *Ensign*, May 2011, 96.)

A student said of her parents: "My parent's relationship is strong, and I have seen it grow throughout my life and throughout the trials my family has experienced. One thing I love is how my parents go to the temple together. I don't feel that there are many better ways to strengthen your eternal marriage than by going to the House of the Lord where the sealing took place. This has been an example to me and I know that it is something that I will do with my husband one day." Righteous parents greatly impact their children for good.

Application: If possible, go back to the temple where you married and review the feelings and events of that day. Can you define 'pure love.' How is it a 'potent power for good?'

DECEMBER 21

Elaine S. Dalton: "[mothers] you are your daughters' most important example of modesty and virtue—thank you. Never hesitate to teach them that they are royal daughters of God and their value is not based on their sensual appeal. And let them see your belief modeled correctly and consistently in your own personal attitude and appearance. You are also guardians of Virtue" ("Guardians of Virtue," *Ensign*, May 2011, 124).

A daughter said of her mother: "My mom is a beautiful daughter of God who is the sweetest, most humble, charitable, loving friend I could ever have. My mom and I have such a strong bond and I am so grateful for her. My mom has the strongest testimony of anyone I know. She is a spiritual powerhouse and has always set a strong example for not only me but also everyone in my family including my dad. From a young age, I saw my mom kneeling at her bedside. She takes every opportunity to teach me the gospel and to discuss it with her. She dresses modestly and is an example of purity and devotion to the Lord than I wish to follow."

Application: How did your mother bless your life? What important trait or attribute did you gain from her that is now an important aspect of your character and personality?

DECEMBER 22

Thomas S. Monson: "I recall a time—and some of you here tonight will also—when the standards of most people were very similar to our standards. No longer is this true....Brethren, none within the sound of my voice should be in any doubt concerning what is moral and what is not, nor should any be in doubt about what is expected of us as holders of the priesthood of God. We have been and continue to be taught God's laws. Despite what you may see or hear elsewhere, these laws are unchanging" ("Dare to Stand Alone," *Ensign*, Nov. 2011, 60).

Have moral standards changed since you left high school or college? Are the standards you see in music, television, and other media, those that you wish for your family? The title of President Monson's address is a challenge to all of us to set our own standards, ones that are in harmony with true principles. Once set, we don't deviate from them regardless of the pressures or circumstances that arise. There are times in our lives when we must stand firm against demeaning fashions, immoral messages, and peer pressure to modify our standards.

Application: Discuss any changes you have seen in moral standards since your school days. What do you consider the most serious changes in the past few decades?

DECEMBER 23

Ezra Taft Benson: "Families must spend more time together in work and recreation. Family home evenings should be scheduled once a week as a time for recreation, work projects, skits, songs around the piano, games, special refreshments, and family prayers. Like iron links in a chain, this practice will bind a family together, in love, pride, tradition, strength, and loyalty" ("Fundamental Principles of Enduring Relationships," *Ensign*, Nov. 1982, 60).

Surely there was wisdom in Church leaders reemphasizing family home evenings far back in 1965. The counsel to gather families together for instruction, prayer, and music, is one of the more important things parents can do. Certainly working together, playing together and enjoying each other in a weekly Monday evening session, should be quality family time. Each family member should participate in some way on the program, whether helping prepare treats, passing out songbooks, or giving part all or part of the lesson. These times yield important blessings for both children and parents. Incidentally, children listen and learn more than you think they do! In any event, it is the *doing* of things together as much as it is the nature of the activity that children remember. This Christmas season is a great time for binding your family together.

Application: Is Monday evening held inviolable by all family members? Nothing short of an emergency should interfere. Establish this as an enjoyable tradition.

DECEMBER 24

Dieter F. Uchtdorf: ". . . be thankful for all the small successes in your home, your family relationships, your education and livelihood, your Church participation and personal improvement.... For example, insisting that you have a picture-perfect family home evening each week—even though doing so makes you and everyone around you miserable—may not be the best choice. Instead, ask yourself, "What could we do as a family that would be enjoyable and spiritual and bring us closer together?" ("Forget Me Not," *Ensign*, Nov. 2011, 120).

This Christmas Eve, you may try for that 'perfect' family home evening wherein the family gathers to read the Christmas story, acting out various scenes with whoever is present. Christmas Eve is a special time in which we reflect on the mission of the Christ Child, the one who condescended to come to earth and experience mortality and carry out the Atonement. His mission is a great blessing to married couples through the events of His life and resurrection. His coming forth from the grave confirmed the reality of life beyond death. Christmas brings renewed hope to mankind while Easter brings with it the promise of eternal life.

Application: Have a traditional family home evening by reading the Christmas story from Luke and Matthew. Watch a version of "A Christmas Carol," ('Scrooge') as a family.

DECEMBER 25

Dieter F. Uchtdorf: "The Christmas season is wonderful in many ways. It is a season of charitable acts of kindness and brotherly love. It is a season of being more reflective about our own lives and about the many blessings that are ours. It is a season of forgiving and being forgiven. It is a season to enjoy the music and lights, parties, and presents. But the glitter of the season should never dim our sight and prevent us from truly seeing the Prince of Peace in His majesty" ("Can We See the Christ?" *Ensign*, Dec. 2010, 4).

Christmas reminds us of the Savior and His mission. Though He came as a babe in Bethlehem to the household of Mary and Joseph, He was the Son of God. Elohim, His Father, is the father of His spirit body and of His earthly body. With the combination of an eternal father and a mortal mother, he was capable of performing an Atonement, something no one else could do. His unique combination of an eternal father allowed him to remain alive until He had completed the Atonement whereas a mere mortal would have died immediately. He inherited the power to die from His mother which made possible His death and resurrection, that supernal gift to all mankind. He took upon Himself the sins of all those who repent. His great suffering came as a result of the Father withdrawing His Spirit from Him, for that is the penalty for sin. Yet, He was sinless; hence His sacrifice was voluntary and love-inspired on our behalf. No wonder Latter-day Saints love this Perfect Man, the very Son of God.

Application: What kind of Christmas will you have today? Is it a commercial onslaught of all the toys in the kingdom, or a spiritual feast which brings the spirit of appreciation for the birth of our Savior?

DECEMBER 26

Neil L. Andersen: "The family is ordained of God. Families are central to our Heavenly Father's plan here on earth and through the eternities. After Adam and Eve were joined in marriage, the scripture reads, 'And God blessed them, and God said unto them, Be fruitful, and multiply, and replenish the earth'…This commandment has not been forgotten or set aside in The Church of Jesus Christ of Latter-day Saints. We express deep gratitude for the enormous faith shown by husbands and wives (especially our wives) in their willingness to have children. When to have a child and how many children to have are private decisions to be made between a husband and wife and the Lord" ("Children," *Ensign*, Nov. 2011, 28).

Latter-day Saints are 'pro-family' by virtue of our theology. We marry not to avoid having children, but to bring to earth those spirits who must be anxious to come and experience their own mortality. We are blessed as married couples to provide a body for them. Though many in our culture shy away from bearing children, Latter-day Saints celebrate the announcement of conception leading to birth. Birth control pills and antibiotics make it possible for people in the world to enjoy the privileges of sex while using a barrier to prevent life. With modern medicine, sexually transmitted diseases can usually be controlled and these medications allow couples to live together and avoid conception or death from diseases. What a far cry this perspective is from the command of the Lord to Adam and Eve to 'multiply and replenish' the earth.

Application: The Christmas season is an exciting time for children who anticipate the gifts of the holiday. Even though in their youthfulness they are more interested in the 'gifts' of the season, be sure they understand the real significance of Christmas.

DECEMBER 27

Boyd K. Packer: "No man receives the fulness of the priesthood without a woman at his side. For no man, the Prophet [Joseph Smith] said, can obtain the fulness of the priesthood outside the temple of the Lord (D&C 131:1-4). And she is there beside him in that sacred place. She shares in all that he receives. The man and the woman individually receive the ordinances encompassed in the endowment. But the man cannot ascend to the highest ordinances—the sealing ordinances—without her at his side. No man achieves the supernal exalting status of worthy fatherhood except as a gift from his wife" ("The Relief Society," *Ensign*, May 1998, 73).

What could more clearly demonstrate the value and significance of a couple's relationship than the act of kneeling before their Heavenly Father, in His House, to make holy their pledge to each other of their love and affection? Exaltation requires that a man and a woman be sealed together by priesthood authority, and to then honor the covenants they enter into on that sacred occasion.

Application: Commit to a schedule in the coming year to attend the temple more frequently and listen carefully to all ordinances associated with the House of the Lord.

DECEMBER 28

D. Todd Christofferson: "When prophets come crying repentance, it 'throws cold water on the party.' But in reality the prophetic call should be received with joy. Without repentance, there is no real progress or improvement in life. Pretending there is no sin does not lessen its burden and pain. Suffering for sin does not by itself change anything for the better. Only repentance leads to the sunlit uplands of a better life. And, of course, only through repentance do we gain access to the atoning grace of Jesus Christ and salvation. Repentance is a divine gift, and there should be a smile on our faces when we speak of it. It points us to freedom, confidence, and peace. Rather than interrupting the celebration, the gift of repentance is the cause for true celebration" ("The Divine Gift of Repentance," *Ensign*, Nov. 2011, 38).

Repentance means to 'turn away,' signifying a change in direction. Repentance follows faith inasmuch as when we gain faith in the Son of God, we realize that 'no unclean thing' can enter His presence or that of the Father. Repentance is the way in which we access the Atonement. Repentance sets us back on the path when we have strayed. In marriage, repentance is usually carried out by genuine, sincere apologies. Most marital sins such as harsh words, criticisms, and sarcastic comments, do not require a bishop's attention, but we do need to commit to not repeat the offense.

Application: Reflect on how readily you apologize when you offend. Genuine apologies heal relationships, while rationalizing stokes the fires of selfishness.

DECEMBER 29

Gordon B. Hinckley: "I am satisfied that if we would look for the virtues in one another and not the vices, there would be much more of happiness in the homes of our people. There would be far less of divorce, much less of infidelity, much less of anger and rancor and quarreling. There would be more of forgiveness, more of love, more of peace, more of happiness. This is as the Lord would have it" ("Living Worthy of the Girl You Will Someday Marry," *Ensign*, May 1998, 51).

'Till death do us part' is the secular promise in contrast to a temple sealing for eternity. Yet, the temple ordinance, alone, is insufficient. As we live our lives, the principles of the gospel become more important than ever and being positive and appreciative are essential elements of a healthy marriage. Every married person should understand that the 'food' that feeds marriage relationships are the positives that we express. The simplest way to brighten another's day is by a sincere compliment. Everyone deserves credit for the good things they do. A compliment acknowledges the efforts of a spouse or a child. Sincere compliments create positive emotions of love and a willingness to reciprocate.

Application: Some grow up in homes where negative comments are more common than were words of appreciation. Discuss the value of compliments and their effect on your own behavior.

DECEMBER 30

Thomas S. Monson: "How blessed we are to have come to earth at such a time as this—a marvelous time in the long history of the world….From a small beginning 182 years ago, our presence is now felt throughout the world. This great cause in which we are engaged will continue to go forth, changing and blessing lives as it does so. No cause, no force in the entire world can stop the work of God" ("As We Gather Once Again," *Ensign*, May 2012, 4).

From the First Vision in the year 1820, to the growth of Church membership that numbers in the millions, it is comforting to know that the work of the Lord will go forward despite continued challenges to Church standards and theology. There is much that lies in the future that will impact the growth of the Church. It is refreshing to hear a prophet tell us that the work of the Lord will move forward. Much of that progress, of course, depends on the quiet daily efforts of Church members who live the gospel and serve others during the unfolding events of these last days.

Application: Find the number of temples the Church presently has in operation, have been announced, or are under construction. How many temples were there when you were born?

DECEMBER 31

David A. Bednar: "In this momentous season of the earth's history, you and I as bearers of the priesthood need to be righteous men and effective instruments in the hands of God. We need to rise up as men of God....Many wives are pleading for husbands who have not only priesthood authority but also priesthood power. They yearn to be equally yoked with a faithful husband and priesthood companion in the work of creating a Christ-centered and gospel-focused home" ("The Powers of Heaven," *Ensign*, May 2012, 51).

This is a momentous season in the planet's history. Review your progress as a couple and family during this past year. Was it a year of growth? What will the coming year hold? Dicken's characterization of the late 18th century remains the same: "It was the best of times, it was the worst of times, it was the age of wisdom, it was the age of foolishness....Each year as we more nearly approach the coming of the Savior to the earth, there will be major upheavals for which we must be prepared (see D&C 88:87-94). Make the stability of your marriage and family your primary focus. The days ahead will require faith and testimony in living prophets, a major effort to spread the gospel worldwide, and in our identifying ancestors and performing ordinance work in their behalf.

Application: Read D&C 88:87-94. Husbands, follow Elder Bednar's counsel. Develop power in your priesthood authority, for your wife and children need a righteous patriarch.

APPENDIX A

BASIC DOCTRINES - SEMINARIES AND INSTITUTES OF RELIGION

1. GODHEAD

There are three separate personages in the Godhead: God the Eternal Father; His Son, Jesus Christ; and the Holy Ghost (see Acts 7:55-56). The Father and the Son have tangible bodies of flesh and bone, and the Holy Ghost is a personage of spirit (see D&C 130:22-23). They are one in purpose and doctrine. They are perfectly united in bringing to pass Heavenly Father's divine plan of salvation.

GOD THE FATHER

God the Father is the Supreme Ruler of the universe. He is the Father of our spirits. He is perfect, has all power, and knows all things. He is also a God of perfect mercy, kindness, and charity.

JESUS CHRIST

Jesus Christ is the Firstborn of the Father in the spirit and is the Only Begotten of the Father in the flesh. He is Jehovah of the Old Testament and the Messiah of the New Testament.

He lived a sinless life and made a perfect Atonement for the sins of all mankind. His life is the perfect example of how all mankind should live (see 3 Nephi 27:27). He was the first person on this earth to be resurrected. Jesus Christ will come again in power and glory and will reign on the earth during the Millennium.

All prayers, blessings, and priesthood ordinance should be done in His name.

THE HOLY GHOST

The Holy Ghost is the third member of the Godhead. He is a personage of spirit without a body of flesh and bones. He is often referred to as the Spirit, the Holy Spirit, the Spirit of God, the Spirit of the Lord, or the Comforter.

The Holy Ghost bears witness of the Father and the Son, reveals the truth of all things, and sanctifies those who repent and are baptized (see Moroni 10:5).

2. PLAN OF SALVATION

In the premortal existence, Heavenly Father introduced a plan to enable us to become like Him and obtain immortality and eternal life (see D&C 14:7; Moses 1:39). The scriptures refer to this plan as the plan of salvation, the great plan of happiness, the plan of redemption, and the plan of mercy.

The plan of salvation includes the Creation, the Fall, the Atonement of Jesus Christ, and all of the laws, ordinances, and doctrines of the gospel. Moral agency—the ability to choose and act for ourselves—is also essential in Heavenly Father's plan. Because of this plan, we can be perfected through the Atonement, received a fullness of joy, and live forever in the presence of God. Our family relationships can last throughout the eternities.

PREMORTAL LIFE

Before we were born on the earth, we lived in the presence of our Heavenly Father as one of His spirit children. In this premortal existence we participated in a council with Heavenly Father's other spirit children. At that council Heavenly Father presented His plan, and the premortal Jesus Christ covenanted to be the Savior.

Blessed with the gift of agency, we made important decisions, such as the decision to follow Heavenly Father's plan (see 2 Nephi 2:27). We prepared to come to the earth, where we could continue to progress.

Those who followed Heavenly Father and Jesus Christ were permitted to come to the earth to experience mortality and progress toward eternal life. Lucifer, another spirit son of God, rebelled against the plan. He became Satan, and he and his followers were cast out of heaven and denied the privileges of receiving a physical body and experiencing mortality.

MORTAL LIFE

The mortal part of our existence is a time of learning in which we can prepare for eternal life and prove ourselves to see if we will use our agency to do all that the Lord has commanded us. Our spirit is untied with our physical body, giving us opportunities to grow and develop in ways that were not possible in our premortal life.

LIFE AFTER DEATH

When we die, our spirits will enter the spirit world and await the Resurrection. The spirits of the righteous are received into a state of happiness, which is called paradise. Many of the faithful will continue to preach the gospel to those in spirit prison.

Spirit prison is a temporary place in the postmortal world for those who died without a knowledge of the truth or those who were disobedience in mortality. Here spirits will be taught the gospel and have the opportunity to repent and accept ordinances of salvation that are performed for them in temples. Those who accept the gospel may dwell in paradise until the Resurrection.

Resurrection is the reuniting of our spirit body with our physical body of flesh and bones (see Luke 24:3-39). After resurrection, the spirit and body will never gain be separated, and we will be immortal. Every person born on earth will be resurrected because Jesus Christ overcame death (see Job 19:2526; 1 Corinthians 15:20-22). The righteous will be resurrected before the wicked and will come forth in the First Resurrection.

The Final Judgment will occur after the Resurrection. Jesus Christ will judge each person to determine the eternal glory he or she will receive. This judgment will be based on each person's obedience to God's commands (see Revelation 20:12-13).

There are three kingdoms of glory (see 1 Corinthians 15:40-42). The highest of the three kingdoms is the celestial kingdom. Those who are valiant in the testimony of Jesus and obedience to the principles of the gospel will dwell in the presence of God the Father and His Son, Jesus Christ.

The second of the three kingdoms of glory is the terrestrial kingdom. Those in this kingdom will be the honorable men and women of the earth who were not valiant in the testimony of Jesus.

The telestial kingdom is the lowest of the three kingdoms of glory. Those in this kingdom chose wickedness rather than righteousness during their mortal lives. These individuals will receive their glory after being redeemed from spirit prison.

3. CREATION AND FALL

THE CREATION

Heavenly Father is the Supreme Creator. Jesus Christ created the heavens and the earth under the direction of the Father. The earth was no created from nothing; it was organized from existing matter. Jesus Christ has created worlds without number.

The creation of an earth was essential to God's plan. It provided a place where we could gain a physical body, be tested and tied, and develop divine attributes. We are to use the earth's resources with wisdom, judgment, and thanksgiving.

Adam was the first man created on earth. God created Adam and Eve in His own image (see Genesis 1:26-27). All human beings—male and female—are created in the image of God.

THE FALL

Adam and Eve's transgression and the resultant changes, including spiritual and physical death, are called the Fall.

In the Garden of Eden, God commanded Adam and Eve not to partake of the fruit of the tree of knowledge of good and evil;

the consequence of doing so would be spiritual and physical death. Spiritual death is separation from God. Physical death is the separation of the spirit from the mortal body.

Because Adam and Eve transgressed and partook of the fruit of the tree of knowledge of good and evil, they were cast out from the presence of the Lord—they experienced spiritual death. They also became mortal—subject to physical death.

As descendants of Adam and Eve, we inherit a fallen condition during mortality in which we are tested by the difficulties of life and the temptations of the adversary (see Mosiah 3:19).

The Fall is an integral part of Heavenly Father's plan of salvation. It has a twofold direction—downward yet forward. In addition to introducing physical and spiritual death, it gave us the opportunity to be born on the earth and to learn and progress.

As a result of the Fall, Adam and Eve and their posterity could experience joy and sorrow, know good and evil, and have children (see 2 Nephi 2:22-25).

4. ATONEMENT OF JESUS CHRIST

To atone is to suffer the penalty for sin, thereby removing the effects of sin from the repentant sinner and allowing him or her to be reconciled to God. Jesus Christ was the only one capable of making a perfect Atonement for all mankind. His Atonement included His suffering for the sins of mankind in the Garden of Gethsemane, the shedding of His blood, His suffering and death on the cross, and His Resurrection from the tomb (see Isaiah 53:3-5; DD&C 19:16-19). The Savior was able to carry out the Atonement because He kept Himself free from sin and had power over death. From His mortal mother, He inherited the ability to die. From His immortal Father, He inherited the power to take up His life again.

Through the Atonement of Jesus Christ everyone will be resurrected and overcome physical death. Through the Atonement those who repent, obey the commandments, receive the saving ordinances, and keep their covenants will overcome spiritual death and receive the gift of eternal life.

As part of His Atonement, Jesus took upon Himself the pains, sicknesses, and infirmities of all people (see Alma 7:11-12). He understands our suffering because He has experienced it.

5. DISPENSATION, APOSTASY, AND RESTORATION

DISPENSATION

A dispensation is a period of time when the Lord reveals His gospel doctrines, ordinances, and priesthood. It is a period in which the Lord has at least one authorized servant on the earth who bears the holy priesthood and who has a divine commission to dispense the gospel to the inhabitants of the earth. The dispensation of the fullness of times is the final dispensation. It began with the revelation of the gospel to Joseph Smith.

Previous dispensations were identified with Adam, Enoch, Noah, Abraham, Moses, and Jesus Christ. In addition, there have been other dispensations, including those among the Nephites and the Jaredites the plan of salvation and the gospel of Jesus Christ have been revealed and taught in every dispensation.

APOSTASY

When people turn away from the principles of the gospel and do not have priesthood keys, they are in a state of apostasy.

Periods of general apostasy have occurred throughout the history of the world. One example is the Great Apostasy, which occurred after the Savior established His Church (see 2 Thessalonians 2:1-3). After the deaths of the Savior's Apostles, men corrupted the principles of the gospel and made unauthorized changes in Church organization and priesthood ordinances. Because of this widespread wickedness, the Lord withdrew the authority and keys of the priesthood from the earth.

During the Great Apostasy, people were without divine direction from living prophets. Many churches were established, but they did no have the authority to confer the gift of the Holy Ghost or perform other priesthood ordinances. Parts of the holy scriptures were corrupted or lost, and the people no longer had the true knowledge of God.

This apostasy lasted until Heavenly Father and His Beloved Son appeared to Joseph Smith and initiated the Restoration of the fullness of the gospel.

THE RESTORATION

The Restoration is God's reestablishment of the truths and ordinances of His gospel among men on earth (see Isaiah 29:13-14; Revelation 14:6-7).

In preparation for the Restoration, the Lord raised up noble men during what is called the Reformation. They attempted to return religious doctrine, practices, and organization to the ay the Savior had established them. They did not, however, have the priesthood nor the fullness of the gospel.

The Restoration began in 1820 when God the Father and His Son, Jesus Christ, appeared to Joseph Smith in response to his prayer (see Joseph Smith—History 1:15-20). Some of the key events of the Restoration were the translation of the Book of Mormon, the restoration of the Aaronic and Melchizedek Priesthoods, and the organization of the Church on April 6, 1830.

The Aaronic Priesthood was restored to Joseph Smith and Oliver Cowdery by John the Baptist on May 15, 1929. The Melchizedek Priesthood and keys of the kingdom were restored in 1829 when the Apostles Peter, James, and John conferred them upon Joseph Smith and Oliver Cowdery.

The fullness of the gospel has been restored, and The Church of Jesus Christ of Latter-day Saints is "the only true and living church upon the face of the whole earth" (D&C 1:30). The Church will eventually fill the whole earth and stand forever (see Daniel 2:44-45).

6. PROPHETS

A prophet is a person who has been called by God to speak for Him (see Amos 3:7). Prophets testify of Jesus Christ and teach His gospel. They make known God's will and true character. They denounce sin and warn of its consequences. At times, they prophesy of future events.

We sustain the President of the Church as prophet, seer, and revelator and the only person on the earth who receives revelation to guide ht entire Church. We also sustain the counselors in the First Presidency and the members of the Quorum of the Twelve Apostles as prophets, seers, and revelators (see D&C 1:38).

7. PRIESTHOOD

The priesthood is the eternal power and authority of God. Through the priesthood God created and governs the heavens and the earth. Through this power He redeems and exalts His children, bringing to pass "the immortality and eternal life of man" (Moses 1:39).

God gives priesthood authority to worthy male members of the Church so they can act in His name for the salvation of His children. Priesthood holders can be authorized to preach the gospel, administer the ordinances of salvation, and govern the kingdom of God on the earth. This authorization comes from those leaders who hold priesthood keys.

AARONIC PRIESTHOOD

The Aaronic Priesthood is often called the preparatory priesthood. The offices of the Aaronic Priesthood are deacon, teacher, priest, and bishop. In the Church today, worthy male members may receive the Aaronic Priesthood beginning at age 12.

The Aaronic Priesthood "holds the keys of the ministering of angels, and of the gospel of repentance, and of baptism" (D&C 13:1).

MELCHIZEDEK PRIESTHOOD

The Melchizedek Priesthood is the higher or greater priesthood and administers in spiritual things. This greater priesthood was given to Adam and has been on the earth whenever the Lord has revealed His gospel.

It was first called "the Holy Priesthood, after the Order of the Son of God" (D&C 107:3). It later became known as the Melchizedek Priesthood, named after a great high priest who lived during the time of the prophet Abraham (see Genesis 14:18; D&C 107:2).

Within the Melchizedek Priesthood are the offices of elder, high priest, patriarch, Seventy, and Apostle. The President of the Melchizedek Priesthood is the President of the Church.

8. FIRST PRINCIPLES AND ORDINANCES

"We believe that the first principles and ordinances of the Gospel are: first, Faith in the Lord Jesus Christ; second, Repentance; third,

Baptism by immersion for the remission of sins; fourth, Laying on of hands for the gift of the Holy Ghost" (Articles of Faith 1:4).

FAITH

Faith is a "hope for things which are not seen, which are true" (Alma 32:21). Faith is a spiritual gift that comes from hearing the word of God. Faith can increase as we pray, study the scriptures, and obey God's commandments. More than passive belief, faith is expressed by the way we live.

Faith must be centered in Jesus Christ in order for it to lead a person to salvation. Having faith in Jesus Christ means relying completely on Him and trusting in His infinite Atonement, power, and other important aspects of the restored gospel. Faith helps us receive spiritual and physical healing and strength to press forward, face our hardships, and overcome temptation. It also gives us peace. The Lord will work mighty miracles in our life according to our faith.

By faith one obtains a remission of sins and eventually is able to dwell in God's presence.

REPENTANCE

Repentance is a change of mind and heart that gives us a fresh view about God, about ourselves, and about the world. It includes turning away from sin and turning to God for forgiveness. It is motivated by love for God and the sincere desire to obey His commandments.

Our sins make us unclean—unworthy to return and dwell in the presence of our Heavenly Father. Through the Atonement of Jesus Christ, our Father in Heaven has provided the only way for us to be forgiven of our sins (see Isaiah 1:18).

Repentance includes feeling sorrow for committing sin, confessing to Heavenly Father and to others if necessary, forsaking the sins, seeking to restore as far as possible all that has been damaged by one's sins, and living a life of obedience to God's commandments (see D&C 58:42-43).

BAPTISM

Baptism by immersion in water by one having authority is the first saving ordinance of the gospel and is necessary for an individual to become a member of The Church of Jesus Christ of Latter-day Saints. Baptism is also necessary for a person to enter the celestial kingdom (see John 3:5).

The word baptism comes from a Greek word meaning to "dip" or "immerse." Immersion is symbolic of the death of a person's sinful life and the rebirth into a spiritual life, dedicated to the service of God and His children. It is also symbolic of death and resurrection.

Because all of the people born on the earth do not have the opportunity to accept the gospel during mortality, the Lord has authorized baptisms for the dead (see 1 Corinthians 15:29). This permits those who accept the gospel in the spirit world to qualify for entrance into God's kingdom.

GIFT OF THE HOLY GHOST

After a person is baptized, one or more Melchizedek Priesthood holders lay their hands on the person's head and confirm him or her a member of the Church. As part of this ordinance, called confirmation, the person is given the gift of the Holy Ghost (see John 3:5).

The gift of the Holy Ghost is different from the influence of the Holy Ghost. Before baptism, a person can feel the influence of the Holy Ghost from time to time and through that influence can receive a testimony of the truth. After receiving the gift of the Holy Ghost, a person has the right to His constant companionship if he or she keeps the commandments.

9. ORDINANCES AND COVENANTS

ORDINANCES

In the Church, an ordinance is a sacred, formal act that has spiritual meaning. Each ordinance was designed by God to teach spiritual truths. The ordinances of salvation are performed by the authority of the priesthood and under the direction of those who hold priesthood keys.

Some ordinances are essential to exaltation and are called saving ordinances. They include baptism, confirmation, ordination to the Melchizedek Priesthood (for men), the temple endowment, and the marriage sealing. All saving ordinances of the priesthood are accompanies by covenants.

There are other ordinances, such as the sacrament, patriarchal blessings, and administering to the sick.

COVENANTS

A COVENANT IS A SACRED AGREEMENT BETWEEN God and man. God gives the conditions for the covenant, and we agree to do what He asks us to do; God then promises us certain blessings for our obedience (see D&C 82:10; 84:33-39).

All the saving ordinances of the priesthood are accompanied by covenants. We covenant with the Lord at baptism and renew those covenants by partaking of the sacrament. Brethren who receive the Melchizedek Priesthood enter into the oath and covenant of the priesthood. We make further covenants in the temple.

10. COMMANDMENTS

Commandments are the laws and requirements that God gives to mankind. We manifest our love for Him by keeping His commandments (see John 14:15). Keeping the commandments will bring blessings from the Lord (see D&C 130:20-21).

The two most basic commandments are "Love the Lord thy God with all they heart, and with all thy soul, and with all thy mind....And...love thy neighbour as thyself" (Matthew 22:37, 39).

The Ten Commandments are a vital part of the gospel and are eternal principles that are necessary for our exaltation (see Exodus 20:3-17). The Lord revealed them to Moses in ancient times, and He has restated them in latter-day revelations (see Mosiah 13:12-24). Other commandments include keeping the law of chastity, paying a full tithe, being honest, praying daily, having a spirit of gratitude, and observing the Word of Wisdom.

11. MARRIAGE AND FAMILY

"Marriage between a man and a woman is ordained of God" and "the family is central" to His plan of salvation and happiness.

"The sacred powers of procreation are to be employed only between man and woman, lawfully wedded as husband and wife." Parents are "to multiply and replenish the earth," "to rear their children in love and righteousness," and "to provide for their physical and spiritual needs."

"Husband and wife have a solemn responsibility to love and care for each other." "Fathers are to preside over their families in love and righteousness," and "to provide the necessities of life."

"Mothers are primarily responsible for the nurture of their children. In these sacred responsibilities, fathers and mothers are obligated to help one another as equal partners."

"The divine plan of happiness" teaches that "family relationships" may continue "beyond the grave." The earth was created and the gospel was revealed so that families could be formed, sealed, and exalted eternally. (see "The Family: A Proclamation to the World," *Ensign*, Nov. 1995, 102.)

APPENDIX B

LOVE NOTES

HUSBAND → WIFE
I will vacuum all the floors at least one day this week.
I will put the little ones to bed and read their story two nights this week
Tomorrow you will have breakfast in bed
I will clean the outside windows if weather permits
Select the movie you would like to see and we'll go together
I will clean out the garage
This love note entitles you to a surprise one night this week
I'll cover home base while you run errands.
I will write a poem, story, or song for you
I will clean off the top of my dresser and closet this week
I will make any repairs needed around the house

I'll move out the fridge and clean under it.
I get to go with you and help you select something for your wardrobe (maximum - $50).
Let's go jogging, swimming, or to the spa together
This note entitles you to a week-end at our favorite hotel
Let's go for a yogurt
Let's go get some pizza (or have it delivered).
Call_____ and let's go bowling (Insert name of friends)
Call_____and let's go miniature golfing (Insert name of friends)
You choose the place and we will have a night out this weekend
Let's go to shopping—mostly window shopping—at the mall. We'll go for ice cream after.
This love note is good for a back rub after I put the kids to bed.
This love note entitles you a dozen kisses (if you are not in the mood—put back in and choose another one!)
Let's sneak off to the dollar movie this Tuesday.
This love note is good for two hours of time running errands together
How about a quiet hour extra this week reading a good book?
I agree to do something I hate to do. You tell me—I'll do it.
Let's visit your folks this week

Let's do something with the kids...go for a ride, to the beach, softball, etc.
Let's sneak away for a couple of hours—your choice—any ideas?
I'll be your slave one day this week—babysitter, window washer, walls, etc.
Let's go for a long walk
Let's go for a bike excursion as a family
Let's go shopping at the DI or thrift store

COUPONS: *(Cash in at the time of your choosing)*
One evening of babysitting
Trip to the ice cream store
Full Saturday of babysitting
Sundaes for two
One sightseeing ride for two
One fancy dinner out
One hamburger spree
One dinner and a movie
A movie of your choice
An evening of games
My services for a Saturday morning
Need a painter?
Need a chef?
Need my kitchen or bathroom cleaning skills?

Tomorrow, you will have breakfast in bed.
This note is good for a back rub!
Pizza sounds great—let's order in!
Let's take your parents to dinner this week.
This entitles you to a game of your choice.
Let's get physical at the recreation center.
Let's go to the temple and have dinner there
Find a recipe you like—and I'll cook it
I'll be your slave one day this week—what do you want, Master?
Let's go for ice cream or yogurt
We'll do an activity of your choosing
Teach me a new sport
Let's go camping—an overnighter
This is a freebee (anything at all)
I'll shine your shoes this week
A movie of your choice
One night out with the boys and no complaining from me
Two scoops of your favorite flavor
Let's go to Redbox/Netflix and pick out a movie

Help me learn some basic car maintenance
Let's go play miniature golf
Let's go bowling together—on me
Let's start a family scrap book together
Let's go for a walk one evening this week
Your own Genie for an activity or event—your wish is my command
I'll fix your favorite snack/treat one night this week
I'll put a bunch of stuff together to de-junk this week
This is good for a massage—at least 10 minutes
This is for a date of your choice
Let's go for a bike ride

COUPONS:
Good for one weekend at the condo/cabin/hotel
Good for one quiet night listening to CDs, a video or TV show
Good for a pair of new pants/slippers—your choice
Good for a haircut (with your close supervision)

Good for a can of Fischer's Glazed Nuts
Good for a wilderness hike (I'll pack a lunch)
Good for a lunch brought to your work by me
Good for 1/2 - 1 hour of browsing in the bookstore
Good for a ride up the canyon/beach/park/historical site.
Good for one bottle of my favorite aftershave
Good for a Church book of your choice
Good for one new tool for your toolbox
Good for a subscription to your favorite magazine
Good for one wash of your car
Good for a long sleep in—on Saturday/Sunday
Good for an evening of popcorn, chips, and a good movie
Good for one Chinese dinner
Good for a new wallet
Good for a batch of your favorite cookies
Good for one request—I'll do it—no matter what it is.

Made in the USA
Columbia, SC
19 December 2021

52145906R00178